Marjorie Harris Carr

UNIVERSITY PRESS OF FLORIDA

Florida A&M University, Tallahassee
Florida Atlantic University, Boca Raton
Florida Gulf Coast University, Ft. Myers
Florida International University, Miami
Florida State University, Tallahassee
New College of Florida, Sarasota
University of Central Florida, Orlando
University of Florida, Gainesville
University of North Florida, Jacksonville
University of South Florida, Tampa
University of West Florida, Pensacola

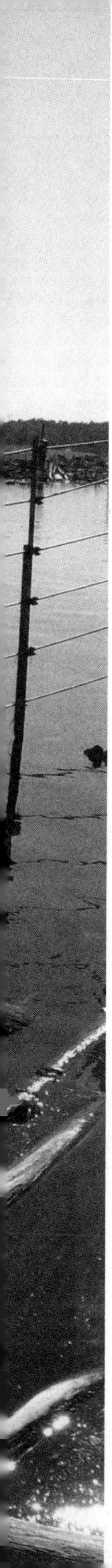

Marjorie Harris Carr

Defender of Florida's Environment

Peggy Macdonald

University Press of Florida

Gainesville

Tallahassee

Tampa

Boca Raton

Pensacola

Orlando

Miami

Jacksonville

Ft. Myers

Sarasota

A Florida Quincentennial Book

Frontispiece: Rodman Dam (now George Kirkpatrick Dam) on the Ocklawaha River. Photo by Peggy Macdonald.

Copyright 2014 by Peggy Macdonald
All rights reserved
Printed in the United States of America. This book is printed on Glatfelter Natures Book, a paper certified under the standards of the Forestry Stewardship Council (FSC). It is a recycled stock that contains 30 percent post-consumer waste and is acid free.

This book may be available in an electronic edition.

19 18 17 16 15 14   6 5 4 3 2 1

Library of Congress Cataloging-in-Publication Data
Macdonald, Peggy, author.
Marjorie Harris Carr : defender of Florida's environment / Peggy Macdonald.
pages cm
ISBN 978-0-8130-4935-9
1. Carr, Marjorie Harris. 2. Women environmentalists—Florida—Biography.
3. Environmentalism—Florida—History. 4. Marjorie Harris Carr Cross Florida Greenway (Fla.)—History. 5. Women and the environment—Florida. 6. Florida—Environmental conditions. I. Title.
GE56.C37M33 2014
333.72092—dc23   [B]   2013038960

University Press of Florida
15 Northwest 15th Street
Gainesville, FL 32611-2079
http://www.upf.com

For Nick, Richard, and Katherine;

for my mother and favorite sounding board, Kit Macdonald;

for my grandparents, Bill and Dorothy Macdonald, who were

like a second set of parents to me and my sister and brother,

Anne (Walton) Alerding and Robbie Walton;

for my uncle, John Macdonald, who has become the head of our family;

for my father and sisters, Bruce Walton, Pam (Walton) Feldman,

and Diana (Walton) Dunn-Roberts;

and especially for Mimi Carr, who made this book possible

Contents

Introduction

Marjorie Harris Carr was a woman who had it all: a loving husband, five children, and a successful career. She devoted her life to protecting a little-known river in the heart of central Florida and in the process played a key role in shaping the modern environmental movement. In a time when women were expected to end their careers after marrying, Carr continued to pursue a career in science, conservation, and environmental activism with the financial and intellectual support of her husband, Archie Carr, a world-renowned turtle scientist and pioneering conservation biologist. Throughout a lengthy and contentious battle over the construction of an expensive U.S. Army Corps of Engineers project that threatened to bisect Florida and destroy the Ocklawaha River, Marjorie Carr and a coalition of academics specializing in science, economics, and the law used the new activist science of ecology to turn a regional struggle over construction of the Cross Florida Barge Canal into a national campaign that helped solidify President Richard Nixon's reputation as an environmental president.[1]

Carr and her allies fought for nearly a decade to accomplish the unprecedented feat of stopping a Corps of Engineers project that was already under way. Despite their success in killing the canal, however, the Rodman Dam remains intact today, disrupting the Ocklawaha's natural course and blocking the migration of aquatic life protected under the Endangered Species Act, including manatees and Atlantic and shortnose sturgeon. Rodman Dam—renamed the George Kirkpatrick Dam in 1998 after the state senator who fought hardest to preserve the dam and Rodman Reservoir, a popular bass fishery—still exists due to the dogged persistence of a handful of local politicians and bass fishermen who have prevailed over a succession of Florida governors, legislators, and activists who have called for the dam's removal.

Even in death, Carr and Kirkpatrick continued to wage war over Rodman. In 1997, after Carr's funeral at First Presbyterian Church in Gainesville, Florida, a "Free the Ocklawaha" sticker appeared on the back of her hearse. At the same church in 2003, during Kirkpatrick's funeral, toward the end of the eulogy, his children placed a "Save Rodman Reservoir" bumper sticker directly on his casket. Carr and Kirkpatrick are both buried in Gainesville's historic Evergreen Cemetery, where they can spend eternity debating the merits of Rodman Reservoir versus a free-flowing Ocklawaha.[2]

Over the years, the defenders of the Ocklawaha sometimes entertained drastic solutions to the problem of removing Rodman Dam, the most important step toward restoring the Ocklawaha to its precanal state. Late in his life, David Anthony, a University of Florida professor of chemistry and botany who worked on the Manhattan Project during World War II and later cofounded Florida Defenders of the Environment (FDE) and Alachua Audubon Society with Marjorie Carr, gave serious thought to blowing up Rodman Dam. According to his widow, Joan Griffin Anthony, David reasoned that by the time the authorities got around to prosecuting him, he would be dead.[3]

JoAnn Myer Valenti, who did public relations work for FDE and lived with the Carrs while Marjorie led FDE's preparation of the environmental impact statement that bolstered the legal case against the Corps of Engineers, recalled that even in FDE's early days, frustrated activists sometimes talked with Carr about blowing up the dam. Valenti said Carr's usual response was, "No, this too shall pass. That's not the way to do it." Carr remained optimistic about the power of the democratic process, and she had faith that if the public and public servants were educated about the dangers the barge canal posed to the Ocklawaha, in the end, Floridians would decide to do what was right for the environment. "But here we are—how many years later—and the damned dam is still there doing its dastardly deeds," Valenti reflected. "I keep waiting for one of those old boys to blow that sucker up."[4]

In 1918, Carr and her parents moved from Boston, Massachusetts, to rural southwest Florida. She lived in her adopted state for nearly eighty years, observing Florida's population explode from less than 1 million at the time of her arrival in the state to close to 5 million in 1960 and almost 10 million in 1980. Carr lived through Florida's transformation from a backwoods frontier state in the early twentieth century to the tenth-most populous state in the nation by 1960. She witnessed firsthand the impact of Florida's rapid population growth on the state's native flora and fauna, which declined dramatically as a result of diminishing habitats. Over the course of an activist career that spanned four decades, Carr used the developing science of ecology to fight for the preservation of Florida's remaining wild places and to challenge the construction of the Cross Florida Barge Canal, which was grounded in the conservation ethos of a bygone era.[5]

In 1962, the Corps of Engineers reached the final stage of its plan to dam the Ocklawaha River at two points as part of the construction of a 107-mile canal that would enable massive barges to travel across inland Florida from the Gulf of Mexico to the Atlantic Ocean. The Ocklawaha is a wild, winding river that flows north toward the Atlantic Ocean (via the St. Johns River). As recently as the 1850s, Seminoles used this ancient river—located in remote central Florida—for transportation. They camped along its banks and hunted black bear, panther, white-tailed deer, and turkey. In 1936, when Carr first encountered the Ocklawaha, its abundant flora and fauna remained relatively unchanged. Because the river was removed from the coast and far from Florida's major cities, it remained largely undeveloped. Its expansive valley and varied habitats supported a diverse variety of native plants and animals. By sheer luck, the Ocklawaha lay mostly undisturbed for another three decades, dodging the massive development that accompanied the state's postwar population boom of the 1940s and 1950s.[6]

Carr first encountered the Ocklawaha River as a new graduate of Florida State College for Women in Tallahassee, the state's capital. Although she had planned to start graduate school in the fall, in the 1930s, women faced discrimination in the graduate admissions process—especially in the sciences. The director of the University of North Carolina's ornithology department told her point-blank that women were not welcome in the field. Fortunately, the New Deal created fresh opportunities for women. Carr started work as the nation's first female federal wildlife technician at the Welaka Fish Hatchery near Palatka.

Through her work at the hatchery, Carr was introduced to the two great loves of her life: the Ocklawaha River and her future husband, Archibald (Archie) Fairly Carr Jr. (1909–1987), who was finishing his doctoral dissertation in biology at the University of Florida. They met when Carr—who had studied ornithology and bacteriology as an undergraduate—traveled to Gainesville to use the university's well-equipped laboratory to determine what had sickened some quail at the Welaka Fish Hatchery's aviary. It was love at first sight. Despite tremendous financial difficulties, the two young scientists eloped and started a fifty-year partnership that combined science, family, and conservation. Nathaniel Reed, who served as the assistant secretary of the interior for fish, wildlife, and national parks during the Nixon and Ford administrations, once described Marjorie and Archie Carr as the "dynamic duo." Marjorie Carr's work to restore and preserve the Ocklawaha and other Florida rivers led Charles Lee of the Florida Audubon Society to give her the honorary title "Our Lady of the Rivers."[7]

Marjorie Carr's story—which cannot be told without also addressing the life of her husband, Archie—bridges the gap between the conservation mindset of the early twentieth century and the nation's growing environmental awareness of the late twentieth century. By the time Carr first heard about the Corps' plan to dam the river, she was forty-seven and the mother of five children. She had studied the Ocklawaha River for decades, first coming to know the river through her work as a biologist at the Welaka Fish Hatchery. Carr later visited the Ocklawaha routinely to conduct research on the river's substantial population of large-mouthed black bass, a species that was the subject of her master's thesis at the University of Florida in Gainesville in 1942.

This book uncovers the story of one of the nation's unsung environmental heroes while also addressing the larger issue of how American women surmounted the obstacles placed in their path during their transition from political exclusion to inclusion in national politics in the late twentieth century. Through her strong convictions, firm command of the new science of ecology, university connections, and phenomenal perseverance, Marjorie Carr championed a pioneering legal battle that provided the environmental movement with a landmark victory that would have far-reaching consequences for federal agencies, real estate developers, private industry, and state and national politics.

Carr grew up in an undeveloped section of the Gulf Coast, where she learned to identify the state's bounteous flora and fauna. She also witnessed the effects of unregulated hunting firsthand, at a time when plume hunters nearly drove several species of Florida's native birds to extinction. When Carr attended Florida State College for Women in the 1930s, women could choose between a feminized curriculum that trained them to fulfill the traditional duties of a wife and mother, or a liberal arts curriculum that prepared women to enter the professions. The discrepancies between these two paths were reflective of competing discourses in higher education. As more women participated in higher education and entered the professions in the early twentieth century, cultural tensions erupted over the nature of women's proper place in society. Carr followed a liberal arts path, studying ecology and other biological sciences. She became a Phi Beta Kappa scholar, was inducted into the science honor society Sigma Xi, and was appointed as a charter member of the Florida Academy of Sciences. Nonetheless, Carr was denied admission to graduate programs in ornithology because of her gender.

Carr was hired as the first female federal wildlife technician through the New Deal's Resettlement Administration, but the opportunity proved to be short-lived. Although the New Deal opened up new opportunities for women, it did not eliminate entrenched biases concerning women's professional abilities. Carr's supervisor was troubled by his superiors' decision to hire a female biologist, and she was soon dismissed from the position. Nonetheless, Carr's resettlement work resulted in her marriage to a fellow scientist who would help her gain admission to the graduate zoology program at the officially all-male University of Florida. Although Marjorie ultimately bore the primary responsibility for the care of their five children while Archie published numerous books and established his international reputation as the world's top turtle man, he generously shared his money and scientific credentials to support her environmental campaigns.

Between 1945 and 1949, the Carr family lived in Honduras, where Archie taught at the Escuela Agrícola Panamericana Zamorano. Although Marjorie and Archie would later embrace an environmental ethos that condemned hunting for sport, in the 1940s they shot thousands of animals for natural history museum collections, research, and to eat. At the time it was considered necessary to kill animals in order to study them. Over the course of the 1950s and 1960s, however, the Carrs would come to realize how fragile the ecosystems of Central America were as they witnessed the rapid deforestation that accompanied the growth of commercial agriculture there.

In Honduras, Carr enjoyed an informal career in science at her husband's side while domestic servants supervised their children. She and Archie adopted more traditional gender roles upon their return to Florida in the fall of 1949, but Marjorie Carr remained engaged in science as much as possible. Throughout the 1950s, Carr continued to assist with her husband's turtle research. By the end of the decade, she was engaged in a variety of conservation projects through the Gainesville Garden Club and the Alachua Audubon Society. Over the course of the 1960s, the focus of Carr's activism shifted from conservation to environmentalism. Rooted in the nineteenth-century view that the earth is composed of natural resources that should be harnessed by humans, conservation was espoused by the Corps of Engineers, which viewed the Ocklawaha River as a resource to be tamed and exploited for profit. Guided by the relatively new science of ecology, the environmental movement gained momentum at the same time that Carr's Ocklawaha campaign was at its peak.

The consequences of the transformation from conservation to environmentalism were profound. Florida was in the vanguard of the environmental revolution of the 1960s and 1970s, when a developing environmental ethos transformed the nation's consciousness and ushered in a wave of pioneering environmental legislation. Inspired at the national level by the 1962 publication of Rachel Carson's *Silent Spring*, and at the state level by a series of near environmental catastrophes that thrust a powerful contingent of citizen activists into the spotlight, the nascent environmental movement was led by a loose-knit coalition of academics, writers, and citizen activists who used the science of ecology to foster a new brand of stewardship of the earth.

Many of Carr's early conservation projects involved local land preservation. As Florida's unchecked growth increasingly encroached upon the state's remaining wild places, Carr and other activists realized that they needed to take action to protect large tracts of land that promoted biodiversity. By the 1960s, Marjorie and Archie Carr had discarded the conservation ethos of their younger days. They had come to represent a new breed of activist scientist. Archie's turtle studies led him to believe that scientists were ethically compelled to take action on behalf of the environment or there would be nothing left to stand up for. Marjorie Carr helped her husband establish a sea turtle research and conservation station at Tortuguero, Costa Rica. In return, Archie supported all of his wife's conservation and environmental campaigns, writing letters to university officials and politicians to explain the ecological reasons that justified land preservation in Florida. Marjorie Carr would make the case that the barge canal was a dinosaur, a product of nineteenth-century thinking that should not be built for economic and environmental reasons.

Construction of a cross-state ship canal had first started during the Great Depression as a means of providing economic relief to Florida. However, America's involvement in World War II halted construction of the canal before much progress was made. In 1942, the canal project received congressional authorization—this time in the form of a shallower barge canal. Yet Congress decided against appropriating funds for construction. For the next two decades, canal proponents pushed for funding. Construction along the Ocklawaha River started in 1964. By that point, Marjorie Carr had led a localized movement to reroute the canal around the Ocklawaha River Valley for more than a year.

In a 1965 *Florida Naturalist* essay, Carr referred to this area as the Ocklawaha Regional Ecosystem. The essay laid the philosophical groundwork for the movement's conversion from a regional movement that centered its efforts on lobbying state politicians, to a national environmental campaign that brought the little-known river to the attention of the nation. The Ocklawaha campaign abandoned its earlier conservation approach that emphasized the natural resources that would be lost if the canal were completed, and embraced an environmental focus that emphasized the threat the barge canal posed to one of Florida's largest uninterrupted, ecologically rich areas of land.

By the late 1960s, the Ocklawaha campaign had attracted the attention of the national media. The *New York Times*, *Reader's Digest*, and other major publications decried the "rape" of the Ocklawaha. After reading about the courtroom success of a new legal organization named Environmental Defense Fund (EDF) in *Sports Illustrated*, Carr contacted the national organization's leaders and convinced them to take on the campaign to save the Ocklawaha. EDF urged Carr and her allies—who were still operating under the auspices of the Alachua Audubon Society—to form an independent, single-issue organization dedicated to saving the Ocklawaha. They dubbed their new organization Florida Defenders of the Environment (FDE, which was EDF reversed), and the two groups promptly started to develop the legal case against the Corps of Engineers.

FDE's first task was to assemble an environmental impact statement that contended that the barge canal should not be completed on economic grounds alone. In the space age, constructing a barge canal made no sense. The interstate system facilitated cheaper, faster shipping via commercial trucking. Moreover, the economic benefits of the canal were exaggerated, especially since the Corps of Engineers had never factored the environmental cost of losing the ecological value of the Ocklawaha River into their calculations when determining the canal's benefit-cost ratio. Finally, FDE's environmental impact statement stressed the catastrophic environmental consequences the canal posed to the Floridan Aquifer, the state's main source of freshwater. Despite the Corps of Engineers' claims to the contrary, FDE's hydrologists and geologists demonstrated that the porous aquifer—which interacts with the surface water along the canal—was vulnerable to saltwater intrusion and pollution from barge traffic.

In the 1960s and 1970s, when the campaign to save the Ocklawaha was at its peak, very few women had penetrated the public sphere in the realm of politics. Therefore, Carr and other women who ventured into this masculine space sometimes used the rhetorical device of describing themselves as housewives, which allowed them to function within the public sphere during a moment of political and cultural transition for women in the United States and other Western countries. The housewife persona served as an effective shield as Carr pressed local, state, national, and military organizations for further information about the canal. She sometimes masked the true extent of her scientific knowledge in her dealings with lawmakers, the Corps of Engineers, and the media. David Anthony, Alachua Audubon Society's copresident (with Carr) and the second president of FDE, explained how Carr exploited people's preconceived notions of her femininity: "She would say, 'I'm just a poor little housewife from Micanopy, but . . .' and then just devastate her opponents with her total command of the subject."[8]

At the dawn of the 1980s, women's presence still was not welcome in politics at the state or national levels. Women first broke into the political arena of the late twentieth century by presenting themselves as traditional women— women who did not appear to challenge the gendered order that excluded them from the public realm—while in reality, they posed a direct challenge to the political order as it then existed. The strategy of presenting themselves as nonthreatening housewives provided Carr—and such contemporaries as Paula Hawkins, the first woman elected to a full term in the U.S. Senate without being preceded in politics by a husband or father—with the moral authority of an earlier wave of female activists. In the late nineteenth and early twentieth centuries, Progressive reformers expanded the confines of the domestic sphere to encompass the larger community, thereby justifying their participation in social work, conservation, nursing, teaching, and other public activities that were new or had previously been the purview of men. In her essays, letters, public appearances, and telephone conversations with politicians, supporters, and opponents, Carr presented herself as a reasonable voice for environmental stewardship. Yet when it suited her cause, Carr downplayed her scientific background and played up the role of unassuming "housewife from Micanopy."[9]

This book seeks to broaden current interpretations of women's leadership styles within the environmental movement to encompass the contributions of professional women and activists such as Marjory Stoneman Douglas, whom Jack E. Davis describes as both a writer and philosopher; and Carr, a scientist and naturalist. Historian Robert Gottlieb differentiates between "male" and "female" leadership styles, contending that the "male" style is based upon facts and science, whereas the "female" style stems from women's direct experiences as mothers and nurturers. The Love Canal activists of the 1970s are characteristic of this experiential form of "female" activism, in which women became environmental activists after their families endured the effects of toxic industrial pollution in their homes and schools. Although Gottlieb acknowledges that the women who engaged in the Love Canal campaign and others like it were transformed from housewives who had previously functioned primarily within the private realm of the home, to politically active public figures, he overlooks the activities of female activists who do not fit into this mold. Women such as Carr and Douglas were not merely adopting "male" leadership styles favoring facts over feelings. They formed single-issue organizations dedicated to studying local environmental issues, used the media to educate the public, and recruited state and federal assistance to achieve their goals.

Another female scientist and writer, Rachel Carson, set the stage for the environmental revolution of the late 1960s and early 1970s. Florida stood at the center of the momentous process that recast nature from a commodity to be exploited to something to be protected. In the early to mid-twentieth century, Carr had mastered an earlier form of ecology that focused on single species within an ecosystem (primarily birds and fish, in Carr's case). In the late twentieth century, she utilized the modern understanding of ecology—which stressed humans' role as either destroyers or stewards of the environment—in her campaign to save the Ocklawaha. Carr's successful campaign to stop construction of the Cross Florida Barge Canal was an important element of the emergence of the American environmental movement in the late twentieth century. In addition, her life story reveals the creative, often subtle ways that women scientists in the twentieth century overcame barriers against their participation in the public sphere and, if they were lucky, transformed the world in the process.

1

Marjorie Harris Carr's Girlhood

A Young Naturalist Growing Up in Florida

Marjorie Harris Carr was born in Boston, Massachusetts, on March 26, 1915. Her father, Charles Ellsworth Harris, was a farmer at heart. Originally from New Hampshire, Charles abandoned a career in law to teach Italian immigrants' children in Boston. Charles and his wife, Clara Louise (Haynes) Harris, were "snowbirds"—northerners who wintered in Florida. In the early twentieth century, south Florida land speculators pitched the benefits of the state's tropical climate to all who would listen, claiming that an industrious individual could retire after running a family orange grove for ten years. In 1918, when Harris was three years old, her father relocated the family to a 10-acre orange grove in remote southwest Florida. Charles built a modest house three miles south of Bonita Springs (formerly known as Surveyor's Creek), near the Imperial River. He built a similar house for his sister and her husband, Mable and Wittgenstein "Vitt" Codwise, who were among a group of eight to ten families who moved with the Harrises from Boston to Fort Myers and regions farther south to grow oranges. Charles and Clara's decision to move to rural Bonita Springs would instill a love of natural Florida in their young daughter, who would later champion the cause of restoring and preserving the state's wild and scenic rivers.[1]

Newborn Marjorie Harris with her mother, Clara (Haynes) Harris (1915).
Courtesy of Mimi Carr.

Two-year-old Marjorie Harris in Boston,
Massachusetts (1917). Courtesy of Mimi Carr.

Marjorie in Fort Myers with her father, Charles Ellsworth Harris (1919). Courtesy of Mimi Carr.

Nine-year-old Marjorie Harris and classmates at Bonita Springs School, Lee County, Florida (1925). Courtesy of Mimi Carr.

Marjorie Harris's childhood home in Bonita Springs (1920s). Charles Harris built this house and a similar one for his sister and her husband, Mable and Vitt Codwise. Courtesy of Mimi Carr.

These transplanted Bostonians attempted to create a small haven for New Englanders in sparsely populated Lee County, in an area formerly occupied by the Calusa people. Massive shell mounds in nearby Estero provide evidence that the Calusa had inhabited the region as early as twelve thousand years ago. About a decade after the Harris family moved to Bonita Springs, the parents of Harris's future husband, Archie Carr, purchased a small orange grove in the town of Umatilla, Florida (located between Ocala and Orlando), providing Harris and Carr with a shared connection to rural Florida. Yet very few small family citrus growers turned a profit in the early to mid-twentieth century. As the citrus industry consolidated, Florida and California farmers formed cooperatives, which left little room for family growers to compete.[2]

Although oranges are actually native to Southeast Asia, Florida promoters had used images of citrus in subtropical Florida to lure tourists and permanent residents to the state since the late nineteenth century. Representing the clash between Florida's native plant life and the state's agricultural industry, the citrus industry was responsible both for improving Americans' health and permanently altering Florida's landscape and wildlife habitats. New World citrus was first planted in Hispaniola in 1493, during Columbus's second voyage to the Americas. It is believed that citrus was first introduced to Florida at St. Augustine in 1565. By 1774, when the naturalist William Bartram traveled up the St. Johns River, he reported finding wild orange groves scattered across the higher regions of land where he camped at night. Early promoters used images and narratives depicting Florida as a land of orange groves and Edenic gardens. The Harrises—originally a farming family—were drawn to the idea of escaping the big-city lifestyle and retreating to a small patch of Florida orange groves. Although it typically takes three to six years for orange groves to reach maturity, and they seldom produce enough fruit to enable a small farmer to turn a profit in less than ten years' time, promoters offered exaggerated visions of instant success.[3]

At the time the Harris family and the other Bostonians who joined them settled in Lee County, southwest Florida was a haven for small family citrus growers. Considered a luxury item since ancient times, oranges attracted such great thinkers as Marjorie Kinnan Rawlings, Harriet Beecher Stowe, Thomas Edison, and Henry Ford to Florida. Rawlings, who won the 1939 Pulitzer Prize for fiction for *The Yearling*, lived on a 72-acre orange grove in north central Florida. Stowe managed a profitable orange grove in Mandarin for almost two decades. John James Audubon sketched Florida birds on orange branches when he visited the state in 1831. Combining images of religion, art, and nature, Florida advertisements and literature tantalized Americans with the promise of paradise. Oranges were frequently at the heart of these images. By 1894, Florida's citrus industry produced 5 million boxes of fruit per year. At the turn of the century, Florida postcards depicted families at work in their private orange groves, but larger citrus operations became the norm as the twentieth century wore on. By the 1920s, large packinghouses and citrus cooperatives had spread across the state. After a series of hard freezes in the late nineteenth and early twentieth centuries, the citrus industry relocated to central and south Florida. Fort Myers was situated far enough south to provide excellent growing conditions for citrus. In 1895, Fort Myers was reported to be the southernmost point at which orange groves had been planted, but subsequent freezes later drove citrus growers farther south.[4]

Although Marjorie Harris's mother, Clara, had descended from Boston urbanites, she and her husband, Charles, taught their only daughter to be close to the earth. Without a radio or telephone (and long before television was invented), members of the Harris family spent much of their free time reading about and exploring their newly adopted homeland. Charles, who was able to trace his lineage to Puritan farmers and planned to carry on the family's farming tradition, was educated in law at Dartmouth College. Charles's parents provided his younger brother, Vincent, with a less august education at the

University of New Hampshire, but Vincent and his wife, Margaret, inherited the family farm in New Hampshire; their sister, Mable, studied at Swarthmore. Charles became a teacher in the Boston school system. This is where he met his future wife, Clara, and her sister Ruth, who were both teachers. In a time of massive urbanization in America, the Harris and Haynes families bucked the trend toward urban life. Charles's decision to purchase a Florida orange grove reflected his longing to return to his farming roots. "His dream was to establish a small farm," Marjorie Harris later recalled. "In those days—this was back in 1918—they felt that having ten acres of citrus would support a person."[5]

The Harris family followed the same Florida dream that would lead millions of Americans to start a new life in the Sunshine State. "My father," Harris explained, "who was really a New Hampshire man, always thought, 'Why should anybody stay up in New England where you can only be out-of-doors for a few months in the year, when there is Florida where you can be out-of-doors all year round?'" Clara's decision to join her husband in Florida seems natural for a new bride. What is more surprising is the fact that so many of Clara's family and friends followed them. Perhaps they needed to combine resources in order to afford the opportunity. Or maybe Charles and Clara's zeal was so infectious that the other Bostonians merely got caught up in the excitement of the adventure. What prompted Charles and Clara's extended family and friends to join them in Florida remains a mystery, but they were part of a growing contingent of northerners who moved to Florida in order to test their luck in the profitable orange industry.[6]

Soon after moving to Bonita Springs, however, Charles realized that his newly acquired orange groves would not provide sufficient income to support a family. Out of economic necessity, Charles continued to teach in Boston seasonally, while his wife and young daughter spent several winters in Florida without him. Charles continued this practice until Harris was seven years old and the family settled in Florida together permanently. As the only child within both her nuclear family and the extended network of New England settlers who had migrated to the region, Harris had a lonely childhood. She turned to nature and literature for companionship, devouring Rudyard Kipling's *Jungle Book* stories and acting out scenes from the book outdoors. Unfortunately, the rest of the Bostonians were unable to cope with the grim realities of managing a small orange grove as readily as Charles had been. According to Harris's daughter, Mimi, the work was too hard and they were too old. Unable to travel north for seasonal work like Charles, many of the other

Boston families chose to return to New England or move to a bigger town in Florida where there were better job opportunities. Only the Harrises and the Codwises stayed in Bonita Springs. In the 1920s, Clara's two sisters and their husbands moved to Fort Myers.[7]

Nonetheless, citrus remained a profitable crop even during the agricultural recession of the 1920s, when prices for citrus remained steady due to the lack of foreign competitors and citrus fruit's special climate and temperature requirements. While many American farmers witnessed a dramatic fall in crop prices after World War I, citrus growers enjoyed a nearly twofold increase in orange prices between 1920 and 1929. However, family orange growers were less likely to reap the record profits that citrus cooperatives experienced in the 1920s. Large packinghouses proliferated in this period, making it possible for cooperatives to sell their crop across the country. Family growers' roadside citrus stands could not compete with the cooperatives' organized marketing and shipping apparatus. "It was very common to have a house and a small grove and sell fruit," Mimi Carr explained. "But nobody could make it. None of the [Boston] families liked it." By 1930, the Depression contributed to a dramatic decrease in the price of oranges. By that time, most of Marjorie Harris's relatives had already left Bonita Springs. Their departure heightened the Harris family's sense of isolation in rural southwest Florida.[8]

In 1922, when Charles Harris stopped teaching in Boston and joined the Harris family year-round in Bonita Springs, the tiny town was little more than a frontier outpost. Surrounded by wilderness, Bonita Springs was home to just 175 residents, according to the 1920 United States census. Its nearby beaches remained undeveloped, and many residents made their living off the sea. The majority of the townsfolk worked on family citrus and vegetable farms. Bonita Springs had a general store, one hotel, a loan and lease business, and a school. Census data indicate that, unlike Marjorie Harris, who was an avid reader, very few of the town's school-age children knew how to read and write. While most Bonita Springs residents were born in Florida, others hailed from regions as far away as Maine, Scotland, Germany, and Portugal. All of the town's residents were white, reflecting the extremely segregated residential patterns in rural Florida.[9]

To the Harris family, Bonita Springs was a naturalist's paradise. Marjorie Harris explored the creeks, rivers, and beaches near Fort Myers (which was still a small town in the 1920s) with her mare, Chiquita. Chiquita was a wild Florida Cracker Horse descended from Spanish stock and caught on the Kis-

Marjorie Harris riding her horse, Chiquita (1920s). Courtesy of Mimi Carr.

simmee Prairie. She was Harris's main form of transportation for several years in grade school. "I could go to Bonita Beach to race along the hard, sandy edge of the Gulf, or go swimming on horseback," she recalled. "I'd take my saddle off and Chiquita and I would go and jump in the waves." Although Lee County made some of its beaches more accessible to tourists during the 1920s boom time through the addition of toll bridges and paved roads, the southwestern coastal areas remained relatively undisturbed until developers and former GIs who had been stationed in the region descended upon south Florida after World War II.[10]

In the 1920s, Bonita Springs was almost like an island unto itself. Harris would later describe south Florida as a naturalist's dream, a place replete with varieties of flora and fauna that were not found in north Florida. She played alone outdoors for hours each day, relating to the wild-boy character of Mowgli in Kipling's *The Jungle Book* as she explored her own subtropical forest "jungle." She encountered a diverse assortment of plants, trees, reptiles, mammals, birds, fish, and insects on her journeys through southwest Florida. The Florida panther, southern bald eagle, eastern diamondback rattlesnake, water moccasin, dolphin, Florida black bear, and prehistoric creatures such as the North American alligator, manatee, stingray, loggerhead sea turtle, and several varieties of shark rivaled the wild animals Mowgli befriended in *The Jungle Book*. In addition to providing companionship on her adventures through wild Florida, Chiquita helped Harris cope with the isolation she felt growing up in a remote coastal settlement. Riding a horse to school lent Harris a certain air of sophistication that she cherished as a Yankee outsider in rural Florida.[11]

Harris was proud of her New England heritage (especially her father's New Hampshire background), but her family's education and relative wealth compared to most Lee County residents made her stand out. Moreover, Harris's schoolmates teased and ostracized her because of her Yankee accent. The wounds of the Civil War were still felt deeply in the South, and Harris and her New England kin were viewed as outsiders. Florida was a Jim Crow state. Endemic racial discrimination continued to plague African Americans, who lived in segregated neighborhoods or in separate small towns divided from nearby towns populated by whites. The reemergence of the Ku Klux Klan following World War I was particularly strong in Florida, where some of the most violent acts of racism emerged. One of the most infamous atrocities occurred in 1923 in the predominantly black town of Rosewood in Levy County, after the alleged assault of Fannie Taylor, a young, married white woman. Local whites presumed that Taylor's unidentified assailant was black; however, Rosewood's black residents maintained that Taylor actually had been assaulted by her white lover and had claimed she was attacked by a black man to conceal the affair. In the massacre that followed, a mob of approximately two hundred to three hundred white people from surrounding areas murdered several Rosewood residents and burned the town to the ground.[12]

Although Marjorie Harris was the child of northerners, her upbringing in rural Lee County made her a witness to the type of discriminatory behavior that occurred throughout Florida. As mentioned previously, Bonita Springs was an entirely white community, and the town's schools, churches, and businesses were all run by whites for the benefit of white patrons. Whether Charles and Clara Harris were cognizant of this fact before they moved to the region is unclear. However, the primary reasons for the Harris family's move to Bonita Springs were to resume the farming life Charles had cherished in his youth and to raise their daughter in the natural surroundings of wild Florida.[13]

The Harris home was well stocked with field guides to the state's flora and fauna, in addition to the works of New England nature writers such as Henry David Thoreau and Ralph Waldo Emerson. Charles's New Hampshire–bred Puritan values molded Harris. These early years shaped her sense of stewardship of the earth, which she believed was a distinctively New England, Puritan trait. "My feeling is that a lot of the environmentalists here in Florida got their stewardship ethics from New England," Harris said in the last decade of her life. "An awful lot of people . . . that are interested in the environmental movement originally came from New England." Environmental historians such as William Cronon have chronicled the Puritans' manipulation of the land, which they viewed as property that belonged to colonists who "improved" it by exploiting its natural resources, even if the land had been hunted for generations by Native Americans. Nonetheless, Puritan teachings stressed the importance of civic service. Charles Harris instilled the ethic of Puritan stewardship in his daughter, who maintained a firm belief in the Democratic process throughout her life and translated this sense of stewardship into an environmental sensibility.[14]

In addition, Charles and Clara Harris were naturalists who taught their daughter how to study, describe, and classify thousands of plants, animals, minerals, and other natural objects. Charles's appreciation for the natural environment began in childhood, when he studied birds and insects. He and Clara collected insects early in their marriage, and they shared their fascination with the outdoors with their daughter. Considering that the naturalists of the eighteenth and nineteenth centuries laid the foundation for the specialist work of modern zoologists, botanists, biologists, and ecologists, it is fitting that Marjorie Harris's first scientific efforts were as a naturalist in Florida. She conducted informal field investigations with her parents and on her own throughout her childhood, preparing for her later career in the "masculine" field of zoology, which involves physical labor, often in subtropical and tropical heat and humidity. Moreover, the zoologists of the early to mid-twentieth century were comfortable killing animals for sport and specimen collecting. Yet the same zoologists who readily combined science with hunting would also be the first to call attention to the degradation of animal habitats as the twentieth century wore on.[15]

Just a few decades before the Harrises arrived in Bonita Springs, south Florida resembled the British North American colonies of the seventeenth and eighteenth centuries. However, as historian Jack E. Davis has observed, this changed in the late nineteenth century, when whites and Seminole Indians killed turtles, bears, wildcats, birds, alligators, deer, otters, and raccoons in south Florida for sale in national and international markets. Their activities took a toll on native wildlife populations, especially alligators and plume birds. Between 1880 and 1894, 2.5 million alligator hides were harvested in

Marjorie Harris (*center*) with a skinned alligator, Bonita Springs (1920s). Courtesy of Mimi Carr.

Florida, rivaling the destruction of bison in the Great Plains. Davis compared the butchery that took place in south Florida in the last quarter of the nineteenth century to the devastation that accompanied each consecutive translocation of the American frontier, from the British colonies along the eastern coast to the western territories to the Florida subtropics. "On each frontier," Davis recounted, "nature rendered the bounty."[16]

The Harris family viewed the effects of rampant, unregulated hunting close to their home near the banks of the Imperial River, where they canoed several times a week. Harris and her parents observed the tragic consequences of the plume trade, which nearly eradicated south Florida's egret and heron populations. "I saw very few herons or waterfowl" along the riverbanks, Harris later recounted. "People would come down and shoot anything that moved for sport." At the time, hunting was unregulated, and any new or existing prohibitions against hunting went unenforced. Passengers on steam ferries traveling along south Florida's rivers shot indiscriminately at wildlife. However, sport was not the only motivation for bird hunting. The egret and other native birds were prized for their plumage, which was used to decorate women's hats in the United States and Europe. The bird trade and the Florida land boom of the 1920s posed a substantial threat to Florida's avian population and wildlife habitats during Harris's youth. Witnessing the carnage firsthand contributed to the formation of Harris's environmental ethos in the years to come, reinforcing her belief that once wilderness was gone, it was gone forever.[17]

Florida's second great land boom, which lasted from 1920 through 1925, had originally been centered along Florida's eastern coast between Palm Beach and Miami, but it soon stretched westward. Developers sold tracts of swampland for exorbitant amounts of money until late 1925, when the national press reported on Florida's scandalous land sales practices and government promotion schemes. Then, on September 19, 1926, a devastating hurricane hit Florida. That same year, a wave of hundreds of bank failures across the United States ensured the end of the Florida land boom of the 1920s. The boom has been characterized as the most prolific example of speculation in new real estate—"both above water and below it," as a contemporary analyst remarked—since land speculators took advantage of settlers moving to the western United States in the late nineteenth century. Financing was no problem in the prosperous 1920s. Exaggerated newspaper and billboard advertisements touted Florida sunshine and the state's lack of income and inheritance taxes, enticing buyers from the cold North and Midwest to purchase small lots sight unseen. Images of Florida as both the final frontier and the fountain of youth tempted buyers to purchase waterfront property along freshly dredged canals and sand-filled mangrove swamps in south Florida. Although southwestern Florida was spared much of the overdevelopment of Miami, Fort Lauderdale, and Palm Beach during the great land boom, the effects of progress had begun to take a toll on Lee County as well. After the 1928 completion of an east-west route (the Tamiami Trail/U.S. 41), traffic from south Florida started to make its way to the Gulf coast, and greater numbers of tourists flocked to the west coast's shell-laden beaches. The 1920s ushered in a new wave of economic prosperity in St. Petersburg and Sarasota. However, the bank failures of 1925 and 1926 turned the newly created subdivisions across south and central Florida into ghost towns.[18]

Florida's second land boom took place before the advent of air-conditioning and mosquito control, and unlike the resort towns of St. Petersburg and Miami, Lee County remained relatively rustic. In 1916, construction was completed on a single-track, shelled road that stretched from Fort Myers south to Naples. The shell roads, which were constructed from rolled oyster shells dug from the extensive Indian mounds along the Gulf coast, fared better in Florida's strong rainstorms than the unsurfaced roads that were characteristic of many parts of the state. Harris recalled that the shell roads became gleaming white after it rained. Florida became a leader in building roads to accommodate automobiles, which by the 1920s brought more tourists to the state than did railroads. In the 1920s, heavy sand trails that were originally designed for horses and ox carts were more common than shelled roads. The sand trails were more difficult to travel on than the shelled roads, which were introduced later and were designed for automobile traffic. According to Harris, the oyster shell roads made excellent horse paths as well. Although few Bonita Springs residents rode for pleasure at the time, Harris delighted in standing out from the crowd. "This gave me a certain prestige with my school mates," she remembered. "Prestige that I needed since I was a Yankee, a girl and wore pants to school." In the 1920s, it was still the norm for middle-class girls and women to wear long skirts or dresses and keep their hair long. But this style of dress did not blend with Harris's outdoor lifestyle, and she kept her hair cropped short.[19]

Harris observed southwest Florida's animal and plant life on daily rides with Chiquita, traveling past palmettos and through cypress and pinewood forests. In time, she was able to classify thousands of species of flora and fauna. "We lived out in the woods," Harris recounted, "and I had parents who could answer your questions about what is that bird, or what is that snake. I grew up with a great appreciation of the natural environment." She also witnessed the steady depletion of southwest Florida's natural resources as controlled burns were conducted to clear space for cattle ranching and the production of sugar and winter vegetables. Commercial farmers had prized the rich muck of the Everglades since the nineteenth century. The U.S. government joined the State of Florida, local developers, and academic thinkers in heralding the exploitation of the Everglades as the best option for the future of the state, describing the marshlands as an "inhospitable and repulsive wilderness" that could be transformed into a "symbol for success in reclaiming waste places of the earth for man's welfare and comfort."[20]

Since the turn of the century, the U.S. Department of Agriculture's newly formed Bureau of Irrigation and Drainage Investigations advocated draining the Everglades to free up "millions of acres which have from time immemorial been regarded as irredeemable and a menace to the healthfulness of the State." In the 1920s, the erection of a levee around Lake Okeechobee and persistent dredging had manipulated the Everglades' natural floodplain significantly. By the 1940s, the same decade that Everglades National Park was established, Congress had been actively encouraging the development of commercial agriculture in the great wetland for a century. By the close of the twentieth century, the Everglades had been reduced to half its original size. The shrinking of the Everglades was palpable to Harris. Lee County's prairie and forest land bordered the Everglades, which developers were clearing for agriculture. After drainage and exposure to the air, the soil would sometimes catch on fire. "In the summers," Harris recalled, "the sky would glow with the Everglades burning."[21]

Charles and Clara Harris considered Floridians' tendency to clear land without reforesting to be both shortsighted and dangerous to the state's fragile ecosystems. "I was brought up with a family that said, 'Isn't it a shame they don't replant any of this?'" Marjorie Harris remembered. "When we would drive to Tampa or Tallahassee, the woods were not very pretty because they had been heavily timbered at that time, and there was no reforestation. There was no fence law, so there were cows. They burned a lot—indiscriminate burning—in order to get more [pasture]. And they had done turpentining, so . . . it looked pretty bad [from the road]." Harris's parents stimulated her intellect through direct observations of nature, field guides, and exposure to works of literature in which nature featured prominently. "I read everything I could find out about the wild things I saw around me," Harris recounted. "Thornton Burgess was one of my favorite authors, and I could recite [Rudyard] Kipling's Jungle Books."[22]

Harris witnessed the effects of commercial exploitation of forests for turpentine production and agriculture. The Lee County town of LaBelle was considered the center of the state's cattle-ranching industry at the time. Timber companies logged Florida's native cypress trees to the brink of complete eradication and exploited native pines for timber and turpentine. Journalist Allen H. Andrews, who wrote about Florida's native and experimental horticulture for the *American Eagle*, reported in 1950 that as a resident of southwest Florida for fifty years, he had seen the "wholesale destruction of Florida's natural resources of timber, game, and marine life" on a scale that was identical to that described by Harvard herpetologist Thomas Barbour in *That Vanishing Eden: A Naturalist's Florida*. Andrews predicted that Florida's flora and fauna would be lost if the state failed to enact aggressive conservation measures.[23]

Northern firms first attempted to drain the Everglades in the 1880s, altering the land for agricultural purposes. The rich, dark muck of the Everglades was ideal for production of winter vegetables and sugarcane. By the time the Harris family moved to southwest Florida, thousands of acres of the Everglades had been transformed into farmland. Meanwhile, developers transformed central Florida's pine forests into orange groves after a series of devastating freezes in north Florida. Witnessing this destruction at such a tender age shaped Harris's worldview, leading her to believe that wherever humans lived, they devastated the natural environment.[24]

In 1928, the Harris family left their small orange grove in Bonita Springs and moved to Fort Myers, where Marjorie Harris attended high school. Although Lee County was the largest county in Florida before it was divided in the early 1920s, remote areas such as Bonita Springs lacked both the financial resources and the population base to establish a solid school system. The Bonita Springs School stopped at the eighth grade. The move to Fort Myers necessitated a move for Chiquita as well. It would not have been practical to keep a horse in the (slightly) more urban setting of Fort Myers, so the Harris family found another home for Chiquita, marking the symbolic end to a bucolic childhood. Harris would always consider her time spent with Chiquita to be "one of my best childhood memories."[25]

In 1930, Harris's life changed instantly and dramatically when her father died from pneumonia. Marjorie Harris was only fifteen years old. Compounding the difficulty surrounding Charles Harris's premature death was the fact that he was just months shy of qualifying for a pension from his former Boston teaching career. A series of bank failures further diminished the family's savings. Left with no substantial means of support, Harris's mother first took a teaching position in a one-room schoolhouse in remote Sanibel Island and later taught in Bonita Springs and Fort Myers Beach. Losing her father at the onset of the Great Depression toughened Harris. According to her daughter, Mimi, Harris internalized her problems and never talked about the challenges she and her mother faced after her father's death. Harris refused to dwell upon the past. She downplayed her family's financial difficulties in her high school and college years, attributing them to the Great Depression. "Lots of folks had to scrabble," Harris explained. These early struggles helped Harris develop an uncanny ability to remain optimistic in the face of defeat and find creative ways to overcome seemingly insurmountable obstacles.[26]

Marjorie Harris, Fort Myers
High School senior picture
(1932). Courtesy of Mimi Carr.

Upon graduating from Fort Myers High School in 1932, Harris, who was still coping with the pain of her father's untimely death, was eager to continue her studies. "Mother wanted to go to college more than she wanted to live," Mimi recounted. Finding the financial resources needed to attend college was a major hurdle. "We didn't have any money," Harris recalled, "and a full year at the college cost about two hundred and fifty dollars, which was really beyond our means." An unexpected inheritance of five hundred dollars (considered a small fortune in the 1930s) from an aunt made it possible for her to matriculate at Florida State College for Women (FSCW) in 1932. Because of the family's financial hardship, it would have been difficult for Harris to finance an education at a private or public college outside of Florida.[27]

Indeed, money was not the only obstacle Harris faced. As a female, her choice of schools was limited. After the passage of the Buckman Act in 1905, Florida's public universities were segregated by gender and race. Just as southern bathrooms were labeled "men," "women," and "colored" through the 1960s, there were three state universities in 1932, when Carr started college: the University of Florida (UF) in Gainesville for white men; FSCW in Tallahassee, reserved for white women; and the coeducational Negro Normal and Industrial School, which would later become Florida Agricultural and Mechanical University (FAMU, or Florida A&M), also in Tallahassee. The Negro Normal and Industrial School, the state's only public university for African Americans,

was always coeducational. After the Buckman Act restructured Florida's public universities, women were prohibited from attending UF, which had previously been coeducational, except during summer school. However, single-sex
education offered distinct advantages for female faculty and students. Since
the 1870s, women's colleges presented women scientists with some opportunities for full-time employment as instructors in their respective fields, whereas
most coeducational institutions in the eastern United States would not hire
women as faculty members, especially in the hard sciences. Female students
benefited from a greater choice of majors than they would have been permitted at coeducational schools.[28]

Between 1900 and 1930, American men and women attended college in
roughly equal numbers at the undergraduate level. Because school teaching
was one of the most popular career choices available to women, however, the
majority of women in higher education were enrolled in normal schools or
other teacher-training programs. When Harris started college, approximately
5 percent of women enrolled in private colleges attended the Seven Sister
schools, and just over 20 percent of women undergraduates were enrolled in
women's colleges. The majority of female college students attended publicly
funded institutions of higher education, and many of these were two-year
teaching colleges. During the Depression, however, the previously feminized
profession of teaching established marriage bars, lowering the value of a
teaching degree for women. Hence, between 1929 and 1935, women's enrollment in teacher's colleges decreased, while men's enrollment increased. Although both of her parents and an aunt had worked as schoolteachers, Harris
elected to study science, a less popular major for female students in the 1930s.
Fortunately, Harris was able to attend a college that emphasized the liberal arts
tradition over vocational training.[29]

FSCW, which was founded in 1905, had a different curriculum from those
of the other southern state colleges for women that were established between
1885 and 1909 in Mississippi, North Carolina, South Carolina, Georgia, Alabama, and Texas, and an outlying state college for women in Oklahoma. Unlike its sister schools, FSCW was established as a liberal arts college. It was
the only southern state college for women that did not include technical and
industrial training among its original purposes. The college's mission was to
"teach the higher branches of education and the arts and sciences which were
taught in similar institutions and which the governing boards might think
necessary."[30]

The FSCW 1909–10 catalogue summarizes its purpose as follows: "The college is not a normal and industrial school, but primarily a college of Liberal Arts. With this is associated a normal school and schools of Art, Music, and Expression. The College of Liberal Arts includes courses in Home Economics, which count for a regular degree." The field of home economics, which was pioneered by Ellen Swallow Richards (who also introduced the term "ecology" to the United States in 1892), opened new opportunities for women in science while simultaneously prohibiting them from making inroads into mainstream science. In the early twentieth century, women scientists were increasingly restricted to a narrow range of feminized scientific fields. Colleges and universities that had previously been reluctant to hire women as full professors welcomed women scientists into the new field of home economics (also known as domestic science or euthenics). In 1911, Cornell University's official policy was to appoint women to professorships solely in the field of home economics, and not in other academic departments. The university would not appoint a woman to an assistant professorship in the College of Liberal Arts and Sciences until 1947, and women were barred from full professorships in the college until 1960. By the 1920s, FSCW offered training in teaching, secretarial work, accounting, music, dietetics (a subfield of home economics), nursing, premedicine, and predentistry. Education was by far the most popular major at the college; women also graduated with degrees in chemistry, mathematics, physics, commerce, liberal arts, English, journalism, history, art, music, foreign languages, sociology, and home economics. By the 1930s, FSCW had become the third-largest women's college in the nation.[31]

During Harris's college years, American women were still struggling to free themselves from the constraints of nineteenth-century cultural norms. Professional women were forced to contend with the remnants of a pervasive domestic ideology that held that a woman's profession should never come before marriage and family life. As an undergraduate student, Harris crafted a unique solution to the problem of whether to pursue a traditionally "feminine" path of study such as school teaching, nursing, or the "feminized" science of home economics, or to follow her dream of entering the "masculine" field of zoology. She chose to double-major in zoology and secretarial science. Her original plan was to train in both fields and seek employment as a secretary at a university zoology department. Harris hoped that one day, when a (male) zoologist became injured in the field, the department would replace him with her, since she would be the only person in the office capable of completing his work. Harris's dream of entering professional zoology through the back door ended when a dean advised her that it was not practical to major in zoology and secretarial science because they both had extensive lab requirements. Soon afterward she dropped the secretarial major and completed a rigorous course of study in the natural sciences, concentrating in zoology, botany, biology, bacteriology, and ornithology.[32]

Although FSCW offered a traditional liberal arts curriculum, the college had no organized graduate school. Advanced degrees for women were not included in the college's mission; consequently, the college offered no courses leading to doctoral degrees. Just as the Florida Legislature had purposefully separated the instruction of white male and female undergraduate students (in addition, the Florida constitution barred the teaching of blacks and whites together), the purpose of women's education at FSCW was designated along gendered lines: "(1) Preparation for home duties; (2) cultivation of formal gentility and grace for their social value through a variety of accomplishments; (3) discipline of the 'mental powers' so that women might be ready for any emergency in life; and (4) more specific preparation for a variety of professional opportunities. Concurrent with all except the last there has been (5) a constant emphasis on religious and Christian purpose."[33]

FSCW's official purpose might have appeared to conflict with the school's practice of offering its all-female student body the opportunity to pursue nontraditional majors. Although the school's education and home economics courses accounted for a significant portion of the total of classes offered, the college also taught many of the same courses offered at its all-male counterpart, UF. Among these were courses in the hard sciences and mathematics. One of Harris's major professors, Herman Kurz, represented the new direction women's colleges had taken in the first decades of the twentieth century. Eschewing the former practice of hiring women professors who published less but were also paid substantially lower salaries than male professors, the women's colleges of the early twentieth century had started to hire more male instructors, whose research and publications could raise the schools' stature. Kurz, a professor of botany and bacteriology with a doctorate from the University of Chicago, published regularly in scientific journals including *Ecology*, the *Science News-Letter*, *Botanical Gazette*, and the *American Naturalist*. In Kurz's field courses, Harris and her classmates learned the fundamentals of ecology, focusing on the relationships of different organisms and their habitats within an ecosystem. In keeping with her naturalist background, Harris made the unconventional decision to major in zoology early in her college career. "It was not a course that many women chose in those days," she admitted, "but I had always been going in that direction."[34]

Harris blossomed in her first year at FSCW. She served as the circulation manager and a writer for the *Distaff, Spinner of Yarns*, the college's quarterly literary magazine, whose main theme was life in Florida. Harris was also a member of the astronomy club. She lived on campus in a residence hall that was supervised by two elderly matrons who monitored students' behavior and enforced a curfew. FSCW was home to eighteen different sororities, but Harris did not join one. The college's 1934 annual featured a sororities section with an illustration of life under Confederate rule in Florida, featuring a plantation house, southern belles, and a prominent Confederate flag. Florida was the third state to secede from the Union during the Civil War, and its publicly funded colleges and universities played "Dixie" at sporting events well into the 1960s, provoking emotional responses among the fans in attendance; students at UF football games sometimes held up oversized, colored cards that formed a giant Confederate flag in the stands while the Fighting Gator marching band played the song. Moreover, students dressed up as Klan members at UF's homecoming parade and Gator Growl pep rally through the 1960s, as depicted in photographs from the UF annual, the *Seminole*. At FSCW, campus life also included athletics. However, instead of competing against rival colleges, FSCW divided its students into two teams: the Evens and Odds. The teams had their own team colors, sporting events, and fans.[35]

Harris was in her element during her first year at FSCW, but she did not know how she would be able to finance another three years of college away from home. Her small inheritance had run out, and Clara Harris was unable to contribute to her daughter's college expenses with her modest teacher's salary. "Then after my freshman year I found out about the National Youth Administration," Harris recounted. "In return for working all summer, N.Y.A. would pay your tuition, room, and board all year, plus fifty dollars in cash for yourself. This was a big break." In 1933, during her first summer with the NYA, Harris performed clerical work at a day-care center near Fort Myers. (Most female NYA participants were restricted to clerical positions.) Hoping to avoid office work the following summer, Harris proposed an experimental naturalist education program that she would offer to preteens and teenagers in Lee County. Drawing upon her knowledge of the county's flora and fauna, she taught the children how to collect specimens and appreciate the region's interconnected habitats. The NYA sponsored Harris's program for two consecutive summers. "I drove around in my mother's old Ford," she remembered. "I could live at home, and it worked beautifully. It was then that I became convinced that people will care for their environment if only they can learn a little bit about it." Harris later explained that these summer programs taught her that anyone could become an environmentalist once they were presented with the "facts." "There is a potential for the public to be very good environmentalists," she maintained, "if we would just give them the information."[36]

At FSCW, Harris refined her understanding of the natural world. In addition to working with botanist Herman Kurz, she studied under zoologist and ornithologist Ezda Mae Deviney, Herbert Stoddard, and other early ecologists. It should be noted that the ecologists of the early twentieth century differed from those of the late twentieth century in their motivation. Although both groups studied the relationships between flora and fauna and their habitats, early ecologists were not averse to applying their studies to the more efficient manipulation and exploitation of the earth, whereas modern ecologists are more likely to use their research to fight the earth's exploitation.[37]

The science of ecology originated in the 1890s, but it did not come to the attention of the general public in America until the 1960s, following the publication of Rachel Carson's best-selling polemic *Silent Spring*, which alerted readers to the dangers of indiscriminate pesticide use. Ecology has traditionally involved the study of interactions between organisms and their environment, but the term "ecology" has come to be associated with concern for the environment. Although the science of ecology has remained constant through the years, the application of this science has changed dramatically. Whereas earlier ecological studies tended to focus primarily on individual species, by the 1950s biologists had started to place more emphasis on the fuller set of interactions between flora, fauna, and habitat within an ecosystem. The acceptance of ecology into the academy in the mid-twentieth century was accompanied by the rise of the activist scientist, who applied his or her ecological expertise to environmental problems caused by human manipulation and exploitation of the earth.[38]

Harris's courses at FSCW were comparable with the science offerings available at UF. In fact, in 1935, FSCW trumped UF by gaining the distinction of becoming the first Florida college or university to receive a Phi Beta Kappa charter. The national academic honor society granted the women's college this honor for its scholastic strength in the liberal arts tradition. Harris's favorite

Marjorie Harris in Florida State College for Women graduation regalia (1936). She was a member of the Phi Beta Kappa and Sigma Xi honor societies. Courtesy of Mimi Carr.

courses were the ones that involved outdoor field trips. "I wanted to work with whole, live animals, preferably birds," she explained, "in their natural surroundings." Harris's professors were among the first to study Florida's forest ecosystems, including the relationship of controlled burns to forest health, which was still an understudied area at the time. Harris assisted Deviney, her major professor, in the zoology lab, and Kurz's botany courses cemented her ability to "read a landscape," she later reflected. She embraced the women's-college experience and excelled in her studies.[39]

In 1936, Harris graduated from FSCW with a bachelor's degree in zoology. Her major professors supported her decision to apply to graduate programs in zoology or ornithology, her chosen field. However, because the majority of eastern universities and private institutions would not admit women to graduate programs in the sciences, Harris was unable to enter graduate school immediately following the completion of her undergraduate studies. This offers a personal example of the dialectic of opportunity and constraint women experienced in the 1930s and 1940s. Harris had received a first-class science education at FSCW. She was inducted into Phi Beta Kappa, the nation's oldest academic honor society, and Sigma Xi, the nation's top honor society for research scientists and engineers. Sigma Xi elects its members based upon their research potential or achievements. The society publishes the award-winning bimonthly magazine *American Scientist*. In 1936, Harris was appointed as a charter member of the Florida Academy of Sciences, the state affiliate of the American Association for the Advancement of Science. The Florida Academy of Sciences publishes *Florida Scientist: Quarterly Journal of the Florida Academy of Sciences*, which Harris contributed to later in her career. Despite these academic accomplishments, Cornell turned down her application for admission to graduate school, and the University of North Carolina at Chapel Hill withdrew an initial offer for funding for graduate studies. At the time of Harris's graduation, the nation's top graduate schools closed their doors to most women scientists. Many schools continued to fight coeducation at the graduate level, especially in the hard sciences. At Cornell, for instance, which had been coeducational since 1872, faculty members remained skeptical about women's capacity for abstract thought.[40]

Those women who succeeded in attaining advanced degrees in science had a hard time finding employment after graduation. Women scientists' education and experience bore little weight in determining their rank or status at coeducational institutions; a man with a master's degree in chemistry automatically outranked a woman with a doctorate. At best, women Ph.D.s were hired as lecturers at coeducational institutions; more commonly, women with doctorates were ranked as "assistants." These hiring and promotion discrepancies stemmed from male scientists' resistance to the increasing tide of female college graduates, who were shunned from graduate school and barred from prestigious "masculine" positions. Aspiring undergraduate women who expressed an interest in science were encouraged to eschew the more "masculine" fields such as physics, chemistry, and zoology, and were funneled into the "feminine" field of home economics. In the 1920s and 1930s, this was the only academic field in which women could be promoted to full professor, department chair, or dean.[41]

Harris's struggle to finish her science education and embark upon what would become a short-lived professional career in zoology mirrored a similar battle among millions of professional women in the United States who had lost ground in their fight to maintain and advance gains for women in education and employment in the 1930s. Polls indicated that educated women preferred marriage to careers in the 1920s, and the Great Depression threatened to eliminate the small gains professional women had made in the previous decade. Moreover, women's membership in professional organizations dropped in the 1930s, as public support for women's careers dwindled.[42]

In 1936, Harris's opportunities for full-time employment in the sciences were limited. Most of the available positions for women combined low-level laboratory work with clerical duties. In this sense, the dialectic of opportunity and constraint was palpable to Harris, who had accomplished the impressive feat of graduating with a science degree and being admitted to the nation's most selective honor societies but was rejected from pursuing an advanced degree in her field. Her experience was shared by the majority of women scientists of her time, who were also unable to find appropriate employment in their field.[43]

Gender was the deciding factor in Cornell University's rejection of Harris's application to its graduate program in science. Arthur Allen, the director of the ornithology laboratory, informed her that there was no place for women in the field. The University of North Carolina at Chapel Hill was slow to respond to Harris's application for admission and financial assistance, but, late in the summer of 1936, Harris was offered a graduate assistantship. Deviney advised Harris to brush up on her typing, learn German, and be a model assistant to ensure that other FSCW graduates would have similar opportunities in the future. "You must remember, constantly, that what you do for the first year there, the first quarter in fact, will determine whether we ever get another assistantship given to one of our graduates," Deviney cautioned. "I believe you are the very first graduate of F.S.C.W. who has ever held a graduate assistantship at U.N.C."[44]

Harris was expected to oversee the zoology department library and provide secretarial assistance to H. V. Wilson, the chair of the zoology department, and William Chambers Coker, the first chair of the botany department. However, the UNC assistantship fell through at the last minute. As mentioned previously, large public universities and prestigious private institutions fought coeducation at the graduate level. Hoping to pursue a professional career in science and earn enough money to enter graduate school in the near future, Harris began searching for nearby positions in government work. This led to a short-lived position as the nation's first female federal wildlife technician with the Resettlement Administration in Welaka, Florida, where she first encountered the Ocklawaha River.[45]

The next chapter chronicles the challenges Marjorie Harris faced in government work and private industry. Her supervisor at the Resettlement Administration was as reluctant to work with a woman scientist as Arthur Allen had been at Cornell University. In her next professional position at the Bass Lab in Englewood, Florida, Harris would fight to remain engaged in scientific pursuits instead of performing the secretarial duties her employer often requested of her. Harris's biggest challenge would be to find a way to combine work and marriage. She and her future husband, Archie Fairly Carr Jr., would enter into a passionate yet tumultuous relationship that posed personal and institutional challenges to the continuation of Harris's career in zoology.

2

Blending Science and Marriage in the New Deal Era

Gender discrimination prevented Marjorie Harris from proceeding directly to graduate work in zoology after she completed her bachelor's in science at Florida State College for Women (FSCW). Soon after graduation, however, the Resettlement Administration hired her as the first female federal wildlife technician. Harris was assigned to the Welaka Fish Hatchery, located near the St. Johns River in north central Florida. This position served three key purposes in her professional and personal life. First, Harris's work at the fish hatchery inspired her later research on the large-mouthed black bass of Florida, which would become the subject of her master's thesis. Second, this position introduced Harris to the Ocklawaha River, whose preservation and restoration would later command thirty-five years of her attention. Third, Harris's work at the fish hatchery prompted her to conduct research at the University of Florida in Gainesville, where she met Archie Carr, who was completing his doctoral dissertation in herpetology. Their meeting prefaced the establishment of a personal and professional partnership that would benefit both scientists in their future scholarly and conservation activities. As the young couple began their partnership, however, Harris would face a series of challenges to her ability to combine marriage with a scientific career.

The Welaka Fish Hatchery was part of America's national fish-hatchery system, which was founded in the late nineteenth century. (Welaka, which means "chain of lakes," was the Timucua name for the St. Johns River.) Today, the national hatcheries, which were originally charged with replenishing fish supplies for recreational purposes, culture more than one hundred aquatic species to replace fish lost through natural disasters, pollution, habitat loss, dam construction, and other events that interfere with the natural life cycles of native fishes. Established in 1926, the Welaka National Fish Hatchery was incorporated into the U.S. Fish and Wildlife Service in 1938. The only national fish hatchery in Florida, the Welaka Fish Hatchery is a warm-water hatchery whose purpose is to raise fish native to the Southeast and release them into rivers, streams, and lakes. The hatchery is located by the St. Johns River, which has been described as the "bass capital of the world." Harris's studies of the fish of the St. Johns would later lead to her selection of bass as the subject of her graduate thesis at the University of Florida (UF), "The Breeding Habits, Embryology and Larval Development of the Large-Mouthed Black Bass of Florida." As a wildlife technician, her duties at the Welaka Fish Hatchery included a mixture of biological research, field research and collecting, and aquarium management.[1]

As the nation's first female federal wildlife technician, Harris benefited from the expanding professional opportunities the New Deal made available to women. The New Deal in particular and Depression conditions in general contributed to the feminization of clerical work. This process benefited employers, who compensated female employees at a lower rate than what they had previously paid male employees who performed the same tasks. The New Deal also played a major role in increasing women's presence in public life in the 1930s.[2]

After American women gained the suffrage, the 1920s witnessed a sharp backlash against women's concerns. Yet the election of Franklin Delano Roosevelt, the hardships brought on by the Depression, and the implementation of the New Deal programs redefined relationships among the federal government, society, and the individual. This resulted in an overall improvement in women's status that would not be matched until the 1960s.[3]

Despite the lack of an organized women's movement, the 1930s ushered in a new era of opportunity for women—especially college-educated women—in public life. Nonetheless, the American public was slow to accept women's entry into public life. Four-fifths of Americans surveyed in a 1936 Gallup poll expressed the opinion that married women should not work if their husbands were employed. The federal government's official policy reflected this public sentiment: Between 1932 and 1937, 1,600 married women whose husbands also worked for the government were dismissed from government service. Still, women benefited from the social and economic restructuring that accompanied the New Deal.[4]

Between 1923 and 1939, the total percentage of women employed by the federal government increased from 15.8 to 18.8, representing an increase of ninety thousand government positions for women. In academic and professional science, women were perceived to be a threat. Since the dawn of the industrial age, women's labor had been compensated at a lower rate than men's, and women had been relegated to sex-typed jobs. As women's presence in science increased, these practices were extended to that field as well. Cultural beliefs about gender difference persisted in the 1930s, when women accounted for approximately 50 percent of the work force.[5]

One unresolved issue at the time concerned the future of the nation's college-educated women. Although some would pursue graduate educations or professional careers in the early twentieth century, most college-educated women who worked after graduation entered the female-dominated (and socially acceptable) positions of schoolteacher, nurse, librarian, social worker, or clerical worker. Yet the Depression era represented a time of social and economic reform, followed by a period of global war. Historically, American women's employment has experienced dramatic upswings during periods of great expansion and national emergencies, leading to important (temporary) progress.[6]

The Resettlement Administration's decision to appoint a woman to the biologist position at the Welaka Fish Hatchery was indicative of this overall shift in women's favor. However, not all government bureaucrats supported the extension of traditionally male-dominated positions to women. After spending four years at an all-female institution, Harris enjoyed the camaraderie of her male colleagues at the Welaka Fish Hatchery; nonetheless, as the only female biologist at the hatchery, Harris encountered some resistance. "The program's director was very uncomfortable with a woman biologist," she recounted. "He didn't know what to do with me." Zoology was an unusual career choice for a woman to make in the 1930s. It involved getting dirty in the field: collecting and preserving insects, spiders, reptiles, fishes, mollusks, birds, and other assorted creatures; hunting for specimens by hand or by rifle; and engaging in a host of activities women traditionally shunned. To Harris, however, exploring rural Florida on rugged collecting trips was second nature.[7]

In addition to working with fish, Harris, who had specialized in ornithology at FSCW, assumed research responsibilities in the aviary housed at the Welaka Fish Hatchery. World War I veterans constructed the aviary during the hatchery's expansion under the New Deal. In the fall of 1936, Harris's colleagues were unable to identify the source of an illness that afflicted the hatchery's quail population. The hatchery's laboratory lacked the equipment required to diagnose the disease, but Harris suspected that it was a condition that also affected chickens. "I had minored in bacteriology," she explained, "so I took the quail over to a laboratory at the University of Florida." Because Harris's supervisor refused to allow her to test her hypothesis during working hours, she made several trips to UF after work, conducted her research at the university's laboratory at night, and drove back to Welaka in time to start work the following morning.[8]

Harris spent several late nights toiling over a microscope in a UF laboratory near the zoology department. The young male scientists at UF were awestruck by the presence of the twenty-one-year-old female scientist who had descended upon the science building in high heels and a lab coat, toting a box of sick quail. One graduate student called Harris the most beautiful woman he had ever met. Another graduate student, Horton Hobbs, reported to his friend Archie Carr that he had just met the love of his life. Archie was intrigued. He made himself presentable, headed to campus to work on his dissertation on the geographic and ecological distribution of the reptiles and amphibians of Florida, and promptly introduced himself to Marjorie Harris. The chemistry between them was instantaneous. It was love at first sight, and alas, there was no hope for poor Horton Hobbs.[9]

Marjorie Harris helped finance their courtship by convincing her supervisor at the fish hatchery to purchase a collection of local fish specimens from Archie, who reciprocated by nominating her for full membership in the Florida Academy of Sciences. Harris was already a charter member of the Academy, but because she was female, her current membership was only at the associate level. (As science underwent the process of professionalization in the early twentieth century, it was customary for women to be excluded from full participation in professional organizations such as scientific academies.) Archie's two-hour drive from Gainesville to Welaka was also assisted by his brother, Tom, who loaned him a truck he had inherited from an aunt. Archie's brother was impressed with Harris's "business-like" demeanor when he first met her, in addition to the fact that she wore boots.[10]

Archie teased Harris for taking a position sponsored by the New Deal. "I love to look at you even if you are a resettlement woman," he wrote in December 1936. "You talk so cute too." Archie, a southerner, was amused by Harris's New England accent. Although the pair had just met in October, Archie already signed his letters with love. Yet Archie's next letter, which he wanted to be a "cheerful, happy first love letter," was instead filled with doubts. Harris had just lost her position at the Welaka Fish Hatchery. She was fired after she challenged a colleague who took credit for her discovery of the cause of the quail illness, which she had investigated independently at the UF laboratory. A frantic search for a new position ensued, driving Archie closer to his love interest while simultaneously leaving him feeling inadequate as a potential provider for Harris. This crisis caused the young couple to make a rushed decision about the future of their relationship.[11]

Archie had already proposed to Harris, but marriage was a risky venture during the Great Depression. Archie feared that she would only agree to marry him because of the turmoil stemming from her dismissal from the fish hatchery. Moreover, he was unable to support her financially, so they would have to live separately while he finished his dissertation. This scenario would only be feasible if Harris could find work as a biologist, and even then, the newlyweds would have to endure more than a half year of separation. Archie advised Harris to heed her mother's advice on the matter and think with her mind, not her heart. Archie, a struggling graduate student, claimed that his love was selfish because he had little to offer her, while what she offered him was priceless. "I have so much to gain," Archie warned Harris. "You are everything I need and want. You will make my life far more important and satisfying than it could be without you. Can I do these things for you? Listen to your mother and stop feeling and think. This is a warning, my dearest, because I'm going to marry you the minute you weaken. I'm going to be a louse and take a wife I can't support, and let her live away from me and work, and ignore the risk of losing her respect—the minute you weaken. You are magnificent. I profit so greatly. I don't want to clip your wings. Think hard."[12]

Although his intentions were serious, Archie did not want to curtail Harris's professional ambitions. He was aware of the implications of their potential marriage for her career in science. This explains why his letter contained both a marriage proposal and a plea to be reasonable and end their affair. He confided that writing a three-ream dissertation left him sleep-deprived and admitted that his letters might be "screwy." The following day, Archie sent Harris a hand-delivered letter that revealed the depths of his insecurity. "Your earthly loveliness is as stable and indomitable as a rainforest," he professed. "I'm too skinny and probably will be bald in a couple of years. My right arm is pretty well wrecked. I have to do almost as much physical work as mental to feel right. I should have been a farmer or a mackerel fisherman, and I'm trying to be a scholar."[13]

Archie's father, Archibald Fairly Carr Sr., was a Presbyterian minister who had relocated the family from Fort Worth, Texas, to Savannah, Georgia, in 1920. While attending college there, Archie developed osteomyelitis in his arm. Although penicillin would have cured the disease quickly, it was not available at the time. As a result, Archie underwent six major operations on his right arm. The surgeries resulted in an immobilized elbow and enormous scars that Archie usually kept covered. "It was a big blow to Archie emotionally," his brother Tom explained, adding that Archie had to decide whether he wanted his arm to be permanently frozen in a straight or bent position. He decided that the bent position would be more functional, so his doctors ensured that his right arm remained in that position for the rest of his life.[14]

Archie spent a year in a cast and weighed a slight 109 pounds upon leaving the hospital in Atlanta. His father promptly found work for him as a manager of a terrapin farm in Tidewater, Georgia. The physically demanding job was therapeutic; every day, Archie caught one hundred pounds of fish to feed the turtles. This early experience with turtles stimulated Archie's interest in the species at a time when very little was known about them. In 1930, the Carr family moved to Umatilla, Florida, where Archie's father planned to enjoy semi-retirement. Archie enrolled at UF, and his father worked part-time as a minister at a small church in Umatilla. He hoped to use the profits from a small orange grove on their property to supplement his modest income from the church. According to Tom Carr, hunting and fishing were his father's true passions. The Carr family's hunting cabin in the Ocala National Forest still stands. In 2007, Tom donated the rustic cabin to the U.S. Forest Service, and its restoration was completed in 2012. As children, Archie and Tom learned about the outdoors and science from their father, who shared the work of Einstein and other scientists with his congregation and enjoyed quoting cosmology in his sermons. Both of the Carr brothers went on to complete doctorates in science.[15]

Archie felt inadequate as a suitor. In particular, he was sensitive about his disabled right arm. He speculated that Harris would meet many men through her work in zoology, men who would value what he described as her great friendliness, beauty, and unique relation to men, "a Whitmanesque camara-derie that is a delight to behold." Archie was nearly six years her senior. He cautioned Harris against settling for him and advised her that she would be better off marrying a more suitable companion. Archie admitted that he had an inferiority complex but claimed that in this case, it was justifiable. "In brief I don't think I'm good enough to hold you," Archie confessed. "You're my destiny but yours is elsewhere. I love you. Goodbye."[16]

Shortly after the letter was delivered to Harris, Archie reversed his position dramatically and ordered her to "burn that damned letter." He wrote that his love for her was more powerful than he ever imagined human emotion could be. He pleaded with her to marry him any way she wished: "Secretly or at your Uncle Adolph's. Down at the fish house. In St. Francis' Cathedral. With you I'll submit to the rites of the Buddhists, the Baptists or the Mormons. I'll take the weird vows of Mb'u'q at the headwaters of the Khablh. Or I'll bring you home and let my dad do it. He's good. Please marry me, Margie. I adore you. If we wait something will happen." Archie was convinced that Harris would meet another man while he finished his doctorate in Gainesville and she worked in another city. He believed the only way he could hold onto her love was to marry her immediately. "Let's take a chance," he begged her. "Let's make everybody miserable. If we don't, and quick, we face a good chance of going through life without each other. That, to me, is the most repulsive and revolting thought that I can summon to consciousness. . . . I'd just as soon die now if I could be resurrected when you decide to marry me."[17]

Harris read Archie's passionate letters over and over. She had fallen hard for the fledgling herpetologist. Archie was not Harris's first lover, but his passion was overwhelming, and they were kindred spirits. She wasted no time accepting his proposal. Just seven months shy of completing his doc-torate, Archie contemplated abandoning his degree in order to find a job that would pay enough for the young couple to live together. He claimed he would leave the university without a single regret if she wanted him to, but if not, she would need to find other employment as soon as possible. Shortly after being fired from the Welaka Fish Hatchery, Harris applied for a posi-tion as a biology technician at the Bass Biological Laboratory and Zoologi-cal Research Supply Company in Englewood, Florida. The Bass Lab, which was the first full-time marine station open year-round on the Florida main-land, was located on Lemon Bay on the Gulf of Mexico, south of Venice and northwest of Fort Myers. Archie had made several research trips there, and he had been friends with the owner, John Foster "Jack" Bass Jr., for several years.[18]

Although Archie encouraged Harris to seek work there, he was initially reluctant to speak on her behalf. If he told the Basses they were engaged, she would not be offered a permanent position, since it was still customary for female scientists to resign their positions upon marriage. Nonetheless, he wrote lab manager Stewart Springer to recommend Harris for the technician position. While they were waiting for a response, Archie asked Harris if she would consider working as a secretary in Gainesville if she was unable to secure a position at the Bass Lab. There were very few opportunities for employment in the biological sciences in Gainesville—especially for women. The university's zoology department had no openings, and the best nonfaculty positions (held by Archie and a fellow graduate student) paid just $43.50 per month. After expenses, this left Archie with only $3.50 to live on each month. He held out hope for the summer, when they might find research fellowships together in Virginia. He was already thinking in terms of the scientific partnership they would develop.[19]

For the time being, Archie was powerless to bring about a positive resolution to their financial dilemma. Instead of dwelling on their looming separation, however, he focused on his overwhelming love for Harris. Archie, whose undergraduate training was in English, penned love lines with the flair of a poet. "My love for you is all-pervading," he gushed. "It's as fundamental to my life as metabolism. It is my life. When I lie awake at night and listen to my heart it beats, 'Margie . . . Margie,' so loud in the dark I think everybody must hear. I think you must hear . . . Oh my darling, we must be going to be awful happy—I love you forever." For the next several days, Archie's love for Harris eclipsed his anxiety over their immediate future. "My love for you is my life these days," he opined. "You are my ultimate choice—the end of my existence. I worship you." And on Christmas Day he put pen to paper as only a smitten herpetologist could: "If I stepped on a dozen rattlesnakes a day I'd step off the last two or three casually—with ennui and a jaundiced eye. I don't know whether I think of you a hundred or a thousand times a day. But I do know, my darling, that the thought of you never ceases to thrill me."[20]

Archie, who later became famous for his creative prose, was a prolific writer who refused to adopt the dry scientific writing style typical of his profession. Archie compared Harris to the beauty of the cosmos. "Sometimes to me you are something tiny and infinitely precious which I must watch over tenderly and keep very close to me forever," he promised. "Sometimes the beauty of you expands and mounts to Andromeda and beyond, and I look up and gasp at the cosmic splendor of it and whimper, and beg you to come back to me. Sometimes you are just the loveliest woman I have ever known. Always I love you . . . I adore you—now and the day I die. . . . When the electrons of the last atoms that have been me fly out of their orbits it will be in quest of you."[21]

Marjorie and Archie's feelings for each other grew stronger, intensified by the reality of their impending separation. Shortly after Archie wrote Stewart Springer to recommend Harris for the opening at the Bass Lab, he received a reply directly from Jack Bass. He and Springer remembered meeting Harris during the last meeting of the Florida Academy of Sciences. Bass asked Archie to encourage Harris to visit Englewood at company expense to discuss the biology technician position further. He informed Archie that the starting salary would range between thirty and fifty dollars per month with all living expenses included. Harris quickly made arrangements to travel to the Bass Lab, and Bass requested that she start work immediately. Afraid that he would lose Harris forever if he did not act quickly, Archie convinced her to elope with him before she moved to south Florida for work. So on New Year's night at 10:00 p.m., Marjorie and Archie told Clara Harris that they were going down to the beach to watch the moonrise. Instead, they drove to the Everglades and woke up Judge Platt, whom they drove to the courthouse to marry them. Archie described the elopement in a letter to his mother.[22]

We had been very gay and casual going down with the moon over the glades and the warm wind blowing. When Judge Platt finished his 90 second ceremony we suddenly became serious, dizzy, and very happy. We rode back slowly without meeting a car. The moon was just a little higher and the warm wind still made the sawgrass sing. A flight of black-crowned night herons lined the middle of the trail from Everglades to Naples. It was a fantastic and ethereal wedding night. When we got home at 2:30 Mrs. Harris woke up and delivered an ominous lecture on the perils of staying out late when in love. Margie contritely went to bed with her mama.

The next morning we tarred the roof and left. That night we stopped at a tourist camp outside of Bradenton. The landlady looked highly skeptical when we registered. We felt the same way. . . . You may have gathered that this is a secret marriage. Either don't tell Daddy or make a liar out of him.[23]

After spending their first night as a married couple in separate beds at Marjorie's mother's house, the Carrs honeymooned for two nights at tourist camps in Bradenton and Gainesville before Marjorie boarded a bus to Englewood to start her new job. Although none of their friends or family had witnessed the ceremony and they were soon separated by hundreds of miles, Marjorie and Archie felt like they were walking on air. "My Archie I am so very glad we were married January 1," Marjorie Harris Carr reflected several months later. "That is ours with all its enchantment, Night Herons, mystery and Saw Grass marshes. It was so beautiful."[24]

Blinded by love, the newlyweds were completely unprepared for the pain their separation would cause them. Moreover, Marjorie Carr's decision to marry Archie would have important short-term and long-term consequences for her professional career. Marriage practically constituted professional suicide for women scientists in the 1930s, when almost three-quarters of female scientists were single and nearly two-thirds of all unemployed female scientists were married. Federal policy undermined married women's tenure in the workforce through section 213 of the Economy Act of 1932, which made spouses (customarily wives) the primary targets of workforce reductions. In addition, universities strengthened their antinepotism rules during the Depression, making it even more difficult for married female scientists to advance professionally.[25]

For these reasons, the Carrs decided to postpone sharing the news of their nuptials with colleagues, friends, or coworkers for as long as possible. To conceal the fact that Archie had just married the young woman he had recently recommended for employment at the Bass Lab, he addressed his letters to his new bride to "Miss Margie Harris." Archie's first letter contained news that the Carrs' elopement had wreaked havoc in the UF zoology department. Archie joked that talk of elopement, rape, and suicide pacts had reached J. Speed Rogers, the department chair and Archie's supervisor, whom Archie reported was in "a hell of a lather." Archie attempted to play down the rumors in the department, but he had little to lose should the truth be revealed, since female spouses were almost always the ones to lose their jobs in such situations.[26]

Meanwhile, at the Bass Lab in faraway Englewood, Carr was in an "utter daze" over becoming Archie's wife. She told Archie she enjoyed her new position there, "but I couldn't have stood it if we hadn't gotten married." Although she handled the separation better than her husband, it was still palpable. "What a heaven we have together," she wrote, "and what utter agony apart.

Neither of us can stand that horror of separation again. What had we better do? See each other more often or farther apart?"[27]

The physical demands of Carr's work at the Bass Lab took her mind off of their separation much of the time. It was not uncommon to preserve hundreds or thousands of the same species throughout the day. "Formaldehyde is not a good skin lotion," she quipped. The work was more than mechanical, however. She also had discretion to choose which animals to collect and preserve, and she sought more sales opportunities, where she could market Bass specimens to universities and museums.[28]

Carr stayed busy at the Bass Lab, where she learned how to pilot several types of boats for use in collecting sharks, dogfish, jellyfish, snakes, eels, turtles, seahorses, and other water creatures. She took special pleasure in classifying rare and possibly new species. After just a few weeks on the job, Carr felt confident enough to try her hand at catching alligators. The next day, she and her Bass colleagues embarked upon a cruise on the *Virginia*, the research boat the Carr brothers had helped Bass sail to Englewood. Carr's excitement over her new job prompted Archie to ask her not to stay away from him for such a long time ever again. He did not want her to become too comfortable with long periods of separation from her husband. On an early expedition at the Bass Lab, Carr collected fifty live cockroach specimens by hand. She expressed the unease she felt watching insects molt, combining scientific observations and illustrations with pledges of devotion. "Oh, how every part of me wants you tonight," she wrote Archie, "for I am your wife." At this point, none of Carr's relatives, friends, or colleagues was aware that she was a married woman. She could only share her excitement about her secret nuptials in her letters to Archie.[29]

Back in Gainesville, however, the Carrs' elopement was the talk of the zoology department. In his next letter to Carr, Archie confessed that he had told Rogers about their wedding. He thought it was necessary to tell Rogers because he had control of Archie's future in the department. Pending the state legislature's approval of the university's budget, Rogers had offered him a full-time instructorship in the department. Archie informed Carr that Rogers's wife was already gossiping about their elopement, and concealing it from Rogers would have been imprudent. Fortunately, Rogers told Archie he was glad that he and Carr were married. Moreover, Rogers offered to help Carr get a job in the department. Due to budgetary constraints, however, the best

Wildlife photographer Luther Goldman and Marjorie Harris Carr with snakes at the Bass Zoological Research Supply Laboratory, Englewood, Florida (1937). Courtesy of Mimi Carr.

Bass Lab owner Jack Bass (*far left*), two unidentified visitors, and lab manager Stewart Springer (*far right*) (1937). Courtesy of Mimi Carr.

The interior of the Bass Lab, where Carr and her colleagues prepared zoological specimens for university research. Courtesy of Mimi Carr.

The exterior of the rustic Bass Lab (1937). Courtesy of Mimi Carr.

the department could offer Carr was part-time employment, so she decided to keep her position at the Bass Lab for the time being.

Carr began to plead with Archie to pay her a visit at the Bass Lab in Englewood, which was three hundred miles away (nearly a six-hour trip by car). Since Archie had been friends with Bass and Springer before he met Carr, however, visiting his new wife would be extremely complicated. Archie had previously obtained a fellowship at the Bass Lab, where he conducted research

The Bass Lab boathouse (1937). Courtesy of Mimi Carr.

toward the completion of his dissertation on the distribution of Florida's reptiles and amphibians. Archie and his brother, Tom, had helped Bass sail a 54-foot, two-masted schooner, the *Virginia*, from Mobile, Alabama, to Englewood in July 1935, when the Carr brothers were both students at UF. Bass purchased the schooner, which was built in Mobile in 1865, for use as a laboratory and collecting vessel. During a hurricane in the Gulf of Mexico, the Carr brothers lost their sense of direction, and Jack Bass spent most of the voyage in his cabin with seasickness. In the years that followed, Bass and his associates took the *Virginia* on many collecting trips.[30]

Archie asked Carr how they could possibly conceal their passion from Bass and his wife, Else. He was worried about how the Basses would react if they found out about the true nature of the Carrs' relationship. Carr could not risk losing her position at the Bass Lab, which paid forty dollars a month (just $3.50 less than Archie's monthly salary), plus room and board. Her new job offered extensive hands-on training in specimen collection and preservation. The Bass Lab supplied some of the East Coast's most prestigious colleges and universities with research specimens. The entry-level position would provide Carr with a broad understanding of a diverse set of native Florida marine and wildlife species, provided that she could contain her excitement over her brand-new marriage and cope with her husband's reluctance to visit her at the lab.[31]

Carr's hidden marriage was not the only problem she faced at the Bass Lab, where she resisted Jack Bass's efforts to demote her to the status of lab secretary. "A young man recommended by Dr. Norris is coming down to act as Jack's secretary," Carr informed Archie. "Jack, however, hints that maybe I'll be swapped for him. I had better misspell some words for him. You'd be impressed at the typist I've turned out to be." Unfortunately, Carr's concerns as an undergraduate at FSCW had been justified: in order to fulfill her dream of working as a zoologist, she apparently had to prepare for a side career in clerical work, due to her gender.[32]

The newlyweds remained cautious throughout the first months of their marriage, seldom seeing each other in person. Instead, the couple sent letters and telegrams to each other at least once each day. From the moment Marjorie Carr arrived at the Bass Lab, she longed for letters from her new husband. "I stay in a state of coma until mail time," she wrote Archie. Yet his communications were not always comforting. Archie's writing blended poetic rhapsodies of love with anxiety and depression over their hasty marriage and painfully long separation. Not to be overshadowed by her literary paramour, Carr's voice grew stronger across the months of separation. In her early letters, Carr sometimes sounded like an infatuated girl, but as she became immersed in her field and laboratory duties at the Bass Lab, her letters began to reveal a newfound confidence. Carr indicated that she desired Archie's approval as she pursued her career ambitions, but she also made it clear that she longed for more than the life of a homemaker.[33]

Archie wanted to keep his new bride close to him, and he worried that she enjoyed her independence at the Bass Lab too much. Carr did her best to assuage Archie's fears, constantly reassuring him that she loved him as much as he loved her. Economic necessity kept them apart, leaving behind a trail of passionate love letters that open a window into the early trials Carr faced as an aspiring zoologist who planned to pursue a career in academia, at her husband's side. While Archie was despondent over his inability to provide for his wife financially, Carr grappled with the challenges her secret marriage posed to her ability to navigate a new position in a scientific field coded as masculine. From the moment Carr started working at the Bass Lab, Jack Bass exploited her clerical talents. Archie worried that Bass would attempt to have an affair with his new employee. On one of her first nights at the laboratory, she was awakened in her quarters and summoned to take dictation (while still in her nightclothes). Archie cautioned Marjorie to handle Bass delicately.[34]

While Marjorie and Archie Carr tackled the problem of concealing their marriage from the Basses, they faced the additional hurdle of coping with their families' reactions to the news of their elopement. Archie revealed the truth to his mother, Louise Carr, within weeks of the wedding ceremony. Although she was chagrined that they had not had a church wedding, Louise wrote her new daughter-in-law promptly to offer her blessing.[35] "Of course I am very sorry you two saw fit to go about it in just that way," she admitted. "I can't even pretend to see any sense in it, unless frankness might jeopardize the job [Carr's job at the Bass Lab]."[36] She scolded Carr for failing to realize how difficult their separation would prove to be. "I make allowances for two poor kids in your states of mind not having more than half of what the lord and a college education gave you," she chided. "Didn't you know, you babes-in-the-woods—or was it the Everglades?—that a boyfriend (ugh!) is a lot easier to stand separation from than a husband?"[37]

Unlike Archie's mother, Marjorie's mother was not privy to the inner workings of the couple's relationship in the beginning. Before they eloped, Marjorie had told her mother, Clara Harris, that she and Archie planned to marry, but Clara and some of Marjorie's aunts reacted negatively to the news. They believed that the recent college graduate should devote her affections to her widowed mother. Marjorie contributed a significant portion of her salary from the Welaka Resettlement Administration and later the Bass Lab to her mother's monthly car payments and mortgage. Clara insisted that Marjorie must not marry any time soon, and when she finally told her mother about the elopement four months after the event, Clara reacted violently. Because Clara had come to depend upon her daughter, she viewed the marriage as a loss. By contrast, the marriage provided Louise Carr with an ally who would help her cope with her son's depression, which grew more severe with each passing week that the couple spent apart. In March, Louise Carr asked her daughter-in-law if she could "get away from business long enough to come and spend a weekend" with Archie at his parents' home. Louise promised to help arrange a visit with a "honeymoon effect" and advised Carr to "come *any time*, just as you would go home."[38]

In a subsequent letter, Archie told Carr that she would have been better off if she had stayed with Kenneth, a scientist she dated after ending a romantic entanglement with another suitor named Jack Young. "I think you were wise to change from Young to him. I think you might have been wiser if you had stuck with him," Archie wrote in his typical self-deprecating manner. "Chemists always make plenty of money. And Kenneth would never have married you until he was in a position to set you in platinum." Archie required endless reassurances of Carr's love for him. She usually tempered his doubts with hopeful visions of their future together, but at times Archie's dark letters required harsher responses. After one particularly disheartening letter, Carr sent an immediate response. "Later I will write again and soothe you," she promised, "but now you see just how I feel this minute. Damn it to hell. I did not make a mistake New Year's night. No. It would not have been better to marry Kenneth. . . . What you need to do is to come and sleep with me. I will kiss your doubt of us away and you will know that you are my husband. Please come."[39]

According to Archie's calculations, the only way he could afford the bus fare to Englewood would be if he stopped eating for a week. In an effort to conserve money, he had already switched to hand-rolling cigarettes instead of purchasing them in packs. After reading about Archie's budget, Marjorie offered to send him cigarettes, which offended him. In his next letter, Archie explained that he had described his financial state to her only to explain why he could not visit that particular weekend. Instead of backing down at that point, Marjorie volunteered to pay his bus fare to Englewood. Moreover, she offered to support him over the summer while he finished his dissertation. Instead of lifting Archie's spirits, however, Marjorie's offer of financial assistance left him feeling emasculated. "Listen," Archie admonished her. "It's unpleasant enough for me to have to meditate on your puttering about in mudpuppy guts all day." Archie was exasperated over his inability to support Marjorie, whose recent tasks at the Bass Lab had included the tedious process of preparing a seemingly endless procession of thousands of mudpuppies. "For you to think you must support me is more than I can bear," Archie complained. "After all, I have my pride. Or I should have anyway. Great God in heaven. . . . You are a good wench Margie. I love you. But a Carr was never supported by a woman. Not financially." Archie viewed his wife's relative financial security at the Bass Lab as a blow to his manhood. When Marjorie asked Archie to let her cover his expenses while he finished his doctorate in the spring of 1937, the new husband made it clear to his wife that she had crossed a line.[40]

Rather than sinking into despair like her phlegmatic husband, Carr began searching for a practical solution to their financial predicament. She hunted for scientific positions first in Gainesville and Tallahassee, and later discovered a potential summer position directing the Key West Aquarium. The job paid $150 per month, which was more than three times Archie's salary at UF. The directorship belonged to Archie's friend Leonard "Gio" Giovannoli, who had asked Archie to fill in for him over the summer. This would have made more regular visits with Carr possible, but Archie needed to remain in Gainesville through the end of July to defend his dissertation. He had already turned down a summer research fellowship in Virginia for the same reason. If the aquarium opportunity fell through, Archie planned to work as a teaching assistant in comparative biology at UF or make lantern slides to meet expenses. The uncertainty of Archie's employment and the weight of his separation from Marjorie plagued Archie. "The whole layout strengthens my conviction that I was a damned impulsive ass for marrying you," he wrote Carr in his characteristic self-flagellating manner. "I cannot but regard my inability to mate with the woman of my choice as a cosmic catastrophe . . . prolonging this torture would be suicide."[41]

Carr proposed a solution: she could take the aquarium directorship for the month of July, enabling Archie to assume the directorship after he defended his dissertation. "Let's both go down to Key West," she suggested. "Couldn't I take care of things [at the aquarium] until you got your degree?" Archie was not amenable to this idea, however. "I think Gio would rather turn over his job to an intelligent gibbon than to a woman," Archie maintained. Archie informed Carr that Giovannoli had said he would leave his position July 1 if he could find a "capable" person to take his place. "Coming from him, that stipulates male," Archie explained. "If he knew you he might be more apt to acquiesce, but he would only foam at the proposition, not knowing you."[42]

Despite Archie's selection of a scientist and naturalist for a mate, he still clung to traditional mid-twentieth-century notions of the breadwinner husband and the domestic wife. Archie was uncomfortable with the idea of Marjorie compensating for what Archie perceived to be his failure to earn a living and support his wife financially, even though she prefaced her offers of financial support with an explanation that this would only be a temporary solution while he finished his dissertation. Archie viewed Marjorie as a young novice and an optimist. Although the couple formed a scientific partnership that lasted a lifetime, they entered this partnership with differing interpretations of their proper roles. In the case of the Key West aquarium position, for example, Archie never seriously entertained the notion that Marjorie could run the aquarium in his stead, even though her education, her prior experience managing the FSCW aquarium, and her work at the Welaka Fish Hatchery made her an ideal candidate for the job. Archie was not comfortable with the idea of his wife taking such a lucrative position. He ignored her repeated requests to intervene on her behalf. "Again," Marjorie implored Archie, "you don't think there is a chance in the world Giovannoli would let me pinch hit for you for a month? I had charge of the Florida State Aquarium for three months. Hell I could do it . . . Chuck I know I could." Archie's letters indicate that he feared his wife would become too independent.[43]

Carr acquiesced to her husband's wishes. She still viewed Archie as a mentor and hoped to learn from him. She expressed an interest in auditing his ecology class and asked him numerous questions about specimen preservation, anatomy, proper dissection methods, and other techniques that her colleagues at the Bass Lab lacked the experience to provide sufficient training in. Marjorie asked Archie if he was sorry he had married "such a young incompetent girl," and she promised to improve with age. However, Archie's feelings of inadequacy eclipsed her own. "I shouldn't have married you," he lamented. "You shouldn't have married me. You married a god damn fool. You married beneath you. You made a mistake. Do you realize it yet? You will before fall." He even referred to their wedding as "your indiscretion of Jan. 1."[44]

In late April, Louise Carr pleaded with her daughter-in-law to come to the family's home in the small town of Umatilla for a short honeymoon. Louise claimed that Archie was "pathetic" and said it would do him a lot of good if Marjorie would visit him there. "I get awfully out of patience with him for being so emotional about the situation [their separation]," Louise wrote Marjorie. "But I do feel very sorry for him. He is most madly in love with you and separation from you is making him prey to all sorts of foolish fears about the future." It was Louise's hope that if Archie could see that his parents accepted his marriage to Marjorie during a visit to the family home, he would feel more secure about their union. She referred to Archie as "the poor distraught lover" and warned Marjorie that she feared the consequences if Archie did not get the full-time instructorship at UF upon graduation.[45]

While Louise planned a therapeutic reunion for her son and daughter-in-law, Marjorie grappled with her third pregnancy scare in thirty days. Archie had come to view these episodes with a sense of humor. "Either you are endowed with the most excessively unorthodox physiology south of the blue ridge," Archie teased Marjorie, "or you are completely unlearned in the ancient and indispensable science of chronology." Carr continued to panic over her irregular periods even though Else Bass had helped her get a diaphragm after a prior pregnancy scare. Carr's letters to Archie during this period contain references to using Ortho-Gynol, a spermicidal jelly or cream intended to be used in combination with a diaphragm. Later in life, however, Carr claimed that she had never used birth control. Nonetheless, the Carrs delayed starting a family for the first six years of their marriage. Between 1943 and 1952, Carr gave birth to five children.[46]

Marjorie and Archie did get together in Umatilla, and the visit restored his sense of well-being for the moment. This was actually Marjorie's second visit to Umatilla; she first traveled there over the Christmas holidays to reassure Archie that their relationship would survive her move to Englewood. In both instances, Archie's mother reached out to Marjorie, affectionately requesting that she visit her son in Umatilla to end his doubts over their relationship and pull him out of his depression. The combined stress of dissertation writing and his distance from Carr took a toll on Archie.

As their separation neared its final stretch, Carr was beginning to see the light at the end of the tunnel. Still, she had become accustomed to deprivation, and the prospect of their reunion seemed intangible. "Being with you is such a state of perfection I start and wonder is it true," she questioned, "or is it some Utopian dream?" Carr continued to immerse herself in her duties at the Bass Lab, even as she prepared for her pending troth-pledging ceremony. She enjoyed her frequent nighttime duties, which helped take her mind off of their separation. "The nights are far the worst," she lamented. "At night it is so alone and so quiet, with only the clams burbling, and it's cool at night and I would love to be in your arms tight with coolness over us." Carr's task on that particular night was clam pegging. "First I place some two hundred Quahogs on the anterior part of their umbo," she explained. "Then armed with pegs I stand in the middle of them and pretend not to notice them. The minute one opens his valves to get a breath of air or slap at a mosquito I swoop down and peg him. However they are quite wary and grow sly as the night goes on. While I am pegging one[,] two or three behind my back burble at me but the minute I turn around they are all smugly closed."[47]

Carr's collecting activities were physically exhausting. One grueling grasshopper-collecting expedition lasted from 4:30 a.m. to 10:30 p.m. "We picked steadily all day and netted nearly six thousand of the beasts," she informed Archie. "I am as sore as the day I tried some of Martha Graham's stunts for three hours without stopping." It is unlikely that Jack Bass considered the environmental impact of his company's collecting expeditions on the marine, insect, and animal life of Englewood. Bass was motivated by financial gain, and his products—the biota of south Florida—were prized by academic biology departments throughout the eastern United States. At the time, studying biological specimens went hand in hand with killing them. Carr became adept at coaxing a variety of animals and insects out of their hiding places, catching many species with her bare hands. "I caught two king snakes yesterday," she boasted. "Big devils and one was a male I know. They both were infested with ticks. They are nice beasts, the snakes, and damn strong aren't they?"[48]

While the other women at the Bass Lab, Else Bass and Vergie Springer, spent the majority of their time entertaining, keeping house, and caring for their respective children, Carr dressed in overalls and boots and worked outside or in the laboratory with the men. Although she viewed herself as an equal at the Bass Lab, not all of her male colleagues and supervisors treated her as such. She voiced her frustration over repeated incidents of sexual harassment to her husband and bemoaned the "lecherousness of scientists":

> May I vent my spleen to you? Men and their damn eyes and god-damn nasty tongues make me sick. Can you realize how utterly weary and worn out one gets after, say, nine years of constantly butting up against it? From the first "old-friend-of-the-family-kiss" of some old fool who you knew damn well tried to squeeze your arm and more. I have so many times wanted to slap 'em . . . but no, must evade and pull away and frown and smile and shake head. If only you knew how damn mad it makes me. When you make a simple statement and have it constantly twisted into a sort of shady lip-licking smokehouse implication. The other night, a simple thing, I was seated on the arm of a chair watching a ping pong game and swinging my feet. A ball went wild and went under the chair. I tried to stop it with my feet. When I said "Gee I should have had my feet together," I hear a sort of shady "Oh, yeah. Why Margie. Not you." . . . Archie, if some day I shock you by insulting some man for some slight remark it will be because of the piling up of many years. Hell I'm not a prude. You know that. Things my family, close friends say are all okay. But it's the freedom and liberty any man thinks he can take that makes me want to draw blood. The lecherousness of scientists is pretty raw at times.[49]

Jack Bass took advantage of Carr's live-in status at the lab. Carr claimed that Bass had misrepresented the facts regarding the full-time nature of the position. She thought her job would provide a useful six-month to twelve-month introduction to practical zoology. Carr viewed the position as a transitional step between undergraduate and graduate work in zoology, which would enable a new graduate to learn the essentials of specimen collection, preservation, and laboratory techniques. She wanted Bass to regard her work as a part-time research fellowship, which would have more prestige than a full-time technician position. Bass had routinely offered research fellowships to visiting scientists, including Archie.[50]

Had Carr's colleagues been aware of her marriage to their good friend Archie, they might have been less inclined to take advantage of her. However, it took three months before the Basses began to suspect the truth. Carr was relieved once everyone at the Bass Lab finally realized that she and Archie were married. Although she did not immediately lose her job, her colleagues at the Bass Lab expected that she would resign her position there and follow Archie wherever his career took him. Carr saw no potential for advancement at the Bass Lab, but since she and Archie would not be able to live together until the summer or fall, she decided to stay in Englewood.[51]

During their continued separation, Carr spent her free time reading and smoking in bed. She became a serious smoker during their separation, a habit that would ultimately lead to her death. Smoking was a popular pastime at the Bass Lab. On one occasion, Bass pushed a practical joke past the boundaries of acceptable behavior, placing the lighted "cherry" of a cigarette down Carr's back in the lab. When it burned her and smoke started billowing from her shirt, he apologized, saying he did not realize it would hurt. This was one of the more visible incidents of sexual harassment that Carr endured at the lab. Although it is now understood that lighting cigarettes and smoking while working around laboratory chemicals is dangerous, it was common practice at the Bass Lab. Carr bided her time at the lab before giving notice that she would resign her position at the end of the summer or early in the fall. "So you see my bridges are burning," she informed Archie, "and I really am going to be your wife next fall."[52]

Meanwhile, Archie had become a rising star in herpetology. When Archie began his studies at UF, his dissertation advisor and committee members were pioneers in the field of zoology. Rogers taught ecology at the university, and his students engaged in pioneering research in the field of herpetology, conducting regular field research in Florida's understudied ecosystems. Historian Frederick R. Davis observed that Rogers and fellow UF professor Theodore Hubbell, who both taught at the University of Michigan before coming to Florida, encouraged their students to incorporate a broader societal concern into their analysis of a particular species and its ecosystem. Rogers and Hubbell's innovative approach to biology, coupled with the abundance of diversity of specimens available for collection and research in Florida, led some of the nation's most influential zoologists to visit UF's zoology department when they traveled to the state on collecting trips.[53]

Thomas Barbour (1884–1946), a Harvard biologist and director of its Museum of Comparative Zoology, became a mentor to Archie after he initiated correspondence with the distinguished naturalist. Archie shared a passion for writing about the natural world with Barbour, who published nearly four hundred articles and several books on naturalist topics, including *That Vanishing Eden: A Naturalist's Florida*, which documented environmental decline in the state. Barbour would come to exert the greatest influence over Archie's professional career. Early in their relationship, Barbour provided Archie with turtle specimens, prints, and professional advice. In return, he asked Archie to wait until his colleague Leonhard Hess Stejneger, who was head curator of the Department of Biology and curator of the Division of Reptiles and Batrachians at the Smithsonian, died before publishing his work. "A very peculiar situation,"

Thomas Barbour, director of the Museum of Comparative Zoology at Harvard (1938). Courtesy of Mimi Carr.

Archie confided in Marjorie. "He is Stejneger's very best friend. It suits me, however."[54]

Archie had become an expert in *Pseudemys* and disagreed with Stejneger on several key points regarding that particular turtle species. Barbour predicted that Archie's work would provide a major contribution to herpetology, and he apparently wanted to shield his friend Stejneger from the effects. Although Archie would do his best to avoid taking on Stejneger, he could not postpone publishing his dissertation forever. Stejneger would not die until 1943, at the age of ninety-one. In 1940, UF published "A Contribution to the Herpetology of Florida," which was based upon Archie's dissertation. In 1942, Archie's article "Notes on Sea Turtles" was published in the *Proceedings of the New England Zoological Club*. In response, Stejneger wrote a lengthy complaint to Barbour in which he rejected many of Archie's taxonomic revisions, especially his revision of the genus *Pseudemys*. Using Barbour as a moderator, Archie dismissed all of Stejneger's claims. After Stejneger's death, Barbour proceeded to incorporate Archie's changes into the fifth revision of *A Check List of North American Amphibians and Reptiles*, a book he had coauthored with Stejneger.[55]

Ironically, although Florida was an ideal location for studying turtles, Harvard actually had the best Florida herpetology collection at the time. In 1937, Archie visited the Northeast for dissertation research and to meet some of the nation's top herpetologists, including Stejneger. In January, Archie had traveled with his colleague Horton Hobbs to Harvard, the Smithsonian, the American Museum in New York City, and the Academy of Natural Sciences of Philadelphia (now the Academy of Natural Sciences of Drexel University). Archie met many professional contacts he had corresponded with for years. Archie explained the value of the trip to Carr.[56]

The trip will be of immense value, not only in rounding out my thesis, but in settling some questions about turtles that have bothered me for a long time. I have great plans for turtles. Nobody knows much about them. *Pseudemys*. But me. And I'll know a lot more when I come back. My thesis is going to be a bitch. A hundred and sixty species and for each at least one page on habitat and biology, a full page map, and another page of distribution data. That makes around 480 pages, which staggers me. It must be finished by April. I'll have to work like the devil. Tell me it's for you. I have two courses: I can let the thought of you drive me insane, and seethe and foment and get nothing done. Or I can think of you lotus-face and the stars in your eyes and the song of your voice and the fierce sweetness of those two nights of ours and the perfect years before us, and think of time and work as distance between us—and run like a fiend. And that's what I'll do, of course. But it's hard, hard—the worst job I ever had, and the most worthwhile.[57]

Thomas Barbour would later invite Archie to return to Harvard for a summer fellowship. His patronage helped establish Archie in the field of herpetology. Archie served as a Thomas Barbour fellow for seven summers, beginning in 1937. Barbour's sponsorship helped him conduct vital research into turtles. The pair began corresponding in January 1934, when Archie sent Barbour a copy of the *Florida Naturalist*, hoping to curry favor with the distinguished and influential scientist. The magazine featured Archie's latest paper, "A Key to the Breeding-Songs of the Florida Frogs." Barbour became increasingly interested in Archie's research. In April 1937, Barbour invited Archie to study the museum's turtle collection for a month that summer.[58]

Meanwhile, Carr remained preoccupied with laboratory and collecting work, which was draining. "Oh wise and venerable spouse," she wrote after a particularly arduous collecting trip, "I am battered. Bruised in a hundred places. Two large black spots designate the place my hip bones gouged through my flesh. All this from eeling. But by golly what eeling. At present 85 are slithering around in a Shedd can." She boasted about the challenges of collecting in south Florida, claiming that most biologists limit their forays to the Apalachicola and lake regions, "as if the peninsula ends there. I hate that sort of professional timidity," she asserted. "It takes a brave soul to dip down into south Florida." She had grown confident in her collecting abilities after joining excursions for large predators such as wolves and alligators.[59]

As Archie's dissertation defense grew nearer, the couple felt pressured to arrange a Christian wedding ceremony for the benefit of their families. Archie's father presided over a troth-pledging ceremony at the Bass Lab on June 11, 1937. Before the ceremony, Marjorie's mother and aunts offered their advice to the bride. "I laughed and laughed," she informed Archie. "[On] June 11 I'll laugh and look at you and wink and you'll laugh too. And it will be sweet. Aren't you glad?"[60]

Although they had already been married for more than five months, Carr donned a white wedding gown and the couple enjoyed all the trimmings of a formal wedding. Carr later referred to the event as "the marriage revealed." The troth-pledging ceremony was held just a few years after Prohibition ended.

Archie Carr and Marjorie Harris Carr's troth-pledging ceremony (June 11, 1937). Courtesy of Mimi Carr.

Tom Carr, who had never been exposed to alcohol before, recalled that Marjorie Carr's aunts kept him well lubricated. After the ceremony, Marjorie worked at the Bass Lab for another month while Archie prepared to defend his dissertation. They spent the weekend of the wedding ceremony at Marjorie's family home in Bonita Springs and took a formal honeymoon to Key West after Archie defended his dissertation in July. With the dissertation behind them, Marjorie and Archie Carr were able to live together as newlyweds at long last. "It will be a new and peculiar feeling to be with you and not have the dread of separation hanging over us," Marjorie Carr had predicted in June. "This has been a scrambled spring. I am glad it is nearly over. You and I, we have been tried."[61]

After the Carrs' troth-pledging ceremony, Marjorie Carr prepared for the transition from her independence in Englewood to married life in Gainesville. "Do you know you've never seen me longer than five days in succession? At Christmas," she reminded Archie. "Can you realize how heavenly it will be to live together? I don't believe either of us can fully realize it or we couldn't exist apart. I want to look at you and look at you and look at you for eternity." Although Archie had pleaded with Marjorie to forget him or, at the very least, to love him lightly over the course of their separation, they emerged from their separation stronger than they might have been otherwise.[62]

In the fall of 1937, after the Carrs had spent their first summer together at Harvard, Marjorie Carr enrolled in UF's graduate program in zoology. She worked as a part-time assistant in the department and audited courses in zoogeography and the history of biology. In that same year, Kathleen Vertrees Wheeler became the first woman to graduate from UF with a bachelor's of science in agriculture. In 1938, Juliet Carrington earned a bachelor's of science in entomology and was the first woman to graduate from the College of Agriculture with high honors. Women were slowly integrating themselves into the student body at UF, but their numbers were small. When the university officially reintroduced coeducation in 1947, there were 601 female students and 8,177 male students (a 14:1 male-to-female ratio). Even fewer women attended UF in the 1930s (especially at the graduate level), and they sometimes encountered resistance to their presence on campus. Although many colleges and universities consigned women scientists to separate laboratories, Carr formed strong professional relationships with her male colleagues in the biology department, joining them on numerous collecting trips and working with them in the laboratory.[63]

Unfortunately, graduate funding opportunities for women at UF remained scant. Although it is now common for professors' spouses and family members to receive free or reduced tuition, in the 1930s and 1940s, the university's antinepotism policies prevented Carr from enjoying this privilege. Consequently, she applied for a graduate scholarship to cover her expenses. "I'm back in school again," Carr wrote Jack Bass. "Next semester I'm applying for a scholarship. There are four open and I hope to receive one." Deviney and Kurz from FSCW provided two of the required letters of recommendation, and Carr asked Bass to write the third. Bass's response to Carr exemplified the gender discrimination that she and other female scientists faced in the 1930s.[64]

In a letter dated one week after the scholarship deadline, Bass expressed the frustration he had experienced upon learning that Carr had secretly married Archie before starting work at the Bass Lab. Although she had considered her position to be a scientific fellowship, Bass viewed her primarily as a laboratory assistant and secretary. "Last spring, I was terribly disappointed to hear that you and Dr. Carr were going to [sic] get married," he replied, "as I felt that we had a laboratory assistant, technician, and secretary who would fit into permanent plans for expansion of the Laboratory. It is very understandable that you cannot live in Englewood while your husband teaches in the University of Florida. If it were not for the fact that Dr. Carr has visited us often, here at the Laboratory, we would hold a grudge against him for taking you away from us."[65]

Carr left behind no letters in which she expressed her frustration with Jack Bass's reluctance to assist her with the scholarship application. However, given the fact that she had devoted a half year of service to the Bass Laboratory, it is realistic to conclude that she was disappointed by her former employer's actions. Although it must have been reassuring to hear that Bass wanted to retain her services at the laboratory, it had never been her intention to remain in the laboratory technician position permanently. At the same time, Carr was probably frustrated by Bass's failure to meet the scholarship application deadline, in addition to the condescending tone he took in his letter. Bass complained that he could not write a letter of recommendation on Carr's behalf unless she provided him with the name of the person who would receive the letter, although she had made it clear in her initial request that the letter should go to the dean of the graduate school at UF. He then proceeded to list the positive qualities Carr exhibited while in his employ, focusing especially on the clerical tasks she performed.

"While you were here," Bass wrote, "you had a great number of different duties, among them was acting as secretary for me. In this work, you were competent in filing, typewriting, and general office work." Bass also commented on Carr's willingness to work late at night on a variety of specimen preservation tasks. "Your powers of observations, as well as your scientific notes, were always accurate, so that we were able to use them to our full extent," Bass recalled.[66]

Carr had intended to enlist Bass's help in writing a recommendation for a graduate scholarship. Yet the type of letter Bass proposed to write would have been suitable only for another assistant or secretarial position. Carr had been correct in surmising that there was no room for advancement at the Bass Lab. Unfortunately, this was one of her only paying positions in the sciences. The 1930s was an inhospitable time for women scientists, especially in the South.

Marjorie Carr holds an iguana while riding a burro on a collecting trip in Mexico (late 1930s). Courtesy of Mimi Carr.

Marjorie Carr (*far right*) and a group of University of Florida biology department graduate students preserve freshly caught specimens on a 1941 collecting trip in Mexico. Courtesy of Mimi Carr.

After Carr spent six months as Bass's diligent employee, he was reluctant to write her a strong recommendation for a scholarship. As a provider of generous fellowships to (male) graduate students who used his facilities to conduct academic research, Bass was fully cognizant of the qualities that should be stressed in a letter of recommendation for a graduate scholarship. Yet he focused on Carr's secretarial and assistant skills instead of discussing her general intelligence and fitness for advanced study. This was especially egregious since Carr's competition for the scholarship consisted exclusively of men, and a letter touting her secretarial skills would only reinforce stereotypes and diminish her chances of receiving a scholarship.

Bass's reluctance to write an appropriate letter of recommendation for Carr might have stemmed from the controversial circumstances surrounding the end of her service at the Bass Lab. While Carr was still working at the lab, Archie wrote Bass to try to make amends. "I wish to apologize for my temerity and presumption in marrying a member of your staff without your permission. I won't do it again," he wrote the Basses with tongue in cheek. "When I eventually deprive you of your mudpuppy executioner you will no doubt look for a new one. Be careful this time. You may get another wife in sheep's clothing." Although Archie attempted to use humor to diffuse situation, it did little to relieve Bass's disappointment over Carr's departure. Tragically, in December 1939, Bass died in Mexico City after contracting pneumonia and malaria. He was attempting to facilitate cooperation between biologists in the United States and Mexico.[67]

Archie's concerns over clipping Marjorie's wings had been astute. In time, their marriage would effectively end her formal career in zoology. Yet Marjorie Carr's marriage to a successful herpetologist would also help her develop professionally, beginning with her acceptance into UF's graduate program in zoology. Archie's colleagues, including Thomas Barbour, extended their support to Carr as well, enabling her to join a close-knit group of Florida zoologists. Marjorie and Archie would delay starting a family for the first six years of their marriage while she completed her graduate work and accompanied Archie on collecting and research trips in New England and Florida, in addition to several collecting trips to Mexico that the Carrs organized for graduate students from the UF Biology Department. As the next chapter will show, the Carrs' greatest research opportunity presented itself shortly after the birth of their second child, when Thomas Barbour arranged for Archie to take a sabbatical in order to teach at the Escuela Agrícola Panamericana Zamorano in Honduras. While Archie conducted pioneering turtle research, Marjorie became an authority on the birds of Honduras. She carved out a niche in the field of ornithology, which was slow to professionalize and therefore remained open to women practitioners. Marjorie and Archie Carr would function as equal partners in the local zoological community of Honduras.

3

Honduras in the 1940s

A Naturalist's Paradise

etween 1937 and 1943, Marjorie and Archie Carr spent seven summers in Cambridge, Massachusetts, while Archie worked as a Thomas Barbour fellow at the Museum of Comparative Zoology at Harvard. While Archie conducted research under the guidance of Barbour and other prominent herpetologists, Marjorie alternated between performing mundane laboratory work considered appropriate for women technicians and studying in the Ornithology Department. The Great Depression raged on, and Marjorie Carr was delighted to be able to accompany her husband to Cambridge. As grateful as Carr was to find temporary employment at the museum, the tasks she was required to perform were beneath her education and abilities. "One year I changed all the alcohol in the bottles where reptiles were preserved," Carr later recalled, "and another year I took apart owl pellets." She was eventually permitted to conduct research in the Ornithology Department. "I wanted to do [zoological] research," Carr explained, "but I couldn't get a job in research. I eventually was able to do it because my husband had a research job."[1]

On weekends, the couple engaged in regular collecting excursions for adventure and to supplement Archie's fellowship. "We rented a room from a Mrs. Murphy in Cambridge," Marjorie Carr recalled. "On weekends Archie and I collected marine animals off the coast and we filled up Mrs. Murphy's cellar with pickled specimens. We would get dogfish from a fishing boat in Rockport. The Sicilian fishermen took great delight in watching us inject various colored fluids into the circulatory systems of the dogfish. One of the Sicilians had an uncle who was a mortician, and he would make running commentaries on our technique."[2]

In subsequent summers at Cambridge, Barbour opened his house to the Carrs and even offered to finance their trip north on board a Pullman coach. Upon their return to Gainesville each fall, Carr continued her studies at the University of Florida (UF). In the summer of 1939, the Carrs purchased their first house. After the Japanese attack on Pearl Harbor launched the United States into World War II, Archie tried to enlist in the military. However, he was unable to serve the armed forces in a traditional manner due to his osteomyelitis. The necessities of the wartime economy led Carr to take a temporary position as a nurse's aide.[3]

Even during the war, however, Carr remained focused on completing her graduate degree. Carr's graduate specialty within the larger field of zoology was ichthyology, the study of fish. The subject of her graduate research was the large-mouthed black bass, a native fish that was a practical choice to study because of wartime gas rationing, which made it inconvenient to conduct research far from home. In addition, Carr had prior experience with this species at the Welaka Fish Hatchery. She conducted pioneering research, becoming one of the first scientists to discover social parasitism among freshwater fishes. The parasitic chub sucker, Carr revealed, laid its eggs in the nests of the large-mouthed black bass. Because the chub sucker fry bear a strong resemblance to bass fry, Carr demonstrated, bass are tricked into protecting the young chub suckers after hatching.[4]

While Carr completed her graduate work, she and Archie delayed starting a family. Marjorie Carr conducted much of the research for her master's thesis in Hogtown Creek, Bivens Arm Lake near Paynes Prairie, and other local waterways. She also accompanied Archie on local collecting trips, which was how the Carrs first met their lifelong friend J. C. Dickinson Jr. Like Archie, Dickinson would complete his B.A., M.A., and Ph.D. in biology at UF, where he later became the director of the Florida Museum of Natural History.[5]

The Carrs led groups of UF students on holiday collecting excursions in Mexico. They loaded food and collecting supplies onto the back of a large truck with "University of Florida Department of Biology" emblazoned upon the side of the cab. They camped under the stars, with the Carrs sharing a double sleeping bag that Marjorie made. On cool nights, the students asked the Carrs if they could borrow their dachshund, Zep, who made a stellar hot-water bottle.[6]

The Carrs gave some of the specimens they collected and preserved to the Florida Museum of Natural History and shipped others to Thomas Barbour at the Harvard Museum of Comparative Zoology (MCZ), whose patronage increased over the years to include substantial gifts such as a car, a mortgage, and an original print of John James Audubon's *Carolina Parakeets*. The Carrs' sense of indebtedness to Barbour inspired them to initiate collecting trips throughout Florida and Mexico and ship him specimens to express their gratitude for his financial assistance and mentorship.[7]

For many of Archie's young students, these trips were among the highlights of their college careers. For the Carrs, these three exploratory trips into the Mexican wilderness only whetted their appetite for further adventures. Marjorie Carr observed that these trips "had been so satisfying, so exhilarating and provocative, that we were more than ready for the move to Honduras in 1945."[8]

After Marjorie Carr graduated from UF in 1942, Thomas Barbour helped her publish her thesis, "The Breeding Habits, Embryology, and Larval Development of the Large-Mouthed Black Bass in Florida," in the *Proceedings of the New England Zoological Club*. In that same year, Marjorie also coauthored "Notes on the Courtship of the Cottonmouth Moccasin" with Archie. By this point, Barbour had practically adopted the Carrs, according to J. C. Dickinson Jr. Barbour, who was six feet six inches tall and weighed more than three hundred pounds, traveled to Florida regularly during the 1930s and 1940s to meet with fellow herpetologists and expand his museum's collection. He purchased a Florida license plate in an attempt to mask his Yankee heritage, "but when he opened his mouth you knew," Dickinson recalled. Dickinson came to know Barbour while he was writing *That Vanishing Eden: A Naturalist's Florida*; they spent time together at the Fairchild Tropical Botanic Garden in Coral Gables. Barbour made frequent collecting trips to Florida and conscripted the Carrs to send a variety of additional specimens to the MCZ.[9]

Because Archie's position at UF kept Marjorie tethered to the small college town of Gainesville, she had few options for employment after graduation. In the 1940s, professional opportunities for married (female) scientists were limited. Marjorie Carr could have pursued a doctorate in zoology, but the time seemed right to start a family. In 1943, with Barbour's financial assistance, the

Mimi and Marjorie Carr swim in Hogtown Creek near their home in Gainesville, Florida (1944). Courtesy of Mimi Carr.

Carrs purchased a nicer home on a bucolic piece of land where they raised chickens, geese, ducks, and two pigs. The Carrs' house was close to Hogtown Creek, which flows into the Floridan Aquifer through Haile Sink.[10]

On June 20, 1943, Marjorie and Archie Carr welcomed their first-born child and only daughter, Mimi. With World War II in full swing, resources were rationed, and Marjorie Carr helped to defray household expenses by teaching science in Alachua, a small town ten miles north of Gainesville. Approximately one year after Mimi's birth, Carr became pregnant again—a trend that would continue with little interruption over the next decade. Reflecting upon his experiences in Honduras, Archie would later joke, "My wife is a naturalist too, between babies."[11]

In January 1945, acting upon Barbour's advice, Archie Carr traveled to the Escuela Agrícola Panamericana Zamorano (Zamorano) near Tegucigalpa, Honduras. Barbour had suggested that Wilson Popenoe, the school's founding director, might be able to help Archie answer some unresolved questions about turtles. As it turned out, Popenoe, a longtime United Fruit Company employee and former plant explorer for the U.S. Department of Agriculture, possessed no knowledge of turtles (nor a formal university degree), but he offered Archie a teaching position at Zamorano. At the time, the fledgling school had no Ph.D.s on its faculty, and Popenoe realized that the addition of an established university professor would add to its prestige. Archie was surprised that Popenoe was interested in his turtle research, which involved testing an original theory that turtles migrated between Central America and Africa annually to spawn. "I must say I was surprised that he thought the [United] Fruit Company would be interested in hiring an individual whose chief interests are so wholly devoid of practicality," Archie wrote to Barbour. "But Dr. Popenoe thought that Mr. Zemurray and you, the directors of the school, would have no objections. . . . From my standpoint, I am crazy about the place and the possibilities for doing some pioneering work in natural history."[12]

Since Leonhard Stejneger was no longer an obstacle, Barbour encouraged Archie to begin revising the taxonomy of turtles, which was incomplete and flawed. Although a great deal had been published on freshwater turtles, the literature on sea turtles was a mixture of folklore and fact. Archie corrected this problem with his 1952 publication of *Handbook of Turtles: The Turtles of the United States, Canada, and Baja California*. "I decided to become the world's sea turtle man," he explained. "I couldn't decide whether the turtles in the eastern Pacific were exactly the same as those in the Atlantic or slightly different. Since museum collections of sea turtles are inadequate, I began to meditate on the possibility of my going down where the oceans are close together to compare their turtles directly." Archie's pioneering sea turtle research in Central America, the West Indies, Africa, and Australia in the 1940s and 1950s would establish his international reputation as an expert on sea turtle breeding and migration.[13]

Zamorano, tucked away in the high valley of the Yeguare River in the mountains of southern Honduras, had just graduated its first class of agriculture students when Archie visited the school. He fell in love with the campus, its students, and the tropical setting instantaneously. "I walked about the palm-grove campus and through the school buildings and brand-new staff residences," Archie reflected, "all built in gracefully solid colonial style of hand-cut rhyolite from the school quarry, timbered and beamed with Danlí cedar and pine from the mountainside, and roofed with half-round tiles of red school clay." When Popenoe offered Archie a teaching job at the new school, Archie accepted immediately. At the time, Archie was teaching introductory physics (perhaps his least favorite subject) to cadets with the Army Air Force Pre-Flight Program at UF. The Zamorano position would enable him to resume the naturalist's lifestyle that teaching physics had prevented him from

Coyol palms line a dirt road near the faculty housing at the Escuela Agrícola Panamericana Zamorano, Honduras. Courtesy of Mimi Carr.

enjoying full-time. When Archie traveled home to tell Marjorie the good news, she started packing before he even finished the story.[14]

As naturalists, the Carrs had long dreamed of exploring the lower latitudes, and the decision to uproot their family and move to the rural high tropics was an easy one. Among the factors that drove Archie to accept Popenoe's job offer so quickly was the deprivation that he and Marjorie had experienced since the start of the Great Depression. For instance, wartime rationing had forced most Americans to go without quality meat and produce for years. When Archie toured Zamorano, he was particularly impressed by the school's vast stores of fresh steaks that animal husbandry students delivered to the faculty, in addition to the handsome, newly constructed faculty residences. World War II was coming to a close, the Carr family was expanding, and their Honduran sojourn would provide them with a high quality of life that would never be matched.[15]

The Carrs could explore the forests on quality horses that were available for purchase at twenty-five dollars apiece. Archie received an initial three-year leave of absence from UF, and the Carrs sold their house in Gainesville. Archie moved to Honduras in April to prepare the way for his family. Marjorie was near the end of her second pregnancy, and she decided it would be better to give birth in Florida than in Honduras. Archibald Fairly Carr III (Chuck) was born on May 10, 1945, and in July, Marjorie made the trip to Honduras with two young children in tow. "The school gave us a pleasant house and cheerful servants to run it," Archie later recalled, "and we had a strawberry bed and no morning classes and three months out of the year to collect and explore and get to know the tropics." Archie's responsibilities included teaching two classes per semester at the agricultural school and conducting a biological survey of Honduras for the United Fruit Company.[16]

Zamorano was established in 1942 under the direction of Samuel Zemurray, who was then the United Fruit Company's top executive. The school's mission was to provide training in modern agricultural techniques to rural men from tropical America. Zamorano provided students with free tuition, board, clothing, and funds to defray other educational expenses without requiring them to work for the company after graduation. Zemurray had influenced the United Fruit Company to use its $200 million wartime surplus to construct the agricultural school in Honduras, which lacked an agricultural education program. Wilson Popenoe helped realize Zemurray's dream of establishing a practical school with a hands-on agriculture program. Popenoe created a handsome school on a parcel of rural land covered by a forest of native palms and pastureland. Zamorano had an international student body, a strict code of discipline, and a hands-on curriculum that required students to assist with campus agricultural production.[17]

Thomas Barbour served as the original eminent conservationist on Zamorano's first board of directors. Barbour and David Fairchild—a wealthy botanist, naturalist, and plant explorer—had played a major role in raising public awareness of the problems of habitat loss and dwindling flora and fauna populations in Florida and the tropics. In *That Vanishing Eden: A Naturalist's Florida*, much of which was written in the Carrs' backyard, Barbour argued that the state's remaining wildlife was in dire need of protection and preservation.[18]

Barbour documented the effects of habitat destruction on Florida's birds and other animal species, citing the state's unchecked commercial growth as the main culprit. He also faulted the government for its maltreatment of the Seminole Indians, showing a level of concern for both nature and culture that was rare among naturalists. Barbour recommended several books on Central America to Marjorie Carr soon after Archie accepted the position at Zamorano. None of the books, however, provided any references on the flora and fauna of Honduras, which only increased her excitement over the prospect of collecting there. "You know how I have always wanted to spend at least a few years in South or Central America," she wrote Barbour, "but I never dared hope for such an opportunity as this." Barbour expected the couple to provide the MCZ with many scientific skins, including some rare species that were not represented in the museum's collection. By March 1945, he had completed two-thirds of a book on Central America, but he said his notes would be of little use to the Carrs. This unpublished manuscript, tentatively titled "The Stars Differ," addressed the problems of deforestation and habitat loss in Central America. In October 1945, Marjorie Carr read a completed version of "The Stars Differ," which would be Thomas Barbour's final manuscript. It does not appear to have been published after his death, but it is possible that sections of the manuscript were included in *A Naturalist's Handbook*, which Harvard University Press published in 1946. Barbour's influence on Archie can be seen in *High Jungles and Low*, which Archie began writing while in Honduras; in it, Archie expresses equal concern for the native Honduran peoples and their natural surroundings.[19]

When Archie arrived in Honduras in April 1945, he oversaw the completion of his family's villa. "It is a jewel of a house and I wish you could see it," he informed Barbour. "It's the same basic plan as the other three faculty houses but with improvements." Having been able to identify all of the frog songs of Florida, Archie marveled at his unfamiliarity with Central American frogs. "The rainy season has begun here and the frogs are singing—lots of them," he wrote, "and I don't know a single one."[20]

In addition to being ignorant of Honduran frog songs, the Carrs had to sharpen their Spanish, of which Marjorie Carr knew very little. She began taking lessons immediately, first learning common commands to use with the servants. Mimi's knowledge of Spanish outpaced Marjorie's, however. Soon two-year-old Mimi was able to translate whatever her mother wished to tell the household help. In fact, Mimi spoke in Spanish so well and so often that Marjorie frequently had to ask Archie to translate Mimi's sentences. Only days after arriving in Honduras, Marjorie hired a nanny for Mimi, "a pretty fifteen-year-old girl who does nothing but care for Mimi from six to six." The Carrs wasted no time making use of their new domestic servants. On their first weekend together in Zamorano, they climbed Mount Uyuca. "We drove the first 2000 feet, about six miles, in 45 minutes and climbed the last 1000 feet in about 30 minutes," Marjorie Carr wrote in the first of many letters she sent her mother from Honduras. "The latter part goes straight up and is covered with a cloud forest at the top. The big trees—all damp and dripping—are covered with epiphytes including lots of orchids." Cloud forests are rain forests located on high, tropical mountains. A climb up to a cloud forest begins in the hot, steamy lowlands and changes as one climbs higher through changing vegetation zones, which become cooler as the elevation increases. The highest zone is typically covered in mist and fog; the high moisture levels foster the growth of epiphytes, ferns, and mosses. In Honduras, the Carrs developed their knowledge of tropical ecology, immersing themselves in the study of the local ecosystems and the flora and fauna. As Frederick R. Davis pointed out in his biography of Archie Carr, *The Man Who Saved Sea Turtles: Archie Carr and the Origins of Conservation Biology*, for years, Thomas Barbour had shared stories of his adventures in the tropics with the Carrs. Now, it was the Carrs' turn to explore the relatively uncharted ecosystems of Honduras.[21]

When Marjorie and Archie Carr moved to Honduras, they were thirty and thirty-six years old, respectively. Despite Archie's relatively young age, he would soon become one of the earliest advocates and most powerful voices for conservation of tropical rain forests and sea turtles. Yet Archie advanced scientists' understanding of tropical ecology at the expense of the same fauna he sought to protect. Although modern birders shoot their subjects with a camera, the naturalists of the late nineteenth and early twentieth centuries commonly shot and killed specimens for scientific study or to prove that a particular species was sighted in a specific region. "With respect to my attitude toward varmints," Archie admitted, "I have always been afflicted with a Dr.-Jekyll-and-Mr.-Hyde complex—an altogether unresolved conflict between the instincts of a naturalist and the urge to shoot things." The Carrs shot and killed thousands of animals for science, sport, and sustenance, preparing scientific skins for use in research collections at Barbour's Museum of Comparative Zoology at Harvard; the American Museum in New York; the Florida Museum of Natural History in Gainesville; and Zamorano in Honduras. Barbour was eager to add the Carrs' specimens to the MCZ collection, and he agreed to furnish them with firearms, ammunition, technical advice, and whatever other tools were necessary for killing and preserving specimens.[22]

Much to Barbour's dismay, the Carrs' collecting was delayed in the first months of their Honduran sojourn. They had to wait longer than they had anticipated for their firearms to arrive from the States. Archie joked that he and Marjorie were trying to import such a large quantity of ammunition and firearms that the Honduran government must have feared that they were attempting an insurrection. Two weeks after Marjorie Carr arrived in Honduras, she wrote Barbour that she was "impatient to find out what the birds are here. Practically all are strange to me," Carr confessed. She complained that gun shells were nonexistent in Honduras, "and everything cries out to be shot—ducks, deer, pigeons to eat and many others to skin."[23]

Three months after Carr's arrival in Honduras, the firearms and ammunition required for collecting were still missing. "Our guns haven't come yet," Carr complained to her mother. "It is infuriating, for I can't do anything but slobber at the mouth over the birds." Another item she was missing was pants. When Carr prepared for the family's move to Honduras, she had not realized that it was still not acceptable for women to wear pants in Central America. Yet they were a necessity given the Carrs' daily rides on horseback. Pants and other American-style items of clothing were not readily available in the outlying towns near Zamorano, and most goods cost two to three times more in Honduras than they did in the States. Out of necessity, Marjorie Carr learned to design and sew most of her own clothing and outfits for her growing family.[24]

While the Carrs waited for Barbour's initial shipments of weapons and ammunition to arrive, they borrowed firearms from colleagues at Zamorano. Carr started to prepare bird skins within weeks of her arrival in Honduras, while Chuck was still a newborn. She and Archie also hunted a variety of wild game. "The rice field is ripe and the doves and rice birds come in droves all day long," Carr informed her mother. "We go down every day and shoot a few pigeons to eat. The States doves are thick now and then there are also the big local white-winged pigeons." Archie boasted to J. C. Dickinson Jr. that he had just shot sixty-five pigeons in two days.[25]

The Carrs lived off of the land in Honduras, supplementing the produce from their garden with freshly killed meat. "There was plenty of game to shoot and a little-known wilderness at your doorstep," Archie recalled. "The volcano-set Pacific shore was sixty miles to the south and the hot, lush banana coast a hundred miles to the north; and you could climb a mountain three miles away and find any sort of weather you hankered after." The Carrs hunted and ate macaws and other tropical birds, sea turtle meat and eggs, iguana, monkeys, manatee, rodents, and many other animals. As Archie's turtle conservation efforts increased in the 1950s, critics pointed out his hypocrisy in arguing for the conservation of sea turtles while continuing to consume them. "I appear to be at one moment dejected over the precarious survival state of

The San Antonio de Oriente mining town near El Zamorano, Honduras. Photo by Margaret Hogaboom. Courtesy of Mimi Carr.

sea turtles," he explained, "and at the next drooling over the thought of eating them. Today I try to do better."[26]

While in Honduras, however, the Carrs sampled a variety of native animals. One of Carr's favorite dishes was boiled armadillo. "They were elegant," she wrote Barbour. "Like pig I thought. I believe there is more meat for size than any little animal I've eaten." On an early collecting trip along the Choluteca River—Honduras's largest river near the Pacific, located a short drive from Zamorano—Carr acquired her first scarlet macaw. "We crossed two mountain ridges covered with long leaf pine trees," she wrote her mother. "I got an immense thrill when we came upon a flock of Macaws sitting in the pines along the roadside. They were huge and unbelievably brilliantly colored—red, blue and yellow. They were very common in the Choluteca River Valley and we

J. C. Dickinson Jr. (who later became the director of the Florida Museum of Natural History in Gainesville) and Marjorie Carr prepare bird specimens after a collecting expedition. Also pictured are family friend George Hogaboom (*at left*) and Chuck and Mimi Carr. Courtesy of Mimi Carr.

Archie and Marjorie Carr on a collecting trip at Lake Yojoa, Honduras (1946). Courtesy of Mimi Carr.

Marjorie Carr net-fishing at Lake Yojoa (1946). Courtesy of Mimi Carr.

Archie and Marjorie Carr after a successful deer hunt in Honduras (1946). Courtesy of Mimi Carr.

must have seen over 100 during the day." Still lacking her own firearm, Marjorie asked Archie's colleague George Hogaboom to shoot one of the majestic tropical birds for her. She promptly skinned the bird and took it home for the servants to prepare. "It was simply delicious," she wrote Barbour. "Like good duck I thought." The main purpose for the collecting trip was to find specimens of the *Anableps*, or "four-eyed fish," which was common in the Choluteca River. The eyes of the *Anableps* are divided so that they are able to see under and above water at the same time. After collecting several samples of *Anableps*, Hogaboom shot three iguanas. "The largest was over 5 feet long and weighed 25 pounds," Carr observed. She lamented that they had planned to eat the iguanas, "but the buzzards flew off with the bodies when our backs were turned."[27]

In the 1940s, Honduras boasted not only diverse animal life, but also what Archie described as an "almost infinite variety" of plants. High mountains and steaming lowlands provided the right conditions for numerous habitats to flourish. Over a period of several years, the Carrs explored the cloud forests of the high mountains surrounding Zamorano: Uyuca, Monte Crudo, El Portillo, El Volcán, Rancho Quemado, Peña Blanca, San Juancito, and others. Some of their collecting expeditions led to the discovery of new species of fish and other animals. In contrast to the Colombian rain forests, which had been cleared and cut back for agriculture by the 1940s, the Honduran rain forests contained as many as five layers of tree canopies with 200-foot specimens that blocked direct sunlight. The ocelot, puma, and jaguar hunted there, joining such jungle fauna as the sloth, several species of monkey, the quetzal, mountain goat, and myriad parrots, among other species. The valleys were home to the coyote, numerous snake and frog species, the armadillo, tarantula, fox, deer, skunk, and more. Yet the high cloud forest was relatively devoid of flora, a condition Archie considered a mystery.[28]

Archie's light teaching schedule allowed him to join Marjorie and a rotating assortment of visitors and colleagues on regular collecting and research trips. He taught chemistry and biology in Spanish, which improved with time. Archie's lectures blended traditional science with conservation, making him an anomaly at Zamorano. He attempted to raise his students' awareness of the connection between traditional agricultural methods and environmental degradation, encouraged them to consider the impact of agriculture on forests and fauna, and helped them appreciate the benefits of sustainability in food production. In the 1940s, Honduras still had an abundance of "virgin," or old-growth, forests, and the concept of biodiversity was rarely considered in relation to tropical agriculture. Archie challenged his students to practice visionary agricultural techniques so that the consequences of Honduran agriculture would not be as catastrophic as they had been elsewhere in the tropics.[29]

Over the course of the Carrs' first year in Honduras, Archie struggled to balance his turtle research with his other obligations to Zamorano and the United Fruit Company. Although his teaching load was not demanding, the time requirements nonetheless interfered with his ability to travel across Central America to research turtle migration. Marjorie assisted Archie with his turtle research whenever they were able to get away from campus. These trips were also beneficial to Marjorie's research; she collected and preserved approximately two thousand scientific skins between the summer of 1945 and the fall of 1949. At the time, there were no adequate field books to help her identify the birds. Little was known about the species she collected, increasing the value of her research and specimens.

Marjorie Carr prepared scientific skins at a rapid pace, shipping them to Barbour for use in his museum and elsewhere. "We go collecting ahorse nearly every day," Carr reported to Lucy Dickinson. "I finished 52 bird skins last night. We have a mountain of bats too. Also a weasel, skunk, rabbits, squirrels and so forth. Sunday Archie and I went caving. Nothing there. We want to find a bat cave. A week ago we rode up to Uyuca (I do mean rode—didn't look at the view a single time). We had lunch in the highest milpa and then caught grasshoppers for Hub [Dr. Theo Hubbell at UF]. I felt not unlike Heidi."[30]

The older Carr children have some memories of their mother's preservation activities. Chuck's are mostly impressionistic. Mimi, the eldest of the five Carr children, has stronger memories. One of the earliest is of her mother's brown hands—tanned in the Honduran sun—working with German-made dissection tools to preserve specimens. Carr stuffed cotton in the birds' gutted bodies until it came out of their eyes, her daughter recalled, mimicking the repetitive motions she used to see her mother make so often. Mimi also has many fond memories of the long walks they took with the nannies each afternoon, passing more ox carts than automobiles. After the deprivation of the long Depression years, the Carrs enjoyed their comfortable lifestyle in Honduras. "It was a lovely life and they knew it," Mimi explained. "The war was ending and things were calming down. If you were an outdoorsy type, it was beautiful."[31]

Mimi and Chuck Carr play with sea turtles (1946). Courtesy of Mimi Carr.

The Carrs' nanny, Tina, feeds Chuck and Mimi by candlelight (1947). Courtesy of Mimi Carr.

Ruth Haynes Baird, Clara Haynes Harris, Marjorie Harris Carr, and Mimi Carr on horseback (1946). Courtesy of Mimi Carr.

Before the Carrs moved to Honduras, even while Marjorie was caring for Mimi and later became pregnant with Chuck, she continued to accompany Archie on collecting and research trips. However, in Honduras, the addition of household help also made it possible for Carr to complete unfinished work and start new projects. "I'm writing a small fish paper," she wrote her mother two months after reaching Honduras. "I did the work a year ago and haven't been able to write it up since then." Carr published her work the following year in the *Quarterly Journal of the Florida Academy of Sciences*, which later changed its name to the *Florida Scientist*.[32]

Although Marjorie's publications centered exclusively on the Honduran flora and fauna, Archie's work focused on the ecosystems and people of Central America. In the 1940s, Honduras was among the poorest nations in Central America. Aside from its Mayan ruins and the colonial architecture of its capital city, Tegucigalpa, Honduras remained mostly undeveloped. Honduras lacked roads, and outside the airport in Tegucigalpa, cow pastures functioned as landing strips for the small airplanes that provided the only reliable means of transportation throughout the country. A violent underworld thrived in

Marjorie Carr with a toucan she killed
to add to her tropical bird collection (1947).
Courtesy of Mimi Carr.

Tegucigalpa and the nation's rural areas, replete with local warlords. It was common for men to display pistols on their belts for safety and machismo. Throughout much of rural Honduras, the descendants of the Maya experienced extreme poverty.[33]

In a series of letters describing Honduras's culture and nature, Carr discussed her amazement at the industriousness of the local people she encountered in the face of their impoverished living conditions. "The reasons why one country is more successful than another is a constant source of interest to me," she mused. "The smug way we more fortunate blame it on the human beings of these countries certainly is not fair or true. I keep saying to myself, 'There, but for the Grace of God, go you.' I am convinced it is a group of lucky coincidences that has made our country the success she is."[34]

The small towns surrounding Zamorano were filled with people dressed in tattered clothes, and the majority of the young men who studied at Zamo-

Chuck and Mimi accompany their mother on a collecting trip (1947). Courtesy of Mimi Carr.

rano came from farming families who still used primitive tools and antiquated methods. Carr's description of a student project at Zamorano demonstrates the school's incorporation of modern agricultural practices with practical, low-cost techniques and supplies. "Today they are making ensilage for their new trench silo," she explained in another letter to her mother. "Ox carts bring in the corn stalks. While one bunch of boys fills the cutter another bunch tramps the chopped stalks down in the trench. These boys really learn by doing work." Although Carr was impressed with the students' progress, she expressed misgivings about the state of Honduran agriculture given the severe poverty with which its people had to contend. "Honduras is a pitifully poor country, really," she lamented. "Our valley [Zamorano] is a garden in the wilderness. It just shows what could be done with modern methods. While we use machinery here they also teach the boys how to make home made implements that will work on the farm."[35]

Carr was taken with the rugged beauty of Honduras, as her description of the ride from Tegucigalpa to Zamorano reveals:

The roads are out of this world. Hard clay, dried into ruts and strewn with great rocks that fall constantly from the hills. The road out of Teguc [Tegucigalpa] climbs and winds up mountains and then down into the valley of El Zamorano. The ride has beautiful scenery. The pine trees are covered with many varieties of air plants—many blooming. There are many springs up in the mountains and little freshets pass over the road. We passed lots of little caravans of burros, loaded down, on their way to market. Also two trucks and buses. It took one and a half hours to drive the 16 miles. You come down out of the pine covered mountain to a level green valley—almost round. You pass a little native town of Hicorita, cross a rocky stream drive through a grove of coyol palms and then you are at our house—a big cream stucco house with a high steep pitched roof of red tile and a deep front porch.[36]

Just as the horse had been Carr's chosen form of transportation in Bonita Springs, it was the easiest way to get around in Honduras. One of Carr's first explorations of the local flora and fauna was on a horse ride to San Antonio de Oriente, an old silver-mining town located near Zamorano. "The trail led up a deep ravine the sides of which were covered with pines," she recounted to her mother. "A mountain stream rushed along over beautifully colored volcanic rocks. We came to a place where the water seeped down the side of a steep wall and found large blooming orchids—orchids four inches across. We must have ridden twelve miles over very steep roads so we were tired at the end. Saw a big flock of emerald green parrots flying against the dark green forest."[37]

The Carrs routinely left their children in the care of their nanny while they explored the countryside on horseback. Even when Carr was at home—especially in the latter stages of her pregnancy—the household help played with and cared for her children while she prepared specimens. On one occasion, Archie helped out with child care while Marjorie traveled throughout Central America to examine museum bird collections, add to her own collection, and travel with guests. During this trip, a hired driver escorted Carr, her aunt Ruth, and Carr's mother in the Carrs' recently acquired Ford pickup truck to Guatemala and El Salvador. "I had to stay home to take care of Mimi and Chuck," Archie wrote J. C. Dickinson Jr. "Or at least to make Tina take care of them and Tita cook for them and Juan clean up after them and a gal you don't know wash for them."[38]

At the time of the trip to Guatemala and El Salvador, Carr was pregnant. "Mother was pregnant the whole time she was in Honduras," Mimi recalled. She continued to ride on collecting trips until the final weeks of her pregnancy, when riding a horse became too cumbersome. At that point she shifted her focus to preserving specimens and preparing notes on her collection. "Pregnancy is no obstacle," Archie wrote Lucy Dickinson, hoping to encourage Lucy—who was also pregnant—and her husband, J. C., to visit them again before they left Honduras. "Nothing ever happens to women as near full term as you'll be then, Lucy. Nothing could. As for your self esteem, eschew it. You should feel no shame over basic function. Jesus, you ought to see Margie; and she is this way nearly all the time."[39]

Giving birth in Honduras posed its own unique challenges. Carr came to prefer natural childbirth, which was the norm in Honduras at the time, even for women who gave birth in a hospital. Carr's first two children were born in the United States, where the standard hospital birth involved the use of heavy anesthetics for the mother. The dosage was often so high that the mother would be unconscious throughout much of the labor and delivery, resulting in a lengthened and more complicated recovery period. In Tegucigalpa, Carr "wasn't given so much as an aspirin tablet and all they did was to turn the bed around and tie two ropes to the posts for me to hold on to," she wrote Lucy Dickinson the week the Carrs' third child, Stephen, was born. "The amazing thing was how good I felt right away. Ten minutes after Steve was born Dr. Lazarus and I were having a cup of coffee together while watching the three nuns cope with Steve. I do believe I could have walked right out of the hospital that morning and felt fine." After the birth of her fourth child, Thomas, Carr wrote Dickinson about the advantages of natural childbirth. "You know what you are doing and can cooperate and do more and much, much faster," she explained. "The best thing is your feelings afterwards." Carr told Dickinson that in hindsight, she wished she had given birth to Chuck in Honduras instead of delaying her departure to Honduras so that she could give birth in an American hospital.[40]

The Carrs named their fourth child after Archie's brother, Tom, who had kidney disease and was not expected to recover. In 1946, Tom, who had a physics scholarship to the University of Chicago during World War II, conducted research for the U.S. Navy during the Bikini Atoll atomic bomb tests. He developed and set up instruments to measure the blast pressure on ships after two 23-kiloton atomic bombs were detonated in the atmosphere. After one of the blasts, Tom was exposed to radioactive water. The following year, he was diagnosed with nephritis (kidney inflammation) and was hospitalized for approximately eight and a half months. Nonetheless, Tom's doctors assured him that his illness was not related to the blasts. After a lengthy recovery in Umatilla, Tom resumed his Ph.D. program at the University of Florida, where in 1958 he became the first UF graduate to receive a Ph.D. in astronomy. Tom's illness prevented him from visiting the Carrs in Honduras. In 1948, when Tom learned that Marjorie and Archie had named a child after him, it depressed him instead of cheering him up; in the end, he outlived them both.[41]

A major factor that shaped Carr's glowing endorsement of natural childbirth and motherhood in general was the constant presence of domestic workers in her home. Toward the end of the Carrs' Honduran sojourn, Felipa—whom they had invited to move to the United States with them—accompanied the family on a camping trip to Agua Azul, Cortes. "We are ideally fixed up here," Carr wrote the Dickinsons. "Felipa and the four [children] have bunk beds in one room and Archie and I and a lab table have the other room. We go out on the Lake at least twice a day. In one two-hour jaunt around the south end of the Lake saw about fifty wood ibis, fifty American egrets, three spoonbills, thirty pichichis, thirty least bittern, sixty jacanas and one hundred cormorants. Twenty little blue herons—a few each [male and female]—coots, Florida gallinules, Little green herons, snowy egrets, Muscovy ducks, ringed kingfishers, rails, pelican (one). Saw only about twelve grebes and sixteen big crocs."[42]

The Carrs had become accustomed to life with household help, and as they prepared for their return to Florida, they were reluctant to give up their comfortable lifestyle. "I'm pleased with the servants," Carr wrote her mother shortly after their arrival in Honduras. "We are really quite a tranquil family. I'm enjoying having free time immeasurably." Carr set her own schedule in Honduras, devoting more time to work than to child care or domestic chores. "Our cook prepares delicious soups for lunch and supper and she bakes bread every day," she wrote. "This is really the easiest life I will ever lead. Imagine arriving at six after being away all day to find one's house all in order, a fire burning, babies fed and put to bed and asleep, supper ready and waiting, the bed turned down and plenty of hot water for the bath—and all your clothes clean and ironed!" However, the Carrs were well aware that this dream of a life could very well turn into a nightmare—especially for Marjorie Carr—with four children and no help.[43]

The Carrs' expenses were remarkably low at Zamorano. They grew some of their own produce, hunted and fished near their home, paid no utilities, and had few bills, so they were able to save much of Archie's two-hundred-dollar (U.S.) monthly salary. The Carrs paid each of their domestic workers approximately six dollars per month. Carr appears to have devoted more time to specimen collection and preservation than she spent with her children. Baby Chuck's first words were "Tina" and "Tita," the names of the nanny and cook, respectively. The Carrs had become so dependent upon household help that they invited two of their workers to return to the States with them in 1949. The salary of a UF professor was not substantial enough for the Carrs to afford domestic help at standard American rates. However, if the Carrs could convince some of their Honduran servants to accompany them to the United States, they would benefit from relatively inexpensive domestic service. The Carrs asked the Dickinsons if they would be willing to pay Juan a twenty-dollar monthly salary plus boat fare from Honduras, but this plan never came to fruition. Tina left her position with the Carrs to further her education, and she later married the dean of students at Zamorano. Felipa, who became the Carrs' nanny after Tina was married, and Juan, the gardener, were interested in working for the Carrs in Florida. Unfortunately for the Carrs, however, Felipa was unable to pass an English test required of all Central American immigrants to the United States. Juan spoke better English than Felipa; nonetheless, he remained in Honduras as well.[44]

By the time the Carrs returned to the States, Archie had become the world's foremost authority on sea turtles. In 1952, he published *Handbook of Turtles*, followed in 1953 by the publication of *High Jungles and Low*, which established his international reputation. Following the example of conservationist Aldo Leopold, Archie used his writing to educate the public about the importance of species and habitat preservation. Davis documents Archie's transition from natural history to conservation and ecology in *The Man Who Saved Sea Turtles*. Archie's experimental turtle-tagging program was an example of his practical application of the new science of conservation biology. He blended groundbreaking scientific research into the migration and breeding patterns of sea turtles with compelling nature writing and an effective conservation program that still thrives today. The assistance Marjorie provided to Archie over the course of his career has been largely overlooked. Together they transitioned from naturalists who killed specimens for scientific research and display in museums, to activist scientists—in large part due to Marjorie's attempts to convert Archie from a hunter to a conservationist/environmentalist.[45]

Archie's conservation ethos developed as a result of the influence of his mentor, Thomas Barbour, who died on January 8, 1946; under the tutelage of J. Speed Rogers and other professors at the biology department at UF; and through his encounters with the local people of Central America while he and Marjorie collected animals. The rural mountain folk they met along the way practiced the custom of inviting travelers to dismount their horses and enjoy a cup of coffee in their homes. "Dr. Karl Schmidt, a famous herpetologist, once wrote that naturalists make the best ambassadors because folks are pleased with your interest in their land, and therefore their natural suspicions toward a stranger are allayed," Marjorie Carr explained. "Perhaps this is why we always felt en rapport with country people—whether in Mexico, Honduras, Costa Rica, or any of the other small nations of the Central American isthmus."[46]

At UF, the Carrs had learned to appreciate the relationships between nature and culture. In *High Jungles and Low*, the people of Central America are as central to the narrative as the region's flora and fauna. Archie was also remembered fondly by Zamorano alumni, many of whom came to hold top political, financial, and academic positions in Central America. The connections Archie formed with his students and colleagues at Zamorano blossomed into lucrative partnerships that helped him accomplish his research and conservation goals in the decades to come.[47]

One of the most important partnerships Archie developed in Honduras stemmed from his professional relationship with Zamorano founder and United Fruit Company executive Sam Zemurray, whose daughter Doris Zemurray Stone became a distinguished archaeologist in Costa Rica. Stone's research along Costa Rica's Atlantic seaboard made her familiar with Tortuguero, which is Spanish for "region of turtles." Stone, along with Billy Cruz, a Tico (native of Costa Rica) who studied at Zamorano, introduced Archie to this small village on the northeastern Caribbean coast of Costa Rica, which is home to what Chuck Carr has described as the "mother lode" of nesting sea turtles, making it the most important nesting site of the endangered green turtle in the Western Hemisphere.[48]

Archie visited Central America (particularly Costa Rica) yearly for about four decades as he established and directed the Green Turtle Research Station at Tortuguero on the Caribbean coast, where the Costa Rican government established a national park on a 20-mile stretch of green turtle nesting beach. The Carrs had faith that conservation would work in Central America. "Conservation takes a lot of education anywhere," Marjorie Carr observed. "It requires people to take the long view. In Latin America it takes a special kind of message, and it is needed in massive doses, immediately." Although the pressure to clear land for agriculture and develop the beaches for tourism remains strong in the twenty-first century, the respective governments of the Central American isthmus are cooperating to preserve a wildlife corridor, known as the Mesoamerican Biological Corridor (MBC). In 1990, the Wildlife Conservation Society (WCS) and its partner, Archie's Caribbean Conservation Corporation (recently renamed the Sea Turtle Conservancy), started work with funding from USAID on a project they called Paseo Pantera, or Path of the Panther. It would become the prototype for the MBC. Chuck Carr, who was the coordinator of WCS projects in Mesoamerica and the Caribbean at the time, helped promote regional cooperation in Central America to make the wilderness corridor a reality. The purpose of Paseo Pantera, Chuck said, was to address the economic health of the respective nations and local peoples of Central America while also preserving a series of ecosystems stretching from Mexico to Panama.[49]

In *High Jungles and Low*, Archie described Zamorano as being "at a crossroads of inter-Americanism" in the 1940s. "The war was on, and funds for buying the favor of our neighbors flowed freely. Projects to court the people with the promise of technical or agricultural enlightenment sprouted like mushrooms." Most of these programs flopped, prompting Archie to recommend the following steps in Central America: improve the quality of the personnel the United States sends to the tropics; stop underestimating the intelligence and sensitivity of the rural Latin American people; avoid irresponsible spending for unnecessary technical assistance; increase opportunities for Latin American students to go to the United States for training; support the expansion of public health programs; accelerate and expand agricultural research and education; and encourage and help the Latin American countries in establishing and maintaining campaigns of conservation and restoration of renewable resources. "Of the three principal areas in which technical help from us is most badly needed—nutrition, public health, and conservation," Archie continued, "the last seems to me at once the most basic and the field in which the least is being done. It is surely the most difficult."[50]

Archie promoted an ecologically sensitive solution rather than an outdated conservation program based solely upon regulation of hunting. Explaining the scientific basis behind the decline in Honduras's environmental sustainability, Archie noted that the Yeguare River did not produce enough fish to feed the locals, who turned to dynamite or dropping rocks in the river to catch small water creatures. A simple conservationist approach to this problem, Archie suggested, would be to establish a wardenship to regulate fishing. Yet regulation alone would not return the Yeguare River or other Central American rivers to productivity, he explained, because the root of the problem could be found in the region's spring fires and summer rains. These environmental conditions flooded the rivers with soil and sediment, turning them into the equivalent of storm sewers. Because the silt suffocated most aquatic life except specimens that were small enough to take refuge under stones, Archie hypothesized, the river's larger fish populations were in decline.[51]

"Fish depletion is not to be handled as a problem apart but as a symptom of a more general and basic disorder," Archie maintained, emphasizing the connections between organisms and habitats within an ecosystem:

> The river is lean because the land is lean, and the ills of the two cannot be treated separately. Forests, wildlife, and hydraulic heads are all parts of an integrated whole, and none suffers or is restored separately. The river is sterile because the hillside above it is sterile. The firewood famine in the city and the diminishing water supply are not separate afflictions but different signs of the same disaster. Fishing is poor in the high tropics for the same reasons that a thousand miles of night driving on the highways shines no eyes of wild things.
>
> The idea that tropical America is still an unspoiled wilderness dies hard. The average North American is surprised to learn that the Latin countries have any depletion problems at all, and is frankly incredulous when told of their urgency. . . . A workable plan for restoration and maintenance of a landscape is not easy to devise. The factors involved are complex and their interrelationships almost endless. An immense amount of data on the physical and biological makeup of the region must be gathered before anything that the public can see can be done.[52]

Archie had a talent for distilling complex scientific processes into simple yet lyrical prose. *High Jungles and Low*, which issued an ecological wake-up call for Central America, predated Rachel Carson's *Silent Spring* by nearly a decade. Half a century after the publication of *High Jungles and Low*, Archie's recommendations for U.S. involvement with Central America were still considered on target.[53]

Unfortunately, environmental conditions have deteriorated significantly in

Honduras. The coyotes that used to howl outside the Carrs' faculty residence at Zamorano are rarely if ever heard on campus now. Most of the coyol palms surrounding the school and throughout Honduras were eliminated by a lethal palm disease introduced to the region in the 1960s. Most of the rain forests the Carrs knew in the 1940s are vanishing or no longer exist. Although Marjorie Carr had reported spotting more than one hundred scarlet macaws at a time, not a single macaw has been seen near Zamorano since the late 1960s. New roads and unrestricted hunting are thought to have driven the macaws to eastern Honduras, where there is less human encroachment upon the birds' habitat.[54]

After her family returned to Gainesville in the fall of 1949, Carr started to compile her notes on the tropical birds of Honduras. She prepared a catalogue of the region's birds with notes on their habitat preferences and available habitats in the area. Carr worked on the project sporadically in Honduras, completing her work in the final months leading up to the family's return to the States in August 1949. In 1951, she coauthored "The San Geronimo Swift in Honduras" with J. C. Dickinson Jr. In addition, Burt L. Monroe Jr. included multiple references to Carr's research in his 1968 study of Honduran birds, *A Distributional Survey of the Birds of Honduras*. After the 1951 publication of "The San Geronimo Swift in Honduras," however, Carr did not publish her own research for fourteen years, when she first wrote about the Ocklawaha River. Without domestic help, raising a large family commanded most of Carr's attention. She also assisted Archie with his turtle research and taught biology and chemistry in public and private schools. Not until 1995 did Carr finally find the time to publish her findings from the Honduras trip, "Notes on the Birds of Honduras for the Years 1945–49, With Special Reference to the Yeguare River Valley, Department of Francisco Morazán."[55]

In the 1950s, Marjorie Carr faced the challenge of combining child rearing and science. In keeping with the gender norms of the times, she assumed the role of primary caregiver for her family, which increased to five children in 1952 with the surprise addition of David. Nonetheless, chapter 4 shows that Carr remained active in zoology, albeit on a smaller scale than in Honduras, where she had domestic help. She devoted as much time as possible to the Florida Museum of Natural History at UF, where she was named an associate. When Archie embarked upon lengthy international research trips, Marjorie was often left behind on her own with the children. In 1952, when Archie made a research trip to Africa, Marjorie stayed home with their five children.

She kept them busy by taking them to some of the region's abundant lakes, rivers, and beaches, where she taught them how to identify Florida's flora and fauna, as her parents had taught her. Carr also shared this knowledge with her daughter's Girl Scout troop in the early 1950s.

By the late 1950s, when all her children were of school age, Carr embarked upon a conservation career that focused primarily on land preservation. As postwar development and an influx of millions of residents inundated Florida, the state's natural spaces were being developed at an unprecedented rate. Carr's conservation efforts—which were conducted through the local Garden Club and Audubon Society—marked the beginning of her lengthy career as an environmental activist. Although she was unable to blend caring for a large family with a full-time position in science while her children were young, she kept up with the advancing field of ecology through extensive reading and through her land-preservation activities. The seeds of Carr's later environmental activism were planted long before she learned that the U.S. Army Corps of Engineers was planning to build a barge canal that would bisect the state of Florida and destroy the Ocklawaha River.

4

Marjorie Harris Carr's Early Conservation Career

Marjorie Carr's conservation career began at the local level in the 1950s. Like many of her female contemporaries, Carr's volunteer service started with town-beautification work. From there she branched out into land-preservation campaigns in Gainesville and neighboring Micanopy. Carr's activism took a more controversial turn with her opposition to the construction of three proposed highway projects that would cross environmentally sensitive lands: Interstate 75; a cross-campus throughway and two-thousand-car parking lot on the University of Florida (UF) campus; and a proposed turnpike that would have connected Jacksonville and Tampa. Carr's initial activist projects helped her develop successful grassroots leadership strategies that would prove instrumental to her success with the campaign to save the Ocklawaha River. Unlike her early projects, Carr's opposition to the turnpike took place in the 1980s. Yet it is briefly examined in this chapter—in conjunction with a discussion of her leadership of two earlier campaigns designed to protect the environment from the encroachment of major road projects—to show the progression of Carr's leadership style over the course of her long career in conservation and environmental activism.

Each of the three highway projects that Carr opposed was designed without considering its impact on the environment. Developers failed to engage in land planning as they transformed Florida's environment. The emergence of the state's Interstate Highway System is a prominent example of this lack of foresight. Carr and her colleagues were outraged by the rampant destruction of Florida's landscape. "The nation's road builders have needlessly damaged or destroyed a shocking amount of unique American landscape, not so much because they build unnecessary roads, but because of their narrow-minded attitude in selecting the location of new roadways," Carr observed. "The state highway directors are responsible for selecting the routes which our highways follow, and cheapness of right-of-way apparently has been their main criterion. Too often this has resulted in roadways ripped straight through National and State Parks and unique areas of natural beauty."[1]

By the 1950s, Carr's interest in conservation had been stimulated by her observations of a series of profound changes in Florida's environment over more than thirty years as a Florida resident. Hundreds of thousands of soldiers who had trained in the state during World War II moved there permanently after the war. Florida's inexpensive housing and low cost of living made it an ideal place to raise a family, and the gradual introduction of air-conditioning helped residents tolerate the state's subtropical climate. Carr and others who witnessed the decline of Florida's natural landscapes challenged the dominant pro-business ideology that was central to the state's rapid, unchecked growth. Women's clubs and other organizations with strong female memberships provided female activists with the institutional support required to launch effective conservation campaigns.[2]

The land preservation campaigns Carr spearheaded in the 1950s and 1960s stemmed from her awareness of the importance of biological diversity to the health of an ecosystem. Other noted female environmentalists of the mid- to late twentieth century include Rachel Carson, who blended science and writing to increase awareness of ecosystems and pollution; and Marjory Stoneman Douglas, a writer turned environmental activist who championed the cause of the Everglades. Both Carr and Douglas were Florida transplants who embodied a strong sense of environmental stewardship in their adopted state. Another transplant who used the power of the pen to draw attention to the Florida landscape was Marjorie Kinnan Rawlings, who—along with Carr and Douglas—is fondly known in Florida history circles as one of the "three Marjories."[3]

Unlike Carson, Douglas, and Rawlings, Carr married a fellow scientist and conservationist who supported her activist career. Carson adopted her nephew but never married. Douglas and Rawlings were divorcées who never had children; although Rawlings married a second time, Douglas decided that one marriage was enough. Carson, Douglas, and, to a lesser extent, Rawlings maintained their independence emotionally and financially. Carr, as the mother of

Like her parents before her, Marjorie Carr (*center*) taught her children about Florida's flora and fauna. Marjorie and her five children (Mimi, Tom, David, Chuck, and Steve) at Cedar Key (1953). Courtesy of Mimi Carr.

five children, sacrificed the financial independence the aforementioned environmentalists and writers experienced, but she gained the emotional support of a close-knit family and, perhaps most importantly, the intellectual support of a husband who supported her activist work financially and by offering his scientific expertise publicly and privately.[4]

Carr's conservation activities helped her develop the leadership skills needed to apply her understanding of complex ecological issues to the environmental challenges of the late twentieth century. The path she forged in the 1950s combined the traditional responsibilities of a wife and mother with the aspirations and abilities of an ecologist. Not all married women who raised families in the postwar era subscribed to the ideology of domesticity. However, scholars have couched women's reform work in this period (especially in the first half of the twentieth century) in terms of "domestic feminism" or "municipal housekeeping," contending that their involvement in the "masculine" public realm was an extension of their duties as wives and mothers in the "feminine" private sphere. Historians have also applied the concept of domesticity to women's conservation and environmental activism, focusing on the differences between men's and women's encounters with nature. Since the 1990s, however, scholars have shifted their focus away from domesticity, revealing the complex economic, social, moral, and scientific arguments women articulated in defense of environmental preservation, justice, and reform.[5]

Women were the foot soldiers of the conservation movement of the late nineteenth and early twentieth centuries, but scholars have characterized the Progressive conservation movement as an example of municipal housekeeping, or women's "attempt to sweep up the city as they would their kitchens." When the Florida Audubon Society was established in 1900, most of its presidents were male, although the efforts of its many female members were essential to the organization's early successes. Women's contributions were responsible for the founding of Florida Audubon and the establishment of bird-protection laws and bird preserves. In the opening decades of the twentieth century, women's involvement in Audubon Society and women's club conservation projects increased their political clout in an era in which women lacked full civic status. Florida women had proven their ability to conduct effective grassroots campaigns that slowed the pace of environmental destruction in their state.[6]

Like that of so many of the women conservationists of Florida who came before her, Marjorie Carr's activism stemmed from her appreciation for the state's scenic landscapes. In fact, Marjorie showed an interest in conservation long before her husband, according to Archie's brother, Tom. "She was a conservationist from the very beginning," he explained, while Archie was a hunter first and became interested in conservation gradually. At the beginning of the Carrs' marriage, Marjorie expressed an early interest in establishing a home in rural Florida. One week after their troth-pledging ceremony, Marjorie asked Archie if living close to campus was truly a necessity. "Are there any places a little away from things?" she inquired. "Wouldn't prices be lower farther from campus? And you could have a turtle pen."[7]

Archie shared his wife's distaste for city living. On a research trip to New York City, he complained to Carr that he hated cities "on principle." Before the Carrs moved to Honduras, they sold their Gainesville home. Upon their return in September 1949, the Carrs decided to relocate their family to the small north central Florida town of Micanopy, located ten miles south of Gainesville. Archie resumed teaching biology at UF and was promoted to full professor. Even after Archie's promotion, the Carrs lacked the resources to purchase a new house, so they started to build one on some forested land near a sinkhole pond they named Wewa, after the Seminole word for water.[8]

The Carr family homestead is located on approximately 200 acres in Micanopy, a town so small that it made Andy Griffith's Mayberry seem like a thriving metropolis by comparison. The Carr children came of age in a different world from their suburban school peers in Gainesville. Lacking the commercial and government infrastructure of nearby Gainesville, Micanopy's charm lay in its rustic location at the edge of Paynes Prairie, where the Carr children were immersed in Florida's natural beauty. For about a year after the family moved to Micanopy, there was no telephone in the house. The Carrs designed their house with just enough room to accommodate four children. On New Year's Day 1952, the Carrs welcomed the surprise addition of their fifth and final child, David. (Mimi Carr suspects that her parents used the rhythm method of birth control.) Carr cared for the children in relative isolation, enjoying a daily routine that was different from those of most other faculty wives in suburban Gainesville.[9]

The Carrs owned one automobile in the 1950s, a yellow Dodge truck with a wooden frame around it. Each weekday morning, Archie dropped the school-aged children off at their respective schools in Gainesville on his way to work. By the time Mimi was in junior high school, the daily commute from the country to the city in a truck that was sometimes filled with livestock offended her preteen sensibilities. "I was about twelve years old and I was embarrassed to be riding in the truck to start with," Mimi explained. One morning she asked her father to drop her off at the corner just before they arrived at school so that her friends would not see her sitting in the front cab with her father and three of her four brothers (David was still too young to attend school). Instead, Archie stopped the truck—which was loaded with two steers from the family's herd that he planned to sell in Gainesville—right in front of the school, where a crowd of her peers were gathered. "And just as we pulled up those poor cows defecated and urine came out all over," Mimi recalled with horror. Her friends still ask her to tell the story at their high school reunions.[10]

At the dawn of the 1950s, Florida—especially the state's rural areas—was

Marjorie Carr and Nellie the dog with Don Quixote the donkey (*at right*) on a rare visit inside the Carr residence (1953). Courtesy of Mimi Carr.

still recovering from the Great Depression. Micanopy's residents were primarily farmers, a section of the population that felt some of the greatest effects of the Depression. The cottage industry of harvesting Spanish moss for use in stuffing cushions and mattresses still thrived in Micanopy. Chuck Carr remembers watching men with long poles collect Spanish moss from the tall trees lining the Carr estate. Many of his childhood memories highlight the strong presence of wildlife inside and outside his home. The Carrs shared Wewa Pond with a female alligator for more than forty years. On one occasion, the alligator treed Archie after he attempted to photograph her, leaving him stranded high in the tree until Marjorie came home. The Carrs kept a pet otter inside their home. The otter would follow the family on long walks to a nearby creek, where it swam freely before following them back to the house. The young otter practiced swimming in the toilet bowl. Although the Carrs loved snakes—Archie had kept an uncaged boa constrictor as a pet in his office in Honduras—they taught their children to avoid Florida's venomous snakes and to keep their eyes on the ground when they walked outside. Chuck recalled spotting a large diamondback rattlesnake near the house when he was a child. He ran inside and got his mother, who came out with a double-barrel shotgun and "shot the rattle right off the snake."[11]

Wewa Pond on the Carr family homestead in Micanopy, Florida. Photo by Peggy Macdonald.

Mimi recounted a similar occasion when her mother's talents were required to quell a disturbance among a pack of dogs outside the house. "I remember thinking how brave she was," Mimi recalled, "going out in her pink nylon pajamas with a broom." Carr experienced a strong connection to nature. "Mother was a real naturalist, I think more than my father," Mimi explained. "I mean to walk with her, she was always so aware of her surroundings. It was just part of her soul."[12]

The Carrs' return to the States affected the entire family, but the transition had the greatest impact on Marjorie Carr. The scientific partnership she shared with Archie did not come to an end in the 1950s, but it became overshadowed by the responsibilities of caring for a large family. Carr remained involved in zoology as much as she could, considering the time constraints of raising five young children without the assistance of domestic workers. With no relatives living nearby—Carr's mother lived in Fort Myers at the time, and Archie's parents still resided in Umatilla—Carr devoted the majority of her time to child care and housekeeping. Although biological conservation gradually became the prime focus for the Carrs, they also wanted to provide their children with a stable home life. The Carr children later explained that their parents never tried to force their beliefs on them. "We would talk about biological conservation around the dinner table," David Carr recalled. "And that was just their normal conversation." Still, the Carrs encouraged their children to find their own path in life. "I recall them bending over backwards to accommodate whatever interests we might have," David remembered.[13]

Carr devoted as much time as possible to each of her five children, balancing the needs of caring for baby David with leading a Girl Scout troop when Mimi reached scouting age. Carr served as a Girl Scout leader from 1952 to 1954 in Gainesville. She also helped each of her sons complete the requirements for their Boy Scout nature merit badges. Ever since Carr had led the summer naturalist tours with the National Youth Administration while in college, she had believed in the importance of educating children about the environment. If people did not learn to appreciate nature as children, she feared, they would be less inclined to act as good stewards of the land as adults. Carr's Girl Scout troop included her daughter, Mimi, and several of her friends and schoolmates. She led the girls on nature tours, taught them camping skills, and held meetings in the Carrs' Micanopy home, where one former Girl Scout recalled that a pet otter, goats, ducks, and other animals wandered freely through the house. One time when Mimi was a teenager, while she was reading in her room with the door closed, she heard the sound of hooves in the hallway. She opened the door to discover that her father had let the family's Mexican burro, Don Quixote, inside the house. Mimi remembers that the donkey spent the rest of its life trying to find a way back inside the house.[14]

The Carr children were aware that their upbringing differed from those of their peers. "We were sort of hermit-like," Chuck remembered. On weekends, while their schoolmates watched movies at the Florida Theatre in downtown Gainesville, the Carr kids went on nature hikes, fished, and explored the woods together. "It was like being landlocked out there [in Micanopy]," David explained.[15]

The Carrs turned to nature, music, and books for entertainment and inspiration. Archie played the guitar and quoted the Bible by verse. The family listened to records (mostly Latin music and show tunes), but they did not own a television until the mid-1960s. "We could watch the news, and news specials, and a half hour after the news we'd shut it off," David recalled. "It was to encourage reading and other, more wholesome things, including homework." Like many Florida households, the Carrs lived without air-conditioning throughout most of their children's youth. Much of their time was spent outdoors. David remembers his father's fondness for the family's 100-pound alligator snapping turtle named Jasper, who lived in a small koi pond near the house. "When you'd come home with another kid, Daddy'd be in the kitchen, cutting up strips of calf's liver," David recounted. "He'd put it in a coffee cup and go out and dangle it over the pond. He loved to show anybody who came around how he could dangle the calf's liver over, and this great big turtle would come up." Archie would howl with laughter as he dropped the dripping meat into the turtle's mouth to the amazement of his children's young friends.[16]

Although the Carrs were isolated in Micanopy, the idyllic setting of the family homestead provided Carr with a refuge from the social obligations that preoccupied faculty wives living in Gainesville. The daily routines associated with cooking, cleaning, and caring for a family of seven consumed much of Carr's time, but being removed from the Gainesville social scene freed her to pursue intellectual activities. During the four-and-a-half years she spent in Honduras, Carr had become accustomed to spending her time outdoors with Archie, working on her specimen collection, and reading. By comparison, the move to Micanopy made Carr less of a recluse than she had been in Honduras. Marjorie and Archie spent much of their free time reading books that shaped their growing conservation ethos, including Fairfield Osborn's 1948 book *Our Plundered Planet*; Aldo Leopold's *A Sand County Almanac* (1949); Eugene P. Odum's *Fundamentals of Ecology* (1953); Marston Bates's *The Prevalence of People* (1955), and *Man in Nature* (1964); Rachel Carson's *Silent Spring* (1962); Barry Commoner's *Science and Survival* (1966); Raymond Dasmann's *Environmental Conservation* (1959), and *A Different Kind of Country* (1968); and Paul Ehrlich's *The Population Bomb* (1968). Each of these books examined the growing threat that humans posed to the environment through overpopulation and the manipulation and exploitation of nature. These works also stressed scientists' social responsibility, emphasizing their obligation to provide the citizenry with accessible scientific information that would help them make responsible decisions for the planet. Carr would later convince the authors of several of these groundbreaking environmental works to lend their support to the campaign to save the Ocklawaha River.[17]

The Carr family's Micanopy retreat was intended to serve as a source of inspiration for Archie's writing. In addition, it furthered the development of the Carrs' conservation ethos and provided a constant source of entertainment and education for their children. David, the baby of the family, required his mother's attention more than the four older Carr children, who were like a tribe, Chuck observed. The Carrs' rural homestead and the many lakes, ponds, and creeks that surrounded it functioned as an expansive playground for the Carr children. When Archie traveled to the Caribbean, Brazil, West Africa, or Portugal to research the breeding grounds and migration patterns of sea turtles, Marjorie was sometimes left alone with the children for weeks or months at a time (although she and the children accompanied Archie on several trips to Costa Rica). Between June and September 1952, when David was still an infant, Archie traveled to the Shire River Valley of Nyasaland in East Africa to take part in a medical survey of insects. During Archie's lengthy research trips, Marjorie used nature as an ally to keep the children occupied. She took the family to the UF–owned Lake Wauburg (at Paynes Prairie), where the children swam and played along the shore for hours while Carr read the latest works in the biological sciences and conservation.[18]

Carr learned to manage her time carefully so that she could blend parenting with professional and volunteer work. Soon after returning from Honduras, she started to catalogue the bird skins she had donated to the Florida Museum of Natural History and the UF biology department, most of which were new to their collections. Carr had amassed a sizable collection of more than two thousand tropical birds in Central America. She had an advanced degree in zoology, had published in the field, and was an expert in Florida and Central American ornithology. Carr's work had been incorporated into the ornithology collections of the Escuela Agrícola Panamericana Zamorano in Honduras; the acclaimed American Museum of Natural History in New York City; and the Museum of Comparative Zoology at Harvard University. Carr began donating to these museums while she was living in Honduras, where she discovered species that had not yet been catalogued in natural history museums. She shipped her early skins directly to Thomas Barbour at Harvard, who kept many specimens for the Museum of Comparative Zoology and forwarded others to the American Museum of Natural History.[19]

In March 1954, John Allen, UF's interim president, invited Carr to join the Board of Associates of the university's Florida State Museum of Natural History (now the Florida Museum of Natural History). "As an Associate of the Museum," Allen informed Carr, "you would be in a position to help in the task of its reorganization and would also find its facilities at your disposal for the furtherance of your own studies. The association would appear to be mutually beneficial, since it would promise to contribute to the advancement of Ornithology here."[20]

Although the associate position did not come with a salary or stipend, it provided Carr with an institutional affiliation that helped to advance her career. J. C. Dickinson Jr., who was then serving as the museum's curator of biological sciences before becoming its director five years later, said the board of associates rarely held official meetings, which accommodated Carr's active home life. At this point, the museum had already acquired one thousand of her Honduran bird skins. Although Archie's clout and international reputation likely played a role in convincing the administration that Marjorie Carr would be a worthy addition to the board, his wife's sizable donation of scientific skins certainly improved the museum's collection significantly. Carr's formal affiliation with the Florida Museum of Natural History bestowed on her a level of prestige and professional autonomy that distinguished her from her faculty-wife peers.[21]

Carr assisted with the process of relocating and reconceptualizing the museum, which moved from the flooded basement of the Seagle Building in downtown Gainesville to the UF campus. By this point, the four oldest Carr children had reached school age, but David was still at home. Whenever she could get Archie to watch David, Carr would head to the museum to catalogue specimens and contribute to the museum's transition. Although a professor's schedule tends to be somewhat flexible, Archie supplemented his regular teaching and research duties with substantial writing projects. Between 1952 and 1956 alone, he published three books: *Handbook of Turtles*; *High Jungles and Low*; and *The Windward Road*. This high level of productivity left Archie with very little time to assist Carr with child-care duties. Much of Archie's time at home was spent writing, and he complained to J. C. Dickinson Jr. that this was an extremely difficult task to accomplish with a large family. Still, Archie enjoyed spending time with the children in the garden and wooded grounds outside their house. He taught them to decipher different frog songs and insect chirps as they explored the woods together. The Carrs instilled an appreciation of Florida's flora and fauna in their children. The abundant wilderness that surrounded their home functioned as an outdoor laboratory for Marjorie and Archie Carr and an amusement park for their children.[22]

In August 1956, the Carr family relocated to Costa Rica, where Archie established a research station at Tortuguero and served as a technical advisor and director of the biology department at the University of Costa Rica through November 30, 1957. Marjorie Carr taught biology and chemistry in English at the Escuela Metodista. The Carrs' sabbatical in Costa Rica was not as luxurious as their stay in Honduras. Costa Rica's hot, sandy climate was less hospitable than the temperate Honduran mountains. Whereas the Carrs had enjoyed the assistance of several domestic workers in Honduras, in Costa Rica they were only able to afford a part-time laundress. Most of Marjorie Carr's time was consumed by the responsibilities of teaching, which enabled her to work while her children were in school. This would be the last time the Carrs would uproot their family. Archie normally traveled alone on subsequent international trips while the children were still living at home, but Marjorie continued to assist him with research at Tortuguero, where they monitored nesting green sea turtles. The Carrs published their findings jointly in several prestigious scientific journals, including *Ecology*, *Biological Conservation*, and the *Bulletin of the American Museum of Natural History*. Upon reaching age twelve or thirteen, each of the Carr children spent a couple of summers at their parents' research station on the Costa Rican coast.[23]

By December 1957, when the Carr family returned to Micanopy, all five of their children had reached school age, which freed Carr to engage in volun-

Marjorie and Mimi Carr on the beach in Puntarenas, Costa Rica (1956). Courtesy of Mimi Carr.

teer work during the daytime. One of her early acts of conservation was to pressure Micanopy's town council to preserve the towering canopy of Spanish moss-covered live oaks that shaded Micanopy's historic downtown streets. In March 1962, the town council issued a proclamation declaring that the live oak trees were "a living memorial to the foresight and appreciation of natural beauty of early settlers of Micanopy" and therefore deserved to be "cared for, protected and designated wards of the town." More than one thousand large live oak trees growing within Micanopy's corporate limits (and several nearby nineteenth-century shops) were protected from demolition. Developers erected modern buildings in other sections of Micanopy, but Carr's beautification work helped preserve the historic charm of the pedestrian-friendly downtown. An avid reader, she also worked to expand the small-town library's natural history and literature collections.[24]

Carr soon moved from beautification work to larger conservation projects. Her first major project proved to be a painful failure. As Eisenhower's Interstate Highway System expanded across the nation, several parcels of rural Micanopy farmland lay in the proposed path of Interstate 75, a highway that would connect south Florida to north Florida (and extend as far north as Michigan). Archie's longtime friend and former colleague Leonard Giovannoli (whose Key West Aquarium position had intrigued Marjorie in

1937) informed the Carrs that the proposed route for Interstate 75 would cross their Micanopy property and divide nearby Paynes Prairie. The local courts designated the Micanopy parcels as farmland for the purpose of compensating landowners. Before the Carrs bought their homestead, it had been used for tobacco farming. The Carrs, however, had purchased the land as a nature retreat where Archie could write and they could raise their children in natural surroundings.[25]

Carr decided to take a stand against the construction of Interstate 75 through sections of Micanopy and Paynes Prairie. Archie was busy writing *The Windward Road*, and he decided not to get involved in what he was certain would be a losing battle. Although Carr realized there was no stopping the multi-billion-dollar Eisenhower Interstate Highway System—which funneled nearly $200 million into Florida during the first three years of construction—she wanted to voice her opposition to the highway planners' decision to build the road through Micanopy, Paynes Prairie, and her own backyard. At this point in their careers, Archie's conservation activities were primarily limited to his writing and academic research, but Marjorie's approach was becoming more confrontational and political in nature. She went to court to challenge the state's classification of all of the Micanopy lands that the Interstate would cross as farmland. She sought a higher rate of compensation for the 15 acres of her family's homestead that had been condemned for the purpose of building the Interstate.[26]

Carr's challenge served as a powerful lesson for her children, as Chuck recalls:

> My mother went to the judge here in Gainesville and made this appeal that it wasn't just rural farmland as far as she, and especially her husband, was concerned. It was a wild area, and it was bought for a higher use than just watermelon farms and cattle. It was a retreat for a man whose writing was very important to his income, if you will. She made this case, and the judge rejected her argument. And I have this vivid memory of her at the stove that evening, and there are tears in her eyes. Then she explained this thing, and it was the first time I had ever seen my mother defeated by any damn thing. It left an impression about my mother, and about challenging the system, and about the power of the U.S. government, and a whole lot of things.[27]

The standard procedure for right-of-way acquisition was for the state to pay property owners for the condemned land. Because the federal government reimbursed the state for only 90 percent of the cost of the right-of-way, the judge was reluctant to reimburse the Carrs at a higher rate than what had already been determined to be adequate compensation for Micanopy farmland. By the time Interstate 75 opened in 1964, almost 15 acres of the Carrs' peaceful nature retreat were interrupted by the incessant noise of high-speed traffic along the interstate highway. In that same year, eighteen thousand snakes were killed by automobile traffic along Paynes Prairie.[28]

To Marjorie Carr, the tremendous noise pollution from Interstate 75, which crossed the Carrs' homestead and isolated approximately 10 acres of their land, was a daily reminder of the mounting threat Florida's rapid postwar development posed to the state's rural areas. Although the construction of Interstate 75 forever altered the bucolic setting of the family's nature retreat, it also steeled Carr's resolve and prompted her to fight future proposals to build new highways in central Florida. One of Carr's later and more successful campaigns against the construction of a major highway project was conducted through Florida Defenders of the Environment (FDE), the environmental interest group she cofounded in 1969 to save the Ocklawaha River from the Cross Florida Barge Canal. Carr and FDE argued that a proposed $385 million turnpike linking Jacksonville and Tampa was not necessary. One proposed route would have placed the turnpike close to Gainesville and Micanopy, which was already traversed by Interstate 75 and the four-lane State Road 441, both of which had taken a toll on the wildlife and habitats of Paynes Prairie. The proposed turnpike would have reduced travel time between Jacksonville and Tampa by one hour; in the process, it would have passed through several environmentally sensitive areas in central and north central Florida.[29]

In her later challenges to the construction of major highways that would have had disastrous consequences for some of central Florida's remaining wild places, Carr enlisted the help of established conservation and environmental groups including FDE, the Audubon Society, and the Nature Conservancy. Carr contributed to a new discourse that called for comprehensive land planning and land preservation. This discourse proved effective in killing the Jacksonville-Tampa turnpike in March 1989, when the DOT halted all work on the road. "It is very important that we begin to plan for transportation of human beings and goods for the future in an efficient, environmentally sound way. We need to make those plans now," Carr urged Floridians. "We are losing large amounts of undeveloped land. . . . People do like to have a way to get from here to there. But you don't need three ways to get from here to there. And you don't need to get there a few minutes sooner. I think that's what people are getting upset about, the redundancy."[30]

Carr had revealed that the main driving force behind the construction of toll roads in undeveloped areas was money. In addition to generating revenue through tolls, the proposed turnpike would have opened rural lands for development. The Jacksonville-Tampa turnpike would have transformed Micanopy's historic district into a truck stop. For the most part, Micanopy has resisted the type of development that normally accompanies major highways. Today a few small businesses line the Micanopy stretch of U.S. 441, including Pearl Country Store & Barbecue, a gas station and convenience store with a hometown atmosphere. A sign with the letters "BBQ" inside a neon outline of a pig lights up the store window. Pearl, which David Carr and his wife, Peggy, purchased in 2002, offers country breakfasts, boiled peanuts, Florida nature guides, the *New York Times*, and Wi-Fi access, which makes it arguably the most cosmopolitan feature of Micanopy. Pearl also boasts a self-serve copy machine, which would have pleased David's mother, since Micanopy had no copy machine in the early years of her campaign to save the Ocklawaha River. The pedestrian-friendly, historic downtown area still has no traffic lights, gas stations, fast-food chains, or convenience stores. Several small antique shops, an ice cream store, and an independent book store without air-conditioning are among downtown Micanopy's offerings. Micanopy's historic charm led to its selection as the location for the 1991 film *Doc Hollywood*, in which Michael J. Fox plays a big-city doctor who must adjust to life in a small town.[31]

In contrast to Micanopy's historic downtown area, the garish adult-entertainment complex Café Risqué dominates the scenery near Interstate 75. Other businesses near the Interstate exit include a couple of gas stations, a Knights Inn hotel, a fireworks store, and Smiley's antique mall, which competes with the downtown antique stores. Several closed gas stations and restaurants near Micanopy's Interstate 75 exit attest to the challenges faced by local businesses that must contend with the greater number and more appealing variety of restaurants, strip malls, and gas stations within a stone's throw of nearby Gainesville's four Interstate exits. The majority of the travelers along Interstate 75 pass through north central Florida without noticing Micanopy. Most tourists' only contact with the town comes through their exposure to the many brightly colored billboards featuring pictures of sultry women with the Café Risqué motto "We Bare All" announcing the presence of the town's most infamous attraction. Located approximately two hours from the major metropolitan centers of Jacksonville, Tampa, Orlando, and the Atlantic beaches, Micanopy has escaped the development that would have accompanied the proposed Jacksonville-Tampa turnpike extension.[32]

After the failure of Marjorie Carr's first attempt to oppose the construction of an interstate highway across environmentally sensitive lands, she came to appreciate the importance of collaborating with established statewide and national organizations. She channeled her subsequent conservation activities through the local chapters of the Garden Club and Audubon Society, which had a powerful statewide and national infrastructure that aided Carr and other conservationists in their local campaigns. As an officer and board member of the Gainesville Garden Club and Alachua Audubon Society—which she cofounded along with David Anthony and others in 1960—Carr worked closely with UF experts and government officials on a variety of local conservation projects. She served on the board of directors of the Gainesville Garden Club—whose membership was mostly female—from 1958 through 1962. By contrast, the majority of the Alachua Audubon Society members were professional men, including UF faculty and prominent local businessmen. Carr served as president and a longtime board member of the Alachua Audubon Society.

As the Carr children witnessed the emergence of their mother's activist career, they offered their support. Combining full-time conservation work with the demands of caring for a large family was a challenge. Carr scheduled face-to-face meetings when her children were in school and conducted other business at home over the telephone. The Carrs' conservation activities were a regular topic of dinnertime conversation. Although the children did not always grasp the scientific terms and theories their parents discussed at the dinner table, these talks shaped their understanding of the world and encouraged them to become involved in conservation, first through their parents' projects and later in their own professional and volunteer activities.[33]

Marjorie Carr's first major project with the Gainesville Garden Club involved the preservation of Paynes Prairie, a 17,346-acre prairie made famous by the naturalist William Bartram in the late eighteenth century. The Carrs had read Bartram's *Travels through North and South Carolina, Georgia, East and West Florida* and considered Paynes Prairie (which Bartram had dubbed the Great Alachua Savanna) to be a natural treasure. In 1964, Archie provided an ecological description of the prairie in *Ulendo*:

Paynes Prairie is fifty square miles of level plain in north-central Florida let down in the hammock and pinelands south of Gainesville by collapse of the limestone bedrock. It drains partly into Orange Lake to the south and partly into a sinkhole at its northeast side. The sink used to clog up occasionally, and for years or decades the prairie would be under water. The people called it Alachua Lake in those times and ran steamboats on it. . . . Nowadays the prairie is mostly dry, with shallow ponds and patches of marsh where ancient gator holes have silted up but never disappeared, and with patches of Brahma cattle here and there out into the far spread of the plain, like antelope in Kenya. The prairie is about the best thing to see on U.S. Route 441 from the Smoky Mountains to the Keys, though to tell why would be to digress badly. But everybody with any sense is crazy about the prairie. The cowboys who work there like it and tell with zest of unlikely creatures they see—a black panther was the last I heard of—and people fish for bowfins in the ditches. There used to be great vogue in snake catching on the prairie before the roadsides became a sanctuary. People from all around used to come and catch the snakes that sunned themselves along the road shoulders. When William Bartram was there the prairie wrought him up, and his prose about the place was borrowed by Coleridge for his poem "Kubla Khan." The prairie has changed since then, with all the wolves and Indians gone. But still there are things to make a crossing worth your while, to make it, as I said, the best two miles in all the long road south from the mountains.[34]

Long ago, massive pachyderms, llamas, several varieties of camel, bison, sloths, glyptodonts, giant tortoises and the robust insects they fed upon roamed the prairie. Archie traveled past the prairie daily on his way to and from UF. On one occasion, he spotted 765 snakes during one crossing, but today travelers are unlikely to see even one snake traveling along the road. Although the increased traffic from U.S. 441 and Interstate 75 has played a significant role in the dramatic decline in the population of native snakes, Archie blamed the reintroduction of the armadillo for much of the damage. Florida's native armadillo species had become defunct; however, in the 1920s, between thirty and forty nine-banded armadillos from Central America escaped from two different Florida zoos and an overturned circus truck. Since then they have spread across Florida and into neighboring states, earning the unfortunate distinction of becoming the Sunshine State's most common form of roadkill.[35]

The armadillo, with its protective armor, has few predators in Florida. Those who are able to penetrate its tough exterior include panthers, bobcats, and bears, whose numbers are not strong enough to keep the armadillo population under control in Florida's altered ecosystem. So the nine-banded armadillo remains free to wreak havoc in peninsular Florida. They dig their burrows under orange trees, drying out the roots and destroying them. Through voraciously digging for food, armadillos also destroy the forest floor, whose rich layers are home to an important mixture of mold, organic debris, organic soil, and mineral sand; thus, armadillos make large swaths of the forest floor unsuitable for life. As a result, the state's insect, lizard, salamander, and snake populations have experienced a catastrophic decline in regions inhabited by the armadillo. The reintroduction of one species, Archie lamented, spoiled the natural world in a very subtle yet profound way.[36]

In the 1930s, the armadillo had not reached Alachua County. Even in the 1940s, Archie and his students and colleagues could collect a wide assortment of snakes on Paynes Prairie, which herpetologists from around the globe visited due to its reputation for snakes. "But I drove around here one day last week, made a complete loop, and didn't see a single snake," Archie reported in 1982, "where forty years ago, even twenty years ago, there would have been two hundred. There aren't any! I haven't seen one here in ten years. It seems odd that the only snakes I see anymore in Paynes Prairie are big, six-foot diamondback rattlers," he complained. "Some say that's because rattlers live in the holes made by the armadillos." Archie shot any armadillo he saw near his home in Micanopy, leaving the carcass on the ground to attract bald eagles.[37]

The danger the armadillo poses to Paynes Prairie is matched by the greater threat of development. The prairie was purchased for industrial development at the turn of the century, but through a series of mishaps, it remained relatively undisturbed when Marjorie Carr spearheaded its preservation 1957. Phosphate-mine owner William Camp, who was one of Florida's biggest landowners (in 1907, he owned 150,000 acres of Florida real estate), bought the prairie because he wanted to plug Alachua Sink, re-create Alachua Lake, and harness the lake's overflow to produce electricity. Soon after purchasing the prairie, however, Camp discovered that the plan to flood it was too costly, so he abandoned the idea. While Camp considered how to derive the most profit from his property, he rented grazing rights to cattle ranchers. Since flooding the prairie was not cost-effective, Camp's next plan was to drain it. In November 1911, Camp shared his plans to drain the prairie with Gainesville's city leaders, who were thrilled with the idea. Camp's plans came to a grinding halt just two weeks later, however, when Camp died unexpectedly.[38]

Camp's son, Jack, inherited the prairie and continued his father's practice of renting it out to cattle ranchers. Jack began raising his own livestock and soon had a herd of 3,500 cattle that gave birth to 2,000 additional calves each year. Nonetheless, the younger Camp eventually decided it would be more lucrative to follow through with his father's plan to drain the prairie. When Micanopy's town leaders learned of Camp's plan in 1919, they considered draining Orange Lake and Tuscawilla Lake for development. The water from these lakes would be channeled—along with water drained from the prairie—into the Ocklawaha River, transforming 150,000 acres of "bad lands" into an area suitable for development. Interest in draining the lakes eventually waned, but Camp was still interested in draining the vast prairie. In 1926, local support for draining increased as U.S. 441 (the Dixie Highway) was constructed on Paynes Prairie. Although the outrage Micanopy citizens expressed over the plan to drain the town's nearby lakes pressured town leaders to abandon the idea, the prairie was privately owned, so Jack Camp did not face the same obstacles to his plan to drain the prairie. By 1931, Camp had nearly completed the drainage process. Occasional flooding resulted during heavy rains, but in time the canals did their job and the prairie became dry again.[39]

Camp had free reign over Paynes Prairie until the Gainesville Garden Club—with Carr's assistance—embarked upon a public-education and conservation initiative. The Florida Department of Transportation (FDOT) had launched a program of setting aside roadsides as preserves. Carr and others worked to set aside roadside along U.S. 441 through Paynes Prairie as a preserve. In 1961, the prairie was designated Florida's first official wildlife sanctuary. However, since the majority of the prairie still remained in private hands at that point, the sanctuary only protected a small stretch of land immediately adjacent to the span of U.S. Highway 441 as it crossed the prairie. Not everyone was pleased with the designation of the U.S. 441 roadside as a wildlife sanctuary. "Mr. Camp, who owned the prairie, said, 'Absolutely delightful!'" Carr recalled. "'And if anybody steps off your preserve onto my land, I'll shoot them.'"[40]

Jack Camp's wrath was not the only thing that stood in the way of the transformation of the entire prairie into a wildlife preserve. Alachua County Commissioner Edgar Johnson championed a proposal to flood the prairie and revive the defunct Alachua Lake, and his plan was given serious consideration. The idea of conservation and protection of a unique prairie and wildlife sanctuary lost support among many Gainesville and Alachua County citizens and developers who would have preferred to see the development of a lake for fishing and tourism. Even some members of the Gainesville Garden Club and Alachua Audubon Society approved of the plan. The proposal to flood the prairie eventually ran out of steam after the county commission denied funds for a feasibility study.[41]

Paynes Prairie's fate ultimately rested in the hands of the state. In 1963, Florida established a pioneering land-conservation program with a "bathing suit tax" on outdoor clothing and equipment. In 1968, Republican governor Claude Kirk replaced that tax with a documentary stamp tax that funded the state's land-conservation program with proceeds from all land transactions in Florida. The documentary stamp tax, which was bolstered by the passage of the Florida Land Conservation Act in 1972, evolved into Florida Forever, the nation's largest land-buying program. Florida Forever provides state monies to purchase state forests, state and local parks, water-management-district lands, and state wildlife preserves, banning development on these lands permanently. The program also negotiates preservation agreements with private landowners.[42]

In 1970, the State of Florida used funds from its land-conservation program to purchase Paynes Prairie from Camp for $5.1 million, transforming it into Paynes Prairie State Preserve. The state proceeded to restore the prairie's native flora and fauna, as much as possible, using Bartram's *Travels* as a guide. Several of the species Bartram described had become extinct or only existed elsewhere in Florida by the 1970s, but the state made every effort to restore the prairie's original flora and fauna, including reintroducing bison in 1975. Other species Bartram sketched and described in his *Travels* include wild horses that descended from horses the Spaniards brought to Florida in the sixteenth century; a diverse assortment of reptiles, amphibians, and birds; the Florida panther (which abandoned the prairie and has not been reintroduced there); and other species. The state also purchased a stretch of railway line that ran through the prairie and converted it into hiking trails. Human-made canals and ditches have been harder to eliminate. Today Paynes Prairie is a 21,000-

Bison cool off in a pond at Paynes Prairie Preserve State Park. In the spring of 2012, after Florida Department of Environmental Protection and Paynes Prairie Preserve State Park officials expressed concern over potential safety risks, adult male bison were removed from the herd and young males were gelded. Photo by Charles Littlewood (www.CharlesLittlewood.com).

acre state park and wilderness preserve with open uplands, wetlands, freshwater marshes, and wet prairie.[43]

In the late 1960s, while Carr was working to convince the State of Florida to take action on Paynes Prairie, another one of Gainesville's most important environmental treasures was also at risk. The Carrs had enjoyed viewing the diverse wildlife of Lake Alice on the UF campus since the 1930s. Archie's students wrote ecological descriptions of the Lake Alice ecosystem, wading past alligators while conducting their research. In an essay written shortly before the university community discovered that Lake Alice was being considered as the site of a cross-campus throughway, Archie described the sad state of Lake Alice (which he had long referred to as Jonah's Pond) and Bivens Arm Lake (near Paynes Prairie), which he had explored for decades. "Both used to seem to me to rank among the wonders of the world," Archie reflected, "and much of their old magic is gone. Water hyacinths, in the virulent phase they get into when they grow near civilized man, were the chief cause of the sad change."[44]

Sewage and agricultural runoff had polluted both lakes, adding substan-

tial doses of nitrogen and phosphorous, which caused devastating plankton blooms or submerged plants that depleted the lakes' oxygen levels. Tens of thousands of fish floated to the top of the lake, followed by the growth of a thick blanket of water hyacinths. Occasionally, UF and City of Gainesville officials sprayed herbicides on the hyacinths in Lake Alice and Bivens Arm. The hyacinths died, sank to the lake bottom, and created a different form of pollution that further decimated the biota of the lakes. Regular poisoning eventually killed off the hyacinths at Bivens Arm Lake, which also produced the unintended consequence of distorting the ecology of the lake. At Lake Alice, high levels of nitrogen and phosphorous continued to support the growth of water hyacinths, essentially hiding the lake beneath a thick cover of aquatic weeds for several years.[45]

Archie recommended a more effective and ecologically sensitive course of action for the eradication of water hyacinths in Florida's bodies of water: removal of the nutrients at their source through prevention of agricultural run-off and more effective sewage-disposal methods. "As long as the exudations

Clouds are reflected in Lake Alice on the University of Florida campus. Photo by Peggy Macdonald.

of humanity pour in[,] the hyacinths will riot and grow marvelously tall and crowd together joyously in hydroponic splendor," he cautioned. "And each spring they will celebrate the spread of man with fields of lovely flowers." Today, Florida's standard treatment of the hyacinth problem involves limited use of herbicides and the introduction of two weevils and a moth that feed upon hyacinths, in addition to physical removal of hyacinths when warranted. The goal is to keep the destructive plants at the lowest possible level in the state's rivers, lakes, and ponds, and to prevent the spread of hyacinths before a serious outbreak clogs a body of water.[46]

In the late 1960s, however, UF and FDOT planners envisioned a more permanent treatment for Lake Alice's problems. In the fall of 1969, the university community learned that plans were well under way for the construction of a four-lane, limited-access campus throughway and a two-thousand-car parking lot along sections of Lake Alice. The highway would link West University Avenue with U.S. 441 south of Gainesville. The State Road Department had already completed a preliminary survey at that point, and the project was in

An alligator and a Florida softshell turtle cross paths in Lake Alice. Photo by Peggy Macdonald.

the final planning stages. Marjorie Carr, who was also then heavily involved in the campaign to save the Ocklawaha River—in addition to leading the Paynes Prairie preservation project—helped organize an ad hoc committee to investigate and oppose the proposed cross-campus throughway as soon as she heard about it from Archie and her colleagues at the zoology department. She employed the same grassroots strategies as those she used in her other conservation campaigns, enlisting the assistance of university experts and the Alachua and Florida Audubon Societies, who contacted university and state representatives to express their concern over the imminent destruction of the lake and its surrounding wilderness area.[47]

Opponents shared their outrage at a UF Campus Land Use and Planning Committee meeting, objecting to the proposed highway's route and its effects on the 60-acre campus lake. John H. Kaufmann, an associate professor of zoology who worked closely with Carr on the Ocklawaha campaign, claimed that construction would "immediately and irreplaceably destroy the major wildlife values of the entire lake area," leaving behind "at best a landscaped pond devoid of visible wildlife and surrounded on all sides by roads and parking lots." Kaufmann, Carr, UF law professor Joe Little, and some of their UF colleagues organized the Ad Hoc Committee on Lake Alice within days of learning about the highway. "Many people in the university and Gainesville are aware of Lake Alice as one of the few spots remaining where one can see an alligator or an egret in its natural surroundings," Kaufmann explained. "Relatively few appreciate the functions it serves in the teaching and research programs of the university, or of the potential it has as a scenic and educational facility for both the university and the public."[48]

UF zoology, entomology, and botany professors routinely used the lake and its wooded north shore for undergraduate and graduate research and instruction. Archie wrote UF president Stephen C. O'Connell to convey his dismay over the proposed highway and to inform the president of his and his colleagues' plans to develop the lake and its shore as the site of a campus research station. Throughway proponents maintained that Lake Alice was already damaged by past construction and pollution, rendering it unfit for research and education. Moreover, they contended that the university's predicted growth made the development of Lake Alice at a future date inevitable. Throughway supporters argued that it was pointless to develop the area for biological use, when the university could establish research stations elsewhere on campus. The main reason proponents cited to support construction of a four-lane highway over Lake Alice was that Gainesville was in urgent need of another north-south traffic artery with access to campus facilities, and the proposed route through Lake Alice would best accomplish this goal, from an engineering standpoint.[49]

Kaufmann admitted that Lake Alice had changed over the years, but he disagreed with the idea that its biological usefulness had been destroyed or that it could not be restored. "There are good prospects for repairing much of the damage done so far," Kaufmann informed reporters. "Areas that are set aside soon enough become inviolate because they are the last open areas amid the steel and concrete. The possibility that future expansion will eliminate the wildlife is a poor excuse for irrevocably destroying it now." The speed with which UF and the state were moving forward with plans for construction of the throughway shocked the university community. Kaufmann criticized planners for proceeding with "undue haste and too little publicity."[50]

The Florida Audubon Society pleaded with Governor Reubin Askew, the state cabinet, and the Board of Regents to intervene on behalf of Lake Alice's wildlife. "The campus is in kind of a turmoil over this thing," claimed Martin Northrup, Florida Audubon's assistant executive director. The route favored by university and state planners would cut through Lake Alice Wildlife

Sanctuary, an established refuge for herons. Florida Audubon informed state representatives that more than 40 percent of all of Florida's native bird species had been spotted at Lake Alice. They contended that the highway was "incompatible with the philosophy of a sanctuary."[51]

Both Kaufmann and Little first became involved in conservation through the effort to protect Lake Alice from the proposed cross-campus throughway. They worked closely with Marjorie Carr on the opposition and became heavily involved with FDE. At the start of Little's participation in the Lake Alice campaign, stopping the throughway appeared to be an impossible feat. "The cross-campus highway was a done deal," Little recounted. "Mr. O'Connell himself told me that, face to face." The FDOT and President O'Connell had already signed off on the project when they scheduled a campus hearing on the matter at the J. Wayne Reitz Union, the campus student center. The meeting hall overflowed with protestors, alerting the FDOT and O'Connell to the groundswell of local opposition to the throughway. Before that meeting, campus and state officials had failed to consider the throughway's impact on Lake Alice. Planners had tunnel vision as they prepared to dredge and fill the majority of Lake Alice in preparation for construction. "It was a case of progress versus swamps and alligators," Little explained. "It was real. It was a done deal."[52]

FDOT and O'Connell abandoned the campus throughway project after they became cognizant of the extent of campus and community support for Lake Alice. After the reversal, campus organizers acquired a great deal of respect for O'Connell. Little was an untenured faculty member at the time, but he suffered no professional repercussions from his activism, even though throughway opponents were relentless in their approach to conservation. "Marjorie was absolutely fearless," Little recalled. "She was unremittingly determined, she was brazen."[53]

Marjorie Carr and the other leaders of the opposition worked to inform the community that state and university officials were "putting something over on the public," Kaufmann recalls. Although fellow activists agreed that the cross-campus highway—like the Cross Florida Barge Canal—was a bad idea scientifically, economically, and morally, Carr was the only one who believed that it could be stopped. "Margie," Kaufmann remembered, "from the very beginning, saw this as . . . 'We're going to win this.'"[54]

Once the throughway project was stopped, the opposition shifted its focus to restoration efforts. The university addressed the problem of sewage drainage and agriculture runoff at Lake Alice, and Carr (working through Alachua Audubon Society) coordinated the planting of cypress trees along the edges of the lake. The lake's water-hyacinth population has been reduced significantly. Museum Road, a two-lane road with no shoulders, represents the university's compromise with the opposition. Engineers designed a narrow road that skirts the northern edge of the lake. The plans for a two-thousand-car parking lot on the lake were abandoned. Instead of dredging and filling Lake Alice, it was restored and remains the campus nature retreat that the Carrs struggled to preserve. Today students, Gainesville residents, and tourists stop at Lake Alice to spot alligators, turtles, fish, and birds in the daytime. At dusk, spectators wait outside a bat house located near the lake's north shore to watch thousands of bats fly over the lake in search of mosquitoes and other insects. University students conduct research in an experimental garden next to the bat house. The Baughman Center, a nondenominational chapel and meditation center, was erected on Lake Alice's western edge in 2000. UF students, alumni, and community members use the chapel, which offers a scenic view of Lake Alice, for weddings, funerals, and memorial services. There are no signs at Lake Alice to commemorate the efforts of Marjorie and Archie Carr and their colleagues to save and restore the lake, and few members of the university community remember that the campus landmark was almost destroyed in the name of progress.[55]

Over the course of an activist career that lasted for forty years, Marjorie Carr came to believe that citizen activism was the key to successful environmental campaigns. "It is now abundantly evident that if our Paradise is to be protected, the initiative and force will have to come from the grassroots," Carr wrote in the final years of her life. "The action will have to start at the local level and move upward. That is natural and proper in a democracy. Here in Florida we have indicated over and over again that the public places great value on the preservation of original landscapes, wildlife and ground water. It is the citizen who must lead; and to lead effectively the citizen needs to have certain basic knowledge."[56]

Carr's involvement in beautification work in Micanopy left a living legacy for the town, which recognized her contributions to Florida conservation by erecting a historic marker in her honor, as part of the Great Floridians 2000 program. Carr's inability to stop Interstate 75 from encroaching upon her family's homestead served as a painful lesson. The devastation she witnessed in Micanopy and on Paynes Prairie was magnified many times over when Interstates 4, 10, 75, and 95 facilitated the movement of millions of tourists across the state—especially after the 1971 opening of Walt Disney World in central Florida. Carr's later successes at saving Lake Alice from the campus through-way and preventing the construction of a Jacksonville-Tampa turnpike that would have damaged environmentally sensitive areas were shaped by the sting of defeat in her own backyard. She realized that effective conservation campaigns required an organized, autonomous group of individuals; effective utilization of the media to sway public opinion; persistent grassroots attempts to influence local, state, and national politicians; and competent representation in the court system. These local conservation projects had prepared Carr for the national campaign to save the Ocklawaha River—a battle she would lead for thirty-five years.[57]

5

Protecting Paradise

Marjorie Harris Carr Launches the Campaign to Save the Ocklawaha River

In 1962, one of Marjorie Carr's Garden Club associates advised her that the U.S. Army Corps of Engineers was planning to construct a cross-state canal along a section of the Ocklawaha River in Putnam County. Although the Ocklawaha River was located primarily in Marion, Lake, and Putnam Counties, and Carr's local Audubon Society chapter represented the interests of Alachua County, she had become acquainted with the scenic river while working at the Welaka Fish Hatchery in the 1930s. In addition, Alachua County is part of the Ocklawaha River watershed, which spans six counties (Lake, Alachua, Marion, Orange, Polk, and Putnam) and 2,769 square miles of central Florida. The watershed stretches as far south as the Green Swamp and Lake Apopka in Polk County and as far north as Alachua County, where tributaries from Orange Lake feed into the Ocklawaha River. Therefore, Carr realized that any changes to the Ocklawaha River could potentially affect the rest of the water-shed. Carr and David Anthony, who served as copresidents of the Alachua Audubon Society, invited representatives of the state board of conservation to provide Alachua Audubon Society members with more information about the canal. The November 8, 1962, meeting that followed marked the begin-ning of Carr's involvement in the ongoing campaign to protect and restore the Ocklawaha River.

The Ocklawaha River during a spring 2012 drawdown. The river's water quality and clarity improve during drawdowns. Photo by Peggy Macdonald.

By 1965, the campaign to save the Ocklawaha River Valley consumed Marjorie Carr. "This really did become the most important thing in her life," her daughter, Mimi, recalled. "That's what she did every day." To raise awareness of the plight of the Ocklawaha River Valley, Carr wrote "The Oklawaha Wilderness," which reflected the campaign's new environmental focus. In her essay, which was published in the *Florida Naturalist* in 1965, Carr articulated the damage that the Cross Florida Barge Canal would cause to the Ocklawaha ecosystem. The language of ecology would prove to be a much more effective tool for Carr and her colleagues than their initial campaign strategy, which centered on the natural resources that would be lost should the canal be completed. The next challenge for the defenders of the Ocklawaha River would be to demonstrate the need for a public hearing in which the interests involved could express their opinions, show that the Corps of Engineers was utilizing unsound engineering techniques (including its failure to conduct accurate scientific studies of the canal's impact on the Floridan Aquifer), and demonstrate that the current benefit-cost ratio was unrealistic.[1]

Carr continued to assist her husband with his research and writing on turtles, in addition to leading efforts to transform Paynes Prairie into a state park and save Lake Alice on the University of Florida (UF) campus. Four of Carr's five children had left home by this point in time, freeing her to devote her full attention to her conservation activities. In the late 1960s, the Ocklawaha would attract the attention of a national environmental campaign that awakened America's environmental consciousness. In the mid-1960s, however, the Ocklawaha campaign remained disorganized and regional in focus. Carr and her supporters would suffer a crippling blow at the public hearing they fought so hard to achieve.

Carr's UF connections were central to the success of the Ocklawaha campaign. Marion County's pro-business climate fueled its strong support for the proposed canal, which boosters claimed would provide central Florida with substantial economic benefits. The more liberal Gainesville in Alachua County was populated by a solid base of intellectuals who questioned the canal's alleged economic and recreational benefits. Under Carr's leadership, a growing coalition of UF professors would come to question the logical and moral soundness of destroying a river in order to construct an outdated barge canal.[2]

Canal boosters never stopped to consider the environmental effects of the canal. Politicians and special interests had pushed for the canal since the early twentieth century, first gaining approval for a cross-state ship canal during the Great Depression. However, the public-works project was approved only as a means of providing economic relief. At the peak of the Depression, approximately one-quarter of Americans were unemployed. As the nation turned its attention and economic resources to World War II, funding for construction of the ship canal was canceled, and the canal remained incomplete. However, boosters continued to push for the canal's completion, touting its economic and defense benefits. In 1942, Congress authorized construction of a shallower barge canal, but no funds were appropriated for construction. Years of costly economic restudies followed. In 1958, an economic restudy concluded that the barge canal's recreational and economic benefits justified the cost of construction. With the direct assistance of Presidents John F. Kennedy and Lyndon B. Johnson, funding for the canal was authorized. The Corps of Engineers planned to complete the canal along the same route as the one designated during the Depression—Route 13-B, which crossed the Ocklawaha River.[3]

The Corps of Engineers wasted no time putting their long-awaited canal funds to work. They planned to construct a high-level lock barge canal that would be 12 feet deep and 150 feet wide from the St. Johns River to the Gulf of Mexico with five locks, two earth dams, and several canal crossings. The estimated federal cost of construction was $145,300,000 in 1963 dollars. Congress distributed funds incrementally; canal funding through fiscal year 1963 totaled $1,885,100. Congress authorized an additional $1 million to initiate construction of the canal from Palatka to the St. Johns Lock and from there to Rodman Pool. The leaders of the campaign to save the Ocklawaha realized they needed to take action immediately.[4]

The Ocklawaha River's name comes from the Muscogee (Creek) word *ak-lowahe*, which means "muddy," "miry," or "muddy water." The sand-bottom Ocklawaha is actually crystal clear, although the natural by-products of the dense tree swamp surrounding the river give the water a light-tan stain. The Muscogee and later the Seminole peoples used the river for transportation and hunting. In the 1960s, the Ocklawaha was one of Florida's last relatively undisturbed rivers. The largest tributary of the St. Johns River, the Ocklawaha is among a small number of major North American rivers that flow north, traveling for approximately 78 miles from its source in Lake Griffin, the final lake in the Harris Chain in central Florida, before it joins the St. Johns River approximately 8 miles north of Lake George near Welaka. Silver Springs' massive daily output of crystal-clear water flows into the Ocklawaha River at Silver Springs Run.[5]

Tourists used to travel along the river on steamboats, savoring the exotic beauty and impressive wildlife of the canopied, subtropical river valley. In the 1960s, the Ocklawaha was home to a diverse population of fish species, including channel catfish, chain pickerel, a large variety of sunfish species, speckled perch, and massive largemouth black bass, which were the subject of Marjorie Carr's master's thesis. The river valley also supported several types of herons, limpkins, gallinules, rails, wood ducks, anhingas, snakes, turtles, alligators, deer, raccoons, otters, bobcats, and black bears, and the endangered Florida panther.[6]

Carr had known the Ocklawaha River for thirty years. "The first time I

Turtles bask in the sun to remove algae from their shells at Silver Springs, approximately nine miles from the Ocklawaha River. Photo by Peggy Macdonald.

went up the Ocklawaha," she remembered, "I thought it was dreamlike." The majority of the river is located in Marion County. Carr first learned that the Corps of Engineers planned to build a barge canal along a path that crossed the Ocklawaha River from a board member of Florida Audubon and the Florida Federation of Garden Clubs. After attending a Corps of Engineers hearing in Jacksonville, the woman wrote the district engineer to find out more about the canal route. He informed her that "not much" would happen to the Ocklawaha. The Garden Club advised the leadership of the Florida Audubon Society to research the canal route, but Florida Audubon was reluctant to do so because a member of the Corps of Engineers sat on its board of directors. Thus, the onus fell upon Carr, who—along with David Anthony, a UF professor of chemistry and botany who was related to Susan B. Anthony—added a program on the environmental impact of the Cross Florida Barge Canal on the Ocklawaha River Valley to the Alachua Audubon Society's regular conservation lecture series.[7]

The November 8, 1962, meeting, titled "The Effects of the Cross Florida Barge Canal on Wildlife and Wilderness," featured Dr. John Wakefield of the Florida State Board of Conservation and Dr. Robert F. Klant of the Florida Game and Fresh Water Fish Commission; it was the first public inquiry into

Like the Ocklawaha River, Silver Springs (*pictured*) lay in the proposed path of the Cross Florida Barge Canal. Photo by Peggy Macdonald.

the proposed canal. Ironically, the Board of Conservation was one of the agencies responsible for overseeing the canal's construction. The meeting, which was held in the auditorium of the P. K. Yonge Developmental Research School in Gainesville, focused on the environmental impact of the canal at a time when planners typically failed to address a construction project's environmental impact. The Corps of Engineers had exercised its authority to manipulate Florida's waterways for decades without being requested to justify their actions or examine the environmental repercussions of their work. The organization was neither prepared for nor overly concerned about the potential resistance of a small group of "bird-watchers."[8]

The UF community was outraged by the Corps of Engineers' proposed route for the canal. "They weren't really against the canal," Mimi Carr explained; "they just wanted to protect the river . . . at this point." Marjorie Carr was shocked not only that the Corps of Engineers planned to build the Cross Florida Barge Canal along the Ocklawaha River, but also that the agency had offered only vague explanations of how construction would proceed. "Here, by God, was a piece of Florida," Carr said. "A lovely natural area, right in my back yard, that was being threatened for no good reason." At the Alachua Audubon Society meeting on the barge canal, the two state representatives used an oil painting of the proposed barge canal to describe its route: no detailed explanation, supporting documents, or job specifications. The audience responded with what Carr called a "blizzard" of questions that the state representatives were either unable or unwilling to answer. The members of Alachua Audubon quizzed the representatives of the State Board of Conservation about the canal's potential impact on the aquifer, the benefit-cost ratio, and the damage the canal would cause to the Ocklawaha River. "We were all astounded that they had planned to build the canal right down the Ocklawaha River," Marjorie Carr remembered. "It enraged everybody," Mimi recounted. "And after that, everybody started pulling up their sleeves." Because the Board of Conservation representatives had failed to provide satisfactory answers to their questions at the meeting, Alachua Audubon Society members—under Carr's leadership—launched an investigation into the barge canal's effects on the Ocklawaha.[9]

The Corps of Engineers planned to dam the river at two points and flood 27,350 acres of hardwood forest to create a shallow barge canal and a reservoir that would provide its regular water supply. As Carr and her colleagues researched the Corps' plans for the canal, they began to question the extent of the alleged economic benefits of the canal. None of the Corps of Engineers' economic studies or restudies produced realistic benefit-cost ratios that justified the expense of the canal's construction and maintenance. "It was a ridiculous thing," Carr recalled. "It would destroy a beautiful river and it didn't bring in any money! That really stuck in my craw."[10]

Carr challenged the Corps of Engineers' economic studies of the canal, contending that the Corps had inflated predicted barge traffic and recreation benefits in order to justify the cost of the canal's construction. Canal boosters maintained that the project would enrich the economy of north central Florida. They based their argument upon estimated barge traffic projections and the alleged recreation benefits that would accompany the construction of artificial reservoirs near the canal's dam structures. However, the biggest motivation behind the construction of the canal had always been graft. The Cross Florida Barge Canal was a pork-barrel project designed to funnel congressional appropriations to the Corps of Engineers, line the pockets of construction companies, and draw federal funding to Florida districts in order to keep state lawmakers in office. Carr believed that the ultimate weapon to combat poorly conceived projects that were not in the public's best interest was the democratic process. She played an important part in shaping the discourse of the emerging environmental movement with a coordinated letter-writing and lobbying campaign that targeted state and federal politicians. She later supplemented these efforts with a legal campaign bolstered by the scientific and economic expertise of Florida Defenders of the Environment (FDE), the single-issue organization she cofounded in 1969. One of Carr's main strengths in the campaign to save the Ocklawaha was her use of the media to educate the public and put pressure on state and federal politicians. For nearly seven years before the inception of FDE, Carr led the Ocklawaha campaign under the auspices of the Alachua Audubon Society.

Carr cofounded the Alachua Audubon Society in 1960, along with David Anthony, H. K. Wallace (a colleague from the UF zoology department) and Enid and John Mahon. Its core membership was composed of UF professors who were interested in nature and conservation. Carr held a variety of executive positions with Alachua Audubon, including copresident (with Anthony) and chair of conservation. She also served on the board of directors of Alachua Audubon (1960–67) and Florida Audubon (1960–68; 1972–80). From the inception of the Alachua Audubon Society, Carr observed, its leaders and members were more devoted to conservation than bird-watching.[11]

Carr made it her mission to intervene on behalf of the Ocklawaha. "I felt the destruction of the Ocklawaha was like the murder of the Genovese girl in New York," she later reflected, referring to the 1964 murder of twenty-eight-year-old Catherine "Kitty" Genovese in New York City. (Genovese was stabbed repeatedly, raped, and robbed outside her Queens apartment while her neighbors ignored her screams and cries for help.) "The people who stood by and watched her be killed were not criminals, but they were partly to blame because they refused to be involved. And here, here in Florida, is this beautiful river which was to be murdered. In the beginning, the more I learned about it the stronger I felt that somebody had to do something to prevent its destruction."[12]

Carr wrote the Corps of Engineers to express her concerns regarding the proposed canal route's effects on the Ocklawaha River. The Corps replied that her fears were unfounded; the river would "be left intact except for the part between Sharpes Ferry and Rodman Dam." The Corps of Engineers' response infuriated Carr. "It was like saying that one is just going to cut off the rooster's tail—right behind the head," she explained. "That forty-five-mile stretch was the heart of the river." Alachua Audubon Society members mailed maps of the canal route to conservation groups across the state, wrote letters to their congressmen and state officials, and embarked upon the tedious process of gathering further information on the barge canal. "We were quite sure that if our elected representatives realized the truth," Carr recalled, "they would take appropriate action. Boy, were we naïve. They paid no attention to us."[13]

In the beginning, Carr thought the campaign to save the Ocklawaha would be relatively short and effortless. "I thought when we started out this would be simple," she recalled in the late 1960s. "All it would require, I felt, was to point out a few things to the Corps of Engineers. They would need to understand that the Ocklawaha is a treasure, that there is an alternate route and that a lot of people really want the Ocklawaha River saved. I thought once these things had been explained to them we could get the canal's course changed."[14]

Carr and her fellow activists were aware that the public and most major newspapers at the state and national levels supported the canal. Moreover, the Corps of Engineers had significant political clout, and great amounts of time and money had already been invested in the canal project. Therefore, Alachua Audubon's leaders agreed that it would be impractical to call for an end to the canal project as a whole; instead, they suggested that the canal be rerouted around the Ocklawaha.[15]

F. W. Hodge, then president of Alachua Audubon, attempted to enlist Florida Audubon's help in garnering support and assistance from the state's other conservation groups, but the statewide organization was slow to come on board. Opposition was minimal on the Gulf Coast, where a dam was already in place and Florida Power Corporation had donated the Withlacoochee backwaters area—known as Lake Rousseau—to the Canal Authority. For the moment, Carr and her fellow activists in north central Florida were on their own.[16]

Carr and her allies coordinated a direct-action campaign to increase public awareness of the threat the canal posed to the Ocklawaha. They maintained a "get the facts" strategy that utilized scientific, economic, and legal research; expert testimony; a grassroots letter-writing campaign; and public education. At the same time that Carr and Alachua Audubon spearheaded efforts to save the Ocklawaha, another group of activists launched a separate campaign based in Ocala in neighboring Marion County. Composed of a mixture of Alachua Audubon Society members and locals who lived near the Ocklawaha River, the group assumed the name Citizens for the Conservation of Florida's Natural and Economic Resources. Margie Bielling explained the sense of shock and concern that she and other members of Citizens felt upon learning of the Corps of Engineers' plans for the Ocklawaha River. "The more research I did, the less logical it seemed that they should be building this canal at all, let alone using the Ocklawaha," she recounted. "The land cut would have been disastrous."[17]

Bielling, like Carr, understood the ecological ramifications of the proposed canal. Bielling had a bachelor's in biology from UF and taught high-school science. In 1964, she applied her background in microbiology to her research of the hydrology and geology of the Ocklawaha River Valley, paying special attention to the impact of the proposed canal on local aquifers. Bielling shared her research with Carr and the Alachua Audubon Society, helping to produce a series of brochures that informed the public about the ecological dangers of the canal. Her father, John Couse, a retired Palm Beach County businessman, was another key player in Citizens. Couse's political and business contacts in south Florida proved beneficial to the Ocklawaha campaign. Another important Citizens leader was retired army colonel Walter Hodge, who served as president of both Citizens and Alachua Audubon Society in 1965.[18]

Bielling was already balancing a full-time teaching job and a young family when she first got involved in the campaign to save the Ocklawaha, so she traveled to Gainesville with the goal of finding an existing conservation organization to assume leadership of the campaign. She met with Hodge, whose wife advised her to get in touch with Marjorie Carr. Alachua Audubon Society members worked loosely with Citizens, but Citizens' efforts remained uncoordinated, which ultimately dampened the group's effectiveness. In the fall of 1965, the Federated Conservation Council—an alliance of sixteen nonprofit organizations including Audubon Society chapters, garden clubs, woman's clubs, environmental-education clubs, and river and fishing clubs—expressed its support for the Ocklawaha campaign, with the Alachua Audubon Society continuing to function as the leading organization behind the fight.[19]

Alachua Audubon's approach was to determine the facts about the barge canal and convey them to government agencies and the public. Instead of resorting to emotional attacks, the Ocklawaha campaign was based upon the principle of applying sound scientific and technical information to decisions that affected the environment. Finding accurate details regarding the Corps of Engineers' construction plans proved to be a challenging task, however, because the Corps disseminated very little information about the project to the public. This problem was exacerbated by the fact that newspapers did not yet have environmental writers in the early 1960s. Carr and her Audubon Society colleagues had a difficult time obtaining specific information about Route 13-B and its effects on the Ocklawaha. The group was routinely denied access to information, but things improved after President Johnson signed the Freedom of Information Act into law on July 4, 1966. Early in the process of researching the canal, they discovered that the Corps had not conducted any studies on the canal's potential effects on the lands and wildlife that lay in its path.[20]

Carr's scientific understanding of the Ocklawaha River Valley stemmed from her graduate studies at UF in the 1930s and 1940s. "The young men, and later women, who were in the graduate program could pick out a group of animals that they were interested in, but nobody had ever worked with those in this area [Florida]," she explained. "Eden opened up before you." By the 1960s, UF biologists had developed a sophisticated understanding of the flora and fauna of the river valley and their relationship to the Ocklawaha ecosystem. Professors and students had conducted ecological studies of north central Florida for decades, focusing on the relations of individual species to their respective ecosystems—including the Ocklawaha regional ecosystem. "So when the barge canal came along, which would have destroyed this whole ecosystem," Carr recalled, "you had a whole bunch of people who were very upset and could speak with authority."[21]

Alachua Audubon and Citizens shared members and leadership, often blurring the lines between the two organizations. Bert Dosh, the editor emeritus of the *Ocala Star-Banner*, routinely supported the canal in his columns and reported on the failures of Carr and Citizens. After an unsuccessful Citizens campaign to eliminate a $10 million congressional appropriation for the construction of Rodman Dam and Eureka Dam and Lock along the Ocklawaha River, Dosh informed his readers that "every member of the Florida delegation in Congress is standing firmly in support of the canal." The article included an excerpt from a letter from Representative Syd Herlong Jr. to Marjorie Carr, whom he identified as a director of Citizens. "As much as I admire and respect you and Archie, I regret to advise you that I don't plan to do anything to interfere with the orderly construction of the Cross-Florida Barge Canal," Herlong wrote Carr. "I would be less than honest if I didn't tell you that I'm a supporter of the canal. I do give you full credit for the sincerity of your point, but I think that the overwhelming majority of the people I have the honor to represent are strongly in favor of this waterway and I must respect their views. This is easy to do when I personally agree with them because I believe this project will be most helpful to all of Florida." Carr and her allies faced an uphill battle against formidable opponents: a coalition of state and national politicians, most of the Florida press, and the Corps of Engineers. Even the U.S. Fish and Wildlife Service supported the construction of the barge canal, noting its outstanding recreational advantages if the public had access to the canal bank.[22]

After the passage of the Rivers and Harbors Act of 1899, the Corps of Engineers became the nation's most prestigious engineering organization, charged with oversight of all construction along the nation's navigable waterways. Although Congress was ultimately responsible for decisions related to Corps projects, lawmakers gave serious consideration to the desires of local interests, as demonstrated by the successful lobbying efforts of Congressman Charles E. Bennett and other Florida politicians. The Corps was responsible for flood-control projects that improved agriculture, navigation, and residential areas across the nation. However, the Corps also had a long history of destroying wetlands and manipulating the land without considering the consequences. Since 1802, the Corps had applied Enlightenment-era views of the domination of nature to its engineering projects. Its castle logo is believed to be modeled after the city gates of Verdun, France. Critics have described the Corps as a "ruling class" and an "untouchable empire." The Corps of Engineers, which was initially devoted exclusively to military operations, branched out into civilian projects early on because it was the U.S. government's only organized group of engineers. Before the Civil War, the Corps had assumed responsibility for a variety of civilian canal, river-clearing, drainage, and other waterways projects.[23]

Compounding the fact that the Corps of Engineers obscured the specific details of the canal's pending construction was the challenge of organizing a large-scale environmental movement capable of countering the canal's strong support among politicians, businessmen, and the press. In the early years of the Ocklawaha campaign, Carr continued working through the Garden Club and Audubon Society while a separate group of concerned citizens emerged. The Garden Club provided Carr with early financial assistance, and her leadership of Alachua Audubon lent authority to her correspondence. At first, Florida Audubon was reluctant to support Carr because the organization was fearful that challenging the Corps of Engineers would lead to political repercussions against Audubon in Tallahassee. Eventually, Florida Audubon took a stand against Route 13-B, becoming only the second statewide organization (after the Garden Club) to do so. National organizations including the Izaak Walton League, National Audubon, Nature Conservancy, Sierra Club, and Conservation 70s also supported the Ocklawaha campaign.[24]

Carl Buchmeister, president of the National Audubon Society, considered the Cross Florida Barge Canal to be a national environmental catastrophe. He went so far as to claim that the barge canal was "one of the greatest political and economic boondoggles in the history of the United States," Nathaniel Reed recalled, adding that "boondoggle" was a term that was very "endearing" during the 1960s. "The term 'environmentalist' wasn't in our dictum at that time." Reed later served as the assistant secretary of the interior for fish and wildlife and parks in the Nixon and Ford administrations, and he was on the board of a variety of conservation groups, including the National Audubon Society and the Nature Conservancy.[25]

Ocklawaha supporters found little respect for the sanctity of the Florida environment in Washington, D.C. Congress's reluctance to block $10 million in canal appropriations was not the only setback for the Ocklawaha campaign. In the fall of 1965, Bradford Patton of the Southwest Florida Audubon Society sent a telegram to President Johnson to express his group's concern for the future of the Ocklawaha. Patton's telegram emphasized the river's natural beauty. The official White House response to Patton was that the economic benefits from the canal's construction outweighed the river's scenic value. The Johnson administration reiterated the fact that the matter had been settled for years and construction had already commenced. Under these circumstances, the letter concluded, it was impossible to stop construction of the barge canal.[26]

The political establishment of the early to mid-1960s was devoid of an environmental consciousness; moreover, women like Carr struggled to be taken seriously in a political realm dominated by men. The late twentieth century was a period of political and cultural transition for American women. As their role in formal politics evolved from exclusion to inclusion, two women whose names became synonymous with Florida politics crafted—independently—a subtle strategy that placated critics of women's entry into political spaces that had conventionally been reserved for men, while simultaneously providing the required justification for their admission into those spaces. Marjorie Harris Carr and Paula Hawkins (1927–2009) stood on opposite sides of the Cross Florida Barge Canal debate. Hawkins embarked upon her first and only term in the U.S. Senate in 1981, when the Democrats lost control of the Senate to the GOP. By then, Carr had spent more than a decade lobbying the Florida Legislature and U.S. Congress to kill the canal.

Hawkins, a Mormon, was the first woman elected to statewide public office in Florida, the first woman elected to the U.S. Senate from the South, and the first woman without marital or familial political connections ever to be elected to a full term in the Senate. Nonetheless, the National Organization of Women picketed her appearances because of her opposition to abortion and the Equal Rights Amendment. In Florida, Hawkins raised the ire of environmentalists because she backed legislation that would breathe new life into the canal. Despite their political differences, however, Carr and Hawkins shared the common experience of navigating a political system that was hostile to women. One of Carr's biggest adversaries, state senator George Kirkpatrick of Gainesville, once angered women's groups and grammarians alike when he compared the inevitability of a road-widening project to rape: "If it's inevitable, then you might as well lay [sic] back and enjoy it." He also helped ensure the demise of the Equal Rights Amendment. This larger-than-life politician, who switched his party affiliation from Democrat to Republican after Republicans gained control of the Florida Senate in 1994, embodied the chauvinistic attitude with which Carr and Hawkins were forced to contend in Florida and national politics in the late twentieth century.[27]

Unlike Carr, Hawkins was not a college graduate. The former model became involved in Republican politics as a community activist and quickly branched out into national political campaigns. In the 1970s, she became the first woman in Florida to be elected to a statewide political office, serving two terms on the Florida Public Service Commission. In 1980, Senator Hawkins was swept into office on the crest of the Ronald Reagan landslide. At one of her first national press conferences in Washington, D.C., a reporter from a major television network asked Hawkins who would do her laundry now that she was a U.S. senator. The reporter's question encapsulated the reaction of the previously all-male political establishment to the unexpected presence of women in politics in the late twentieth century.[28]

Carr and Hawkins devised a sophisticated methodology that eased their transition into the male-dominated realm of twentieth-century politics without appearing to challenge the restrictions placed upon women by the gendered social order of their time. Both women were self-described housewives, an occupation that was presumed to be a woman's natural calling. In the early 1960s, when Carr launched her campaign to save the Ocklawaha River, women lacked the full civic status they needed to participate as equals in the American political process—a condition that had not been remedied effectively in the 1970s, when Hawkins first entered politics at the state level.[29]

Carr and Hawkins *performed* femininity as an expedient intended to ease their transition into the male-dominated political realm. Their self-described housewife status offered them relatively safe passage into the previously all-male world of American politics. The tactic Carr and Hawkins employed enabled them to play a central role in state and national politics, where their very presence challenged the established gender order from within.

Carr's and Hawkins's decision to perform domesticity—to use the housewife label as a rhetorical device while they surpassed its limitations in practice—could be interpreted as a conservative response to outdated social norms designed to limit (middle-class) women's activities to the home. However, their adoption of the housewife persona could also be viewed as subversive. Playing the role of a housewife made strategic use of the attitudes of men like Kirkpatrick, who were certain to find a *homemaker* politician to be less threatening than a *feminist* politician who aspired to be treated as an equal.[30]

Carr performed femininity, especially in her private interactions with politicians, when the housewife moniker helped her arrange meetings or lobby on behalf of the environment. She supplemented her housewife persona with a "masculine" knowledge of science, creating a public identity that was palatable to (male) politicians who were sometimes put off by the more militant tactics of other environmentalists. In reality, Carr, who had the composure and commanding presence of a highly educated scientist, considered herself the equal of her (male) peers. From an outsider's perspective, however, Carr and Hawkins appeared to accept their assigned (domestic) role in society, even as they infiltrated the upper echelons of state and national politics at a time when women were grossly underrepresented. Fully cognizant that their presence in the public sphere represented a threat to the gendered order, Carr and Hawkins employed the rhetorical strategy of identifying themselves as housewives as a means to bridge the gap between the safer image of the traditional, domestic woman of the past and the more threatening image of the feminist or modern woman of the late twentieth century, a divide that had become central to late-twentieth-century discourses on womanhood.

The male-dominated news industry appeared to take Carr's self-described housewife status at face value. In 1966, an *Atlanta Journal and Constitution Magazine* article on Carr's fight to save the Ocklawaha was labeled "One Woman's Fight to Save a River," conjuring images of the epic battle between David and Goliath.[31] A 1971 *Houston Chronicle* feature highlighted Carr's sensational success in "Woman Took on Army Engineers to Save River in Florida."[32] In 1974, a *Christian Science Monitor* story on Carr appeared under the headline "Housewife Who Roared."[33] Since 1962, Carr had worked thirty- to fifty-hour weeks (without pay) on the Ocklawaha campaign. Yet these articles stressed that Carr was happily married with five children, which made her successful activist career more tolerable. Even in the 1980s, newspapers continued to use the courtesy title "Mrs." when referring to Carr, Hawkins, and other married women—a title that proved useful during their gradual transition from the sidelines to the front lines of the process of political decision making.[34]

In fact, when the Corps of Engineers finally responded to Ocklawaha activists' repeated requests to reroute the barge canal around the river, they actually asked Carr to propose a more acceptable route and named it "Mrs. Carr's route." With the possibility of stopping the canal's construction seemingly off the table, Carr had suggested a new route for the Cross Florida Barge Canal that would shorten it by 10 miles, reduce the total cost, and—most importantly—steer clear of the Ocklawaha River. "They asked me where I would make the canal," Carr recalled. "*They* were asking *me*. I thought this was ridiculous. I took a pencil and drew a line. Just like that! After that they called it 'Mrs. Carr's route.' I think they were a little upset that they hadn't brought it up themselves, but once they make up their minds on a route they are not interested in any alternates. And they defend their choice to the very last."[35]

A Corps representative later confirmed Carr's suspicions. "To my knowledge, the Corps did not look at any alternative routes in detail or in cost after the '42 study," admitted Sam Eisenberg, who was the environmental impact study manager for the U.S. Army Corps of Engineers. "Everything that was done after that followed along the 13-B route." Eisenberg claimed that the final Corps of Engineers report that triggered congressional funding for construction of the canal in 1964 was "a very minimal type report" that was approximately an eighth of an inch thick, indicating that little consideration was given to the environmental impact of the canal as construction plans were finalized.[36]

"Mrs. Carr's route" would have directed the canal through sand hills sparsely populated with shallow-rooted pines. The channel would have entered the St. Johns River through the Ocala National Forest and Lake George. Moreover, the alternate route would not have required costly reservoirs. The Corps of Engineers decided against "Mrs. Carr's route" because it did not require reservoirs, among other reasons. Without reservoirs there would be no new recreational benefits, and the Corps of Engineers' already inflated benefit-cost ratio would collapse. Congress's July 23, 1942, authorization of construction of the canal was based on a Corps of Engineers benefit-cost ratio that offered a marginal return in exchange for the cost of construction. The benefits included recreation opportunities in the canal's impoundments and alleged enhanced land values along the canal route. The defenders of the Ocklawaha would later argue that recreational opportunities along an unaltered river surpassed those available in a human-made reservoir that is expensive to maintain and plagued by hydrilla, an invasive water weed that was first introduced to Florida in the late 1950s as an aquarium plant. Hydrilla can grow an inch per day and fill a lake or river from the bottom to the surface.[37]

The Corps was only humoring Carr when it asked for her input on the canal route. Both the Corps and the press made light of the opposition. The chief of the Army Corps of Engineers, Lieutenant General W. F. Cassidy, labeled Carr and her supporters "little old ladies in tennis shoes," reassuring politicians and local interests that the canal's opponents were not to be taken seriously. At the time, no active Corps of Engineers project had ever been stopped in its tracks. During the same time frame, pesticide corporations smeared Rachel Carson as a "bird and bunny lover," seeking to discredit her best-selling exposé on the dangers of DDT and other chemical pesticides. Although the Corps belittled canal opponents in public, behind the scenes their strategy was to bypass the opposition by starting construction as soon as possible.[38]

In the 1960s, the Corps of Engineers' current and anticipated projects in Florida—not to mention their other major projects across the United States—

included the channelization of the Kissimmee River, the extension of the Intracoastal Waterway, and flood-control projects in the Everglades National Park and Lake Okeechobee. A January 1965 Corps map depicts a future Florida that resembles Frankenstein's monster, with sections cut apart and stitched back together from Key West to Pensacola. Corps mapmakers severed the Florida Panhandle from the rest of the state and placed it at the southwestern corner of the map, near Key West. For administrative purposes, Florida was divided into three parts: the Mobile District oversaw the Pensacola region; the Savannah District managed a slice of Florida's northeastern edge; and the Jacksonville District supervised projects throughout the remainder of Florida. The map's disturbing dissection of Florida's northwestern tip, combined with the sheer volume of current and proposed Corps projects, speaks volumes about the Corps of Engineers' vision for a redesigned Sunshine State that would place nature firmly under human control. Congress trusted the Corps implicitly. In fiscal year 1964, Congress appropriated more than $1 billion for Corps of Engineers civil-works projects and nearly $1.25 billion for fiscal year 1965, the most Congress had ever designated for Corps projects up to that time.[39]

The fiscal year 1965 appropriations included $14,150,000 in construction funding and $254,700 in operation and maintenance costs for flood-control projects in central and southern Florida; $16,000 for investigations into navigation locks in central and southern Florida; $137,000 for investigations into flood-control projects at Everglades National Park; $250,000 for operation and maintenance of the Intracoastal Waterway from Jacksonville to Miami; $100,000 for investigations of the Intracoastal Waterway from St. Marks River to Tampa Bay (also known as the "missing link"); and $4 million for construction of the Cross Florida Barge Canal, the Corps of Engineers' chief navigation project in Florida. These funds were in addition to the $1 million fiscal year 1964 appropriation for construction of the barge canal. The Corps' fiscal year 1963 estimate for the total cost of construction was $145,300,000, considered conservative by canal opponents. The Corps planned to use the fiscal year 1964 $1 million appropriations to begin work on the canal from Palatka to St. Johns Lock and from St. Johns Lock to Rodman Pool.[40]

Carr embraced the language of congressional funding in her plea for a new route for the barge canal and ultimately demonstrated that the Corps of Engineers had exaggerated the canal's economic benefits. In the first years of the campaign to save the Ocklawaha River, Carr and her supporters called

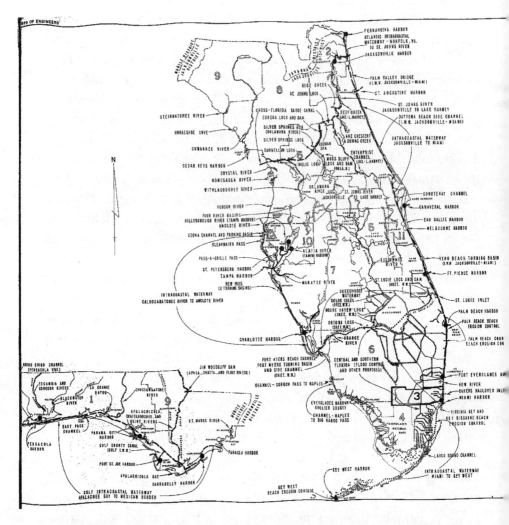

upon state and national politicians to reconsider the economic feasibility of an active Corps of Engineers project—authorized and funded by the U.S. Congress—at a time when it was considered unpatriotic to question the government. Carr thought it was wrong to place a dollar amount on every species, body of water, or forest in Florida. However, if that was what it took to protect the state's unique ecosystems, she was willing to speak in terms of the financial costs of environmental destruction. At first, Alachua Audubon and Citizens placed great importance on the economic value of the wild turkey population that depended upon the Ocklawaha. The groups also stressed the negative impact that the canal would have on hunting and fishing in the river valley. Speaking in the language of nineteenth-century conservation—which viewed

A 1965 U.S. Army Corps of Engineers map detailing the organization's active and planned civil works projects in Florida. The Cross Florida Barge Canal is identified with a thick, black line. Note that Florida is severed, with the Panhandle located near Key West. "Summary of Civil Works Projects under Construction and Studies in Progress," December 1965. Mildred and Claude Pepper Library, courtesy of the Florida State University Libraries, Special Collections and Archives.

nature as a collection of natural resources that should be managed for the benefit of humankind—did little to further the Ocklawaha campaign.[41]

The river was under consideration for inclusion on a national list of wild, scenic rivers that deserved protection from development. In 1963, the Departments of Agriculture and the Interior concluded that the Ocklawaha met the established study criteria and should be considered for inclusion. However, the Corps of Engineers was slated to begin work on the Cross Florida Barge Canal the following year, and such a classification would have forced the Corps to select an alternate route for the canal. When the Corps informed the Senate about its plans to construct the canal along a portion of the Ocklawaha, the river was removed from the list of rivers considered for the wild river study. A

Department of Agriculture administrator later admitted that the barge canal "may have been one reason why the Ocklawaha was not considered in wild and scenic rivers legislation."[42]

Carr pleaded with President Lyndon B. Johnson—who became the canal's new champion after President Kennedy's assassination on November 22, 1963—to prevent the destruction of the Ocklawaha. Her request fell on deaf ears, so she decided to reach out to the First Lady instead. Lady Bird Johnson succeeded in delaying the president's approval of funds for initial construction of Rodman Dam for two days, but the president remained a firm supporter of the canal. In February 1964, President Johnson traveled to Palatka, Florida, to start construction of the Cross Florida Barge Canal with a ceremonial blast of dynamite. Johnson's speech touted the alleged economic benefits of the canal: "Today, we accept another challenge—we make use of another natural resource. We will construct this canal across North Florida to shorten navigation distances between our Atlantic and Gulf coasts. When this canal is completed, it will spark new and permanent economic growth. It will accelerate business and industry to locate along its banks. It will open up new recreation areas. I wish all of you—and the canal—Godspeed."[43]

To canal boosters, the start of the canal's construction was a long-awaited dream come true. Nonetheless, Carr and her colleagues were not ready to admit defeat. In addition to destroying tens of thousands of acres of wildlife habitat through the creation of a series of locks, dams, and reservoirs, salt water and pollution from barge canal traffic would have contaminated the Floridan Aquifer, the state's major source of groundwater. The defenders of the Ocklawaha River sought a public hearing to address the issue, but canal backers ignored their repeated requests. Canal boosters faulted Ocklawaha supporters for waiting until the barge canal was already underway before initiating their protests. "You don't stop something like this after it's started," Congressman Syd Herlong insisted. "The canal is going to be completed."[44]

The Alachua Audubon Society urged Florida politicians and governmental bodies to take strong steps to oppose the completion of the Cross Florida Barge Canal. In a series of letters, Marjorie Carr and David Anthony, acting on behalf of the Alachua Audubon Society, advised their representatives that the "present route of the canal will obliterate the Ocklawaha River and its heavily forested valley from Silver Springs down to its confluence with the St. Johns." Carr and Anthony also voiced their concern over the introduction of heavy industry along the river's banks. "The mere presence of an industrial barge canal in the heart of a section of Florida long dedicated to the various out of door pleasures of man will damage and degrade the character of the entire wilderness area," they warned. "We believe that in years to come the wilderness of the Ocklawaha River wilderness area will mean more to the economy of Florida if it is preserved than if it is destroyed."[45]

In a letter to Florida's congressional delegation, Carr and Anthony suggested an immediate course of corrective actions. First, the letter directed the fourteen congressmen to request the immediate suspension of construction of the barge canal from the Silver Springs area to the St. Johns River. Carr and Anthony also urged the congressmen to direct the U.S. Army Corps of Engineers to offer plans for a new canal route from the Silver Springs area to the St. Johns River, avoiding the Ocklawaha River regional ecosystem. They stressed that the Corps of Engineers should work with the Department of Agriculture and the Department of the Interior to prepare plans for an alternate route. Finally, Carr and Anthony requested that a public hearing on the barge canal be held in north central Florida in order to allow the public to offer input on the new plans before their approval. "The Ocklawaha River will become a symbol," Carr and Anthony predicted, "whether of man's folly or man's wisdom remains to be seen."[46]

Canal boosters ignored the growing opposition movement and proceeded with plans to secure right-of-way for the barge canal. In an *Ocala Star-Banner* article, Bert Dosh had stressed the importance of securing a large crowd for an upcoming Ocala Canal Authority meeting scheduled to address the acquisition of canal right-of-way. To his dismay, those in attendance included a vocal group of Citizens members who asked the Canal Authority why there had been no public hearing on the canal since 1940. Canal Authority chairman L. C. Ringhaver admitted that he was unable to offer an explanation, and he attempted to shift the focus of the meeting back toward the procedure of obtaining right-of-way for the canal. State Conservation director Randolph Hodges accused the questioners of having "ulterior motives," adding that "some people may not be aware of it, but if we take time to have some projects of the canal restudied it would seriously jeopardize construction of the canal in a time in the foreseeable future."[47]

Indeed, stalling construction of the canal long enough to inform the public about its negative environmental impact would have been a major boon for the Ocklawaha campaign—especially since the Corps of Engineers would require the State of Florida to hold the United States free from damages from the canal's construction after it provided lands, rights-of-way, and easements for the canal. Citizens members resumed their questioning, asking what benefits the canal would provide that would counter its harmful effects to the Ocklawaha River Valley. One crowd member asked if the canal was such a "flimsy project" that it could not withstand the close scrutiny a public hearing would bring. An unidentified female attendee asked, "What would be the harm of a public hearing?" At that point, Ringhaver advised the crowd that the canal's feasibility had already been established and reminded those in attendance that the purpose of the meeting was to discuss right-of-way acquisition and not whether the federal project should have further public hearings.[48]

The *Florida Times-Union* (published in Jacksonville, which overwhelmingly favored construction of the canal) reported that the canal opponents' two main objections to the canal—the threat it posed to the Floridan Aquifer and saltwater intrusion—were unfounded. Colonel Giles Evans of the U.S. Army Corps of Engineers assured those in attendance that underground water did not flow long distances through the length of the state. He claimed that the canal would be built in a "sag" in the land and would not affect the state's main source of drinking water. When someone in attendance asked how the Corps planned to handle the issue of oil flecks from the barge canal damaging fishing along the river, officials responded that the switch from a proposed ship canal to a barge canal eliminated the threat of pollution from barge traffic. In addition, the height of the Atlantic and Gulf Coast locks—20 feet above sea level—would eliminate the danger of saltwater intrusion. Hodges admitted that a great deal of concern had been shown over possible damage to the state's wildlife and fish as a result of the canal. He attempted to assuage canal opponents' fears about the canal, informing the crowd that the Board of Conservation—composed of the governor and his cabinet (instead of an independent group of scientists and other appropriate experts)—had studied all aspects of the canal and was certain that it posed no threat to the state's wildlife.[49]

The Corps planned to step up construction efforts in order to complete the canal sooner than early projections of eight years. In order to do so, Congress would have to increase its annual appropriations to more than $20 million per year. Governor Haydon Burns supported this strategy, stating that "the canal is of no value to anyone until the first barge is across the waterway." Increasing the pace of construction would also solve the problem of contending with the canal's opposition, who continued to press for a public hearing to discuss the advisability of completing the canal along Route 13-B.[50]

According to Corps of Engineers literature distributed to Congress, it was standard procedure for all Corps projects to hold public hearings in the initial stages of investigation. "The desires of the people concerned are fundamental in making final recommendations to Congress," a 1965 Corps report stated. According to Corps literature, successful projects included benefits that exceeded costs, featured sound engineering design, met the needs of the people concerned, and made the fullest use possible of the natural resources involved. In addition, projects were designed to improve available recreation opportunities and minimize the loss of existing recreational values. "Plans for recreational development are coordinated throughout the planning stages with local interests and interested State and Federal agencies," the Corps stated. The Corps of Engineers' stated goals for the planning process for its projects contrasted with the way plans for the construction of the barge canal had been realized. Approximately 20 percent of the estimated cost of the barge canal had already been expended by the fall of 1965, but no public hearing had been held, although the Corps maintained that this was standard procedure.[51]

Carr and her fellow activists were beginning to harness the power of the press. Newspapers across the state covered their struggle to schedule a public hearing. Canal proponents were slowly realizing that they would have to address the activists' concerns, at least on the surface. The long-awaited public hearing would prove to be a farce. However, it would also prove to be a turning point in the campaign to save the Ocklawaha, which shifted its focus from conservation to ecology. The Ocklawaha fight began during the emergence of the environmental movement, which reoriented activists' focus from the conservationist goal of preserving natural resources for human use to an ecology-based perspective favoring the maintenance of sustainable relationships with nature.

In the nineteenth and early twentieth centuries, dams and reservoirs symbolized human ingenuity and determination. The structures would "improve" upon nature and serve the needs of a population that increasingly abandoned rural life and embraced the modern city, opening up opportunities for engineers to manipulate natural resources to supply the material needs of city residents. In the late twentieth century, the Corps of Engineers received billions of dollars in annual funding for projects that shaped the land according to human will. Just as manifest destiny had been used to justify America's expansion into the American West in the nineteenth century, in the twentieth century, the prevailing view continued to be that humans were destined to dominate and control the natural world.

However, the American public was on the cusp of a paradigm shift in its environmental consciousness that would begin to give preference to stewardship over exploitation. Ironically, the growth of suburbs after World War II—which in turn fueled Americans' increasing dependence upon the automobile—contributed both to the rapid deterioration of environmental qualities and a new appreciation for nature, which had become more accessible to suburbanites than to city dwellers. Mounting pollution from heavy industry and the electric power industry threatened the nation's water, air, and land. In the absence of strict, national environmental regulations and enforcement agencies, industries regularly disposed of raw sewage and chemicals in waterways, emitted vast amounts of toxins into the air, and disposed of toxic waste near residential areas. The science of ecology—a potentially subversive science that would empower scientists and citizens alike with the ability to discern evidence of environmental degradation—provided activists with the expertise required to mount a successful challenge to some of the more environmentally insensitive programs of federal agencies such as the Corps of Engineers and Bureau of Reclamation. The focus of ecology had gradually evolved from the study of single species to analyses of the complex interactions between species and habitats within an ecosystem—a transition influenced by the 1953 publication of Eugene P. Odum and Howard T. Odum's *Fundamentals of Ecology*. Between 1950 and 1954, Howard Odum taught limnology and biology at UF, and he and the Carrs became friends. The Odum brothers provided environmental activists with a sophisticated new language and philosophy that emphasized the centrality of the ecosystem to all living things.[52]

Ecology's maturation also contributed to the rise of activist scientists who acted on a sense of commitment to their local communities and the country at large by using their scientific expertise to evaluate and comment on deteriorating environmental conditions and challenge irresponsible government programs that lined the pockets of state and local officials and contractors while damaging the environment. Aldo Leopold was in the vanguard of a growing group of writers whose combined scientific and literary talents awakened a new generation of environmentalists. Leopold's early career with the U.S. Forest Service afforded him an insider's perspective on the philosophy and methodologies behind federal conservation programs. He abandoned his career in wildlife management to cofound the Wilderness Society and advocate environmental ethics. His message reached its widest audience after his death with the 1949 publication of *Sand County Almanac*, which espoused a land ethic that emphasized cooperation over competition.[53]

Leopold's *Almanac* set the stage for Rachel Carson's 1962 publication of *Silent Spring*, an indictment of the United States' indiscriminate use of DDT and other pesticides. *Silent Spring* aided in the transition from conservation—or the idea of preserving nature *for* humanity—to environmentalism, whose goal was to protect nature *from* humanity. Carson's message contributed to the growth of the public's awareness of the connections between human actions (including unregulated pesticide use) and ecosystems, or the "web of life," as she so lyrically described the relationships between species and habitat. Carson argued that the ways humans interact with the environment affect all life; poisoning an ecosystem with what she termed "biocide" affects not only the targeted insect, but the species that feed upon it, their habitat, and humans who are also supported by the flora and fauna within the ecosystem. *Silent Spring* empowered citizen groups to challenge pollution and other environmental hazards at the local level.[54]

Aldo Leopold and Rachel Carson were not the nation's first activist scientists, however. Florida led the nation both in terms of the science of ecology and citizen activism. Marjorie and Archie Carr's ecological awareness, which began with their undergraduate training in the 1930s at FSCW and UF, respectively, continued to be refined throughout their graduate training at UF, and in Honduras, Costa Rica, and, in Archie's case, Africa, which became the subject of his *Ulendo*. Like Aldo Leopold, Archie wrote about nature with colorful, accessible prose. His UF training had stressed the importance of including human culture as an important variable in the study of ecosystems. For decades his research had considered the impact of human practices upon the survival of several species of sea turtle. By the time the environmental movement was beginning to flourish, Archie lamented that too few scientists acted upon their ethics and involved themselves in global and local environmental struggles:

> The trouble is not mad scientists destroying the world, but politicians not planning beyond their noses, and chambers of commerce clamoring for growth and profit, and people in general being too passive and far too fertile and abundant. As I see it, the thing to blame scientists for is not what they do, but what they don't do—their leaving to engineers,

politicians and military men the decisions that change the earth and determine the way our descendants will live. Obviously scientists ought to be more active in the struggle to put the strong tools that their discoveries have created into the hands of more responsible, humane, and foresighted planners than those who are now in charge. I believe scientists are coming to see that this is so.[55]

Although Archie was frustrated with the slow pace of environmental activism and awareness, Florida was actually years ahead of the national curve. In 1946, the Florida Audubon Society challenged the state's indiscriminate use of DDT, long before the publication of Carson's *Silent Spring*. Audubon expressed its concerns about the pesticide's fatal effects on Florida's avian and marine life. The state board of health and the Florida Anti-Mosquito Association protested the state's practice of spraying DDT throughout entire cities, which the organizations viewed as a public-health threat of epic proportions. In the 1950s, a popular pastime for Mimi Carr's childhood friends in Gainesville was to chase the mosquito spray truck as it made its weekly rounds, spraying a fine mist of DDT on everything in its path. In 1957, the state created the Florida Air Pollution Control Commission in response to the air pollution generated by its thriving phosphate industry. Concerned citizens offered scientific proof of the phosphate industry's role in polluting Florida's air with sulfur oxides and fluorides and insisted upon government intervention. The year prior, the marine biologist Robert Hutton drafted one of the first environmental impact statements as part of a collective action opposing the dredging and filling of Boca Ciega Bay in St. Petersburg. The bay's sensitive estuarine environment had already suffered the Corps of Engineers' dredging of a 15-foot-deep ship channel and extensive plume hunting. Developers' plans to create fill land in the bay were ultimately approved, but Hutton's study served as a useful prototype for future environmental impact studies. The created land is now home to Eckerd College (formerly Florida Presbyterian College), whose students might be unaware that their waterfront campus was created artificially.[56]

The influence of the science of ecology upon the burgeoning environmental movement could not find a clearer form of expression than Marjorie Carr's March 1965 essay "The Oklawaha River Wilderness," published in the August issue of the *Florida Naturalist*. The essay begins with an ecological survey of the Ocklawaha River Valley and its flora and fauna. It demonstrates a shift in Carr's strategy from a focus on the Ocklawaha River as a valuable natural resource that provided clear economic rewards to humans—measured in terms of such tangible experiences as hunting and fishing—to the view that the Ocklawaha River is of value to humans by virtue of its ecological unique-ness. The Ocklawaha River, Carr contended, was an ancient ecosystem that was home to a unique sampling of flora and fauna that were threatened by the construction of the barge canal. The native flora and fauna supported by the river valley required "a big piece of unbroken woods" in order to continue to exist in the state. "Today, as Florida's population increases and its wilderness decreases, more and more people, with a variety of interests are coming into the Forest," Carr explained. "Students, ranging from grade school to college, come here on field trips; winter visitors, groups of youngsters, Boy Scouts, Girl Scouts and families come for a day or a week, just for the pleasure of being in natural Florida woods." Although Carr stressed the value of the Ocklawaha River Valley to nature tourism, her argument centered primarily on the merits of preserving the Ocklawaha River ecosystem—one of the largest unbroken tracts of land in Florida and one of only sixty-eight wild and scenic rivers remaining in the nation—because of its ecological diversity.[57]

Carr's essay was peppered with details about the damage that a completed barge canal would inflict upon the Ocklawaha Valley. Lake Eaton in the Ocala National Forest "will be wholly drowned along with forty-five miles of the river, if the Cross-Florida Barge Canal construction continues as presently planned," she warned. "Five outstanding Florida springs are located in or very near this natural wilderness area. . . . This valuable complex of wilderness which, mostly by plain good luck, remains as a sample of the original Florida, if saved and cared for could forever serve the enjoyment, inspiration and edu-cation of man." By focusing on the value of the land itself—not as a natural resource fit for consumption, but as a treasure to be protected from human ex-ploitation—Carr changed the composition of the movement to save the river from one of limited scope related to the protection of local hunting interests to a movement of national significance. The environmental movement in Florida and the nation was in its infancy, and speaking in terms of the innate value of nature was a powerful new tactic that would expand the influence and reach of the Ocklawaha campaign. If the Rodman and Eureka Dams were com-pleted, Carr pointed out, approximately 27,000 acres of riverine forest would be flooded and more than 30 miles of the mile-wide Ocklawaha Valley would be converted to a "shallow, snag-filled reservoir." Moreover, Rodman Dam would drastically reduce the flow of water to the last 10 miles of the Ocklawaha River, blocking native fish and manatees from traveling up the river (and resulting in their death in the dam and lock structures), and leading to additional disastrous consequences for the flora and fauna along that section of the river.[58]

Although dredging of the barge canal had already commenced along select portions of the Ocklawaha River, construction of the Rodman and Eureka Dams and reservoirs was not scheduled to begin until 1966. Activists' opposition to Route 13-B intensified throughout 1965, when Alachua Audubon, Citizens, the Florida division of the Nature Conservancy, and other Florida conservation organizations lobbied Florida governor Haydon Burns and the Florida Canal Authority to schedule a public hearing on the Cross Florida Barge Canal—something that had not occurred since the inception of the barge canal project in 1942. "It isn't too late to save the Ocklawaha," Carr insisted. "The canal lives from appropriation to appropriation. It's based on a six-and-a-half-year construction period. The cost of the canal is estimated at one hundred and seventy-one million dollars including interest."[59]

The Florida Canal Authority's chairman, L. C. Ringhaver, repeatedly tabled requests to set a date for a hearing. His actions prompted Mrs. Kenneth D. Morrison—chairman of Florida Bi-Partisans (a civic affairs study group investigating the barge canal)—to warn Governor Burns in writing that if the canal authority did not schedule a meeting that week, Florida Bi-Partisans and other civic organizations from across the state would hold a "protest boat-a-cade" on the Ocklawaha River to draw national attention to their cause. Along with Florida Bi-Partisans, Alachua Audubon, and Citizens, statewide organizations that supported the Ocklawaha included the Izaak Walton League of America's Florida division; the Federated Conservation Council; and the Florida Audubon Society.[60]

Time was of the essence. The Corps of Engineers planned to let contracts for Marion County projects including construction of Rodman and Eureka Dams and reservoirs by February 1, 1966. "The valley will be turned into a reservoir," Carr explained. "In effect that will mean killing 27,000 acres of unbroken forest." Governor Burns invited the defenders of the Ocklawaha to voice their concerns at the January 25, 1966, Annual Water Resources Development Meeting in Tallahassee. "Burns invited us because we had raised so much hell," recalled Bill Partington, an officer of the Florida Audubon Society who served as FDE's first president.[61]

The meeting had originally been scheduled to coordinate the state's water-related public-works projects before presenting an official budget request to Congress, which raised the ire of activists, who had requested a meeting designed specifically to address the planned route for the barge canal. Activists also complained that Tallahassee was an inconvenient location and requested a hearing closer to the proposed site of the barge canal; they encouraged Florida's politicians to visit the Ocklawaha River before deciding upon its fate. Although the Corps of Engineers assured activists that they would do everything possible to preserve the wild and natural state of the Ocklawaha River Valley, the river's defenders claimed that the canal would destroy its wild status and natural beauty. Marion County officials supported the canal, which was predicted to be a boon to the region's economy. Ringhaver admitted that the canal would alter approximately 41 miles of the Ocklawaha River Valley, but he maintained that construction would also improve access to recreation opportunities for the public. The Citizens group was the most vocal in criticizing the state for failing to schedule a hearing that would focus exclusively on the issue of rerouting the canal. At the time, 2 miles of the eastern segment of the canal were already complete. On the western end, extensive dredging and bridge and lock construction were under way.[62]

More than 350 people—ranging from concerned individuals to representatives of every major conservation organization in the nation—converged upon Tallahassee to speak not against the canal, but on behalf of the Ocklawaha River; approximately sixty people made presentations to state officials, requesting an alternate route for the Cross Florida Barge Canal. Most of the speakers assured Randolph Hodges of the Board of Conservation and Secretary of State Tom Adams that they did not oppose the canal's construction, only its present route. Carr had publicized the event in newsletters published by state and regional chapters of the Audubon Society and Garden Club, and in other conservation groups' newsletters throughout the state. Meanwhile, canal boosters resorted to paying supporters to attend. "All these men arrived in their double-breasted suits, and they filled the well of the hall," Carr recalled. "We, on the other hand, were just around on the perimeter and up in the gallery. We outnumbered them. It was fantastic." Canal proponents—including state legislators, county and port officials, waterways officials, and contractors—were given the floor until the early evening. State senator L. K. Edwards of Marion County, a longtime canal supporter, said he would "hate to see anything done to stop the canal now." He pointed out the canal's alleged economic benefits, including increasing land values and cheaper transportation costs for businesses. Although the water resources development meeting was also devoted to projects that were unrelated to the canal, the backers of those projects also expressed their support for the construction of the barge canal along its current route.[63]

Those who favored rerouting the canal around the Ocklawaha traveled from all over the state to share their concerns that the current route would destroy thousands of acres of trees and cause irreparable damage to the river valley. Adams made light of these citizens' concerns, chiding them for failing to realize how difficult it would be to change the route. Adams claimed the only other suitable water source to fill the canal and operate its locks would be Silver Springs, a popular tourist destination and a main source of water for the Ocklawaha River. Tapping into Silver Springs as a water source for the canal would "render the Ocklawaha a stagnant stream," Adams predicted, "from Silver Springs to the St. Johns River." The new route would also cost an extra $13 million and reduce the canal's recreation benefits, he said, reading from a Corps of Engineers report explaining why rerouting the canal was not feasible. Nonetheless, Hodges assured those in attendance that the results of the hearing would be compiled and sent to the Board of Conservation for study, although it would be some time before a recommendation—if any— would be made.[64]

Although river defenders expected to plead their case to the governor or his cabinet, Tom Adams served as the meeting's chair. "He bullied every one of us," Carr recalled. The canal opposition had been scheduled to present their findings early that afternoon, but canal proponents did not cede them the floor until the early evening. Carr had instructed those in attendance not to express any opposition to the canal at the hearing. Instead, they were directed to ask officials to consider the merits of selecting an alternate route that would spare the Ocklawaha. Defenders of the Ocklawaha River Valley made the case that if the barge canal were constructed along its currently planned route, the Ocklawaha's wild state and natural beauty would be ruined. They also predicted that the artificial reservoirs—which proponents claimed would improve upon the river's natural recreation values—would become clogged with exotic water weeds and tree snags. Proponents countered that the Corps of Engineers would preserve as much of the Ocklawaha's natural beauty as possible.[65]

In a stunning blow to the river defenders, activists found out after the alleged public hearing that the real business decisions concerning the canal had already been made in private on the morning of the hearing, without the knowledge or participation of those who had requested a public hearing on the canal project. The committee had dismissed the testimony of the conservationists before even hearing it. Nathaniel Reed called the botched public hearing an epic event that contributed to the growth of Florida's environmental movement. According to Reed, the chief of the Corps of Engineers and his staff "grossly misplayed" the hearing. "And I was there not as an opponent," he added. "I was there to learn. A neutral observer would have been totally aghast at the proceedings. It was the most rigged public hearing that I have ever been to or hope to go to in my lifetime. The opponents were allowed three minutes each at five o'clock in the afternoon. The proponents had the entire day. It was a statewide scandal. Every newspaper picked it up. This thing was totally rigged."[66]

The January 25 hearing had shown that the balance of power favored canal proponents. Although this chapter in the canal story ended with a painful defeat for the defenders of the Ocklawaha, they considered the public hearing to be a watershed. "I learned later," Partington recalled, "that only one copy of the hearing record was made and our arguments never were forwarded to Congress. We went away mad and wounded, but we never forgot. I think of that meeting as the turning point in Florida conservation history, because people from the Florida Keys to the Panhandle met each other for the first time. Splintered groups began talking about organizing a united front."[67]

Although the Corps of Engineers and canal proponents had been reluctant to reconsider their plans to build the canal along the Ocklawaha River, there was a precedent for rerouting Corps navigation projects. At the same time that the Corps was preparing to construct the Cross Florida Barge Canal, it had also been authorized to build the Gulf Intracoastal Waterway from Carrabelle to St. Marks, Florida. The Gulf section of the Intracoastal Waterway would have traversed the Carrabelle, Crooked, and Ochlockonee Rivers, but the Corps agreed to "consider the advisability of providing an alternative route in lieu of the authorized route," according to Corps literature. However, because the Freedom of Information Act was not signed into law until 1966, Carr and her fellow activists were not able to access official Corps of Engineers files. Even after the passage of this crucial law, the Corps obstructed access to official information through a series of delays and failures to reply to the requests of Carr and other activists.[68]

Rebuffed by officials in Tallahassee, Carr retreated to Micanopy to prepare for the next confrontation. In 1966, while the Ocklawaha defenders prepared a new strategy, the Corps of Engineers started work on Rodman Dam, using a massive new machine designed to clear forest as quickly and effectively as possible. F. Browne Gregg, the designer of the experimental "crawler-crusher," estimated that the machine crushed approximately 4,500 acres of trees in five weeks. "They destroyed the forest along the river as fast as they could," Carr remembered. By the fall of 1968, 5,500 acres of Rodman Reservoir had been cleared, Rodman Dam and the St. Johns Lock had been completed, and Eureka Dam was under construction. The Corps closed Rodman Dam on September 30, 1968, and flooded Rodman Reservoir. Thousands of dead trees that the crawler-crusher had bulldozed soon floated to the top of Rodman Pool. Just as activists had predicted, hardwood trees surrounding the reservoir started to die, while hydrilla prospered.[69]

"It was a horrible sight to see," Florida Presbyterian College (now Eckerd College) biology professor George K. Reid observed. "This is a crime against nature." The Corps had destroyed all the trees in a 20-mile section of the

Construction of the St. Johns Lock (late 1960s). During construction of the lock, Florida's terrain was transformed beyond recognition. Courtesy of the State Archives of Florida.

Ocklawaha forest in preparation for the barge canal. A Corps spokesman later admitted that the organization had not anticipated the adverse publicity that followed its use of the crawler-crusher and the flooding of "Lake Ocklawaha" (Rodman Pool). Another chapter in the Ocklawaha campaign had ended in failure for the defenders of the river. After their decisive defeat in Tallahassee, Carr and her allies realized that they had to aim higher. The activists, utilizing a strategy that Audubon societies and club women had used in the early twentieth century, commenced an intensive public-education campaign. They also employed an improved legal strategy backed by an ecological study highlighting the canal's consequences for Florida's environment.[70]

By 1966, Mimi, Chuck, Stephen, and Tom Carr had reached college age. Only David, the youngest of the Carrs' children, was still living at home with his parents. Carr devoted most of her time to the campaign to save the Ocklawaha River, which meant that there were many nights when David and Archie had to fend for themselves at dinnertime. Because the Carrs were both too busy to devote much time to household chores, they employed a part-time housekeeper. David offered occasional assistance to his mother's cause by taking potential supporters on canoe rides along the Ocklawaha or helping with office duties. In 1970, David started his freshman year at UF, but he continued to live at home with his parents. He often called his mother at the FDE office in Gainesville to ask if she was coming home for dinner. Carr later apologized for devoting more time to the Ocklawaha than to her family as the campaign progressed, but Archie was equally preoccupied with his own research and writing.[71]

Carr continued to support her husband's turtle research throughout her campaign to save the Ocklawaha. In 1968, she spent five weeks at the Tortuguero research station in Costa Rica, where she tabulated the results of fifteen years of turtle tagging. This data provided the foundation for several subsequent articles that she wrote with Archie, including two pieces that were published in the prestigious national journal *Ecology*. Just as the science of ecology now informed the debate over the Cross Florida Barge Canal, beginning in 1970, ecology and conservation formed the theoretical framework of all of Archie's research projects, Frederick Davis noted in *The Man Who Saved Sea Turtles*. While Archie's groundbreaking turtle studies directed international attention to the plight of endangered sea turtle populations, Marjorie Carr harnessed the activist science of ecology to raise awareness

Marjorie and Archie Carr at Tortuguero Lagoon in Costa Rica with Archie's former student, Larry Ogren (1970). Courtesy of Mimi Carr.

of the threatened Ocklawaha River and foster environmental stewardship at the national level.[72]

Science remained at the heart of Carr's campaign to save the Ocklawaha, which stands in contrast to certain scholarly interpretations of women's environmental activism in the late twentieth century. Historian Robert Gottlieb makes a distinction between male and female leadership styles within the American environmental movement. He argues that within the antitoxics movement that emerged in the 1970s, women's leadership skills were derived from their experiences "managing their homes, engaging in activities concerning their children's schools, and in holding their families together."[73] Gottlieb contrasts this "feminine" style of leadership with the "masculine" leadership style that leaders of the mainstream conservation and environmental organizations espoused—a leadership style that was grounded in science and policy. He maintains that there were no women leaders of environmental groups at the beginning of the movement; by the 1970s, there were only a handful, and most of these women leaders adopted "male" leadership styles. Gottlieb's history of the environmental movement of the late twentieth century is comprehensive in scope, yet it largely overlooks Florida campaigns and leaders—including Marjory Stoneman Douglas's leadership of Friends of the Everglades and Marjorie Harris Carr's leadership of the campaign to save the Ocklawaha River. Although Gottlieb contends that women seldom served in formal leadership positions within established conservation organizations such as the Audubon Society and the newer professional organizations such as Environmental Defense Fund (EDF) at the start of the environmental movement, Carr and other Florida women activists served at the helm of both types of conservation and environmental organizations.[74]

One of the reasons behind Carr's successful leadership within the male-dominated field of environmental activism was her background in academic science. Unlike the activism that was characteristic of the antitoxics movement—in which women leaders constructed arguments that stemmed from personal experiences with toxic pollution and its effects on their families and communities—Carr's authority was based upon her scientific understanding of the effects of the proposed barge canal upon the Ocklawaha ecosystem. A graduate of UF's zoology department, Carr functioned as a member of the academic community of Gainesville. She drew upon the intellectual resources of UF, an established bastion of professional expertise, to coordinate and disseminate scientific, economic, and legal information that bolstered the Ocklawaha defenders' developing case against the Cross Florida Barge Canal.

Using Gottlieb's model for female and male leadership styles as a guide, Carr's style would have fallen into the "masculine" category—like most of the other women leaders of the early environmental movement—because she emphasized science, economics, and politics over traditional women's concerns. The subtext of Gottlieb's argument on female and male leadership styles appears to be that the expertise and policy-driven approach to environmental activism is male, whereas female activism stems from women's personal experiences within their presumed cultural role as nurturers. As a female scientist, Carr's leadership style does not fit within the gendered constraints of this male/female leadership style dichotomy.

The next chapter examines the role Marjorie Carr and FDE played in the emergence of a statewide and national environmental movement in the late

1960s and early 1970s. Carr's continuing battle to stop construction of the barge canal and restore the Ocklawaha River garnered national media attention and stood as an example of the effectiveness of science and citizen activism in resolving environmental controversies. Her persistence never waned. When Carr reached retirement age, her influence was at its peak, and she remained active in the fight for restoration until terminal illness sapped her energy in the late 1990s.

6

Florida Defenders of the Environment and the Death of the Cross Florida Barge Canal

By the late 1960s, Marjorie Carr and her colleagues had transformed the campaign to save the Ocklawaha River from a regional movement to one of national significance. Carr and like-minded activists questioned the economic and environmental soundness of bringing a nineteenth-century dream to life in the late twentieth century. Florida Defenders of the Environment (FDE) would prove that the Cross Florida Barge Canal would devastate Florida's environment while providing no real economic benefits to central Florida. The organization would show that the U.S. Army Corps of Engineers had in fact manipulated economic data to inflate the canal's alleged economic and recreational benefits. Throughout the twentieth century, a group of politicians and business leaders had kept the dream of the barge canal alive in order to curry favor with political constituents and profit from the construction of the canal, as opposed to its actual operation. FDE proved that the Corps of Engineers inflated estimated barge traffic in order to justify the cost of the canal's construction. Moreover, the nation's Interstate Highway System rendered water transportation obsolete. Rachel Carson had enabled environmentalists to articulate humans' threat to sensitive ecosystems through the language of ecology. Starting in 1965, Carr applied this new language to the Ocklawaha campaign, alerting Florida and the nation to the threat federal agencies such as the Corps of Engineers posed to the environment.

The defenders of the Ocklawaha warned that the Cross Florida Barge Canal would do more harm than good, slicing through the state's main source of drinking water and polluting it further with the by-products of the barge traffic that would travel across the center of the state. Activists raised concerns about the reliability of the benefit-cost ratio the Corps of Engineers had developed, contending that the canal's economic benefits had been blown out of proportion in order to justify the cost of construction. Carr and her allies also challenged the Corps of Engineers' contention that damming the Ocklawaha River at two points and creating a pair of reservoirs to facilitate barge travel along the canal would improve the river's recreational benefits. She stressed that the recreational benefits provided by an unaltered Ocklawaha River Valley surpassed any alleged benefits from the creation of two artificial reservoirs.

At the time of the Ocklawaha campaign, the United States was at a cultural crossroads. Ecology—a science that considered the connections between humans and all aspects of their environment—blossomed amid the backdrop of social unrest, as American citizens began to question their nation's involvement in the Vietnam War and were awakened to the inequalities embedded in their culture's racial and gender hierarchies. The campaign to save the Ocklawaha River Valley helped a growing number of Floridians and Americans redefine the concept of progress.

Boosters maintained that the barge canal would bring trade and profit to central Florida, transforming the small inland city of Ocala into a thriving port city and increasing barge traffic along the Gulf and Atlantic coasts. FDE countered that the benefits of constructing the Cross Florida Barge Canal were debatable. Those who fought against the canal and to protect the Ocklawaha River Valley questioned the legitimacy of the Corps of Engineers' economic projections and considered the environmental gamble of the barge canal to be too great a risk for Floridians to tolerate.[1]

As the 1960s progressed, the science of ecology bolstered and transformed the 1950s preservationist message. The evidence-driven environmental impact statement countered the engineering expertise of federal agencies such as the U.S. Bureau of Reclamation and the Corps of Engineers, which represented an antiquated conservation ethos. The tool of the environmental impact statement lent authority and credibility to the embryonic environmental movement as it challenged the nineteenth-century worldview embodied by such federal agencies as the U.S. Forest Service, the U.S. Fish and Wildlife Service, and the U.S. Department of the Interior, which managed nature as a resource to be altered and consumed at will by humans.

By the 1950s, a wilderness ethos had developed in the United States. Although opponents relied upon scientific techniques to bolster their political campaign against the dam, the science of ecology was still not readily accessible to activists. After Carr and her colleagues suffered a hard defeat in Tallahassee in 1966, they widened the scope of their campaign beyond the limitations of traditional grassroots campaigns, embracing ecology and forthcoming federal legislation to strengthen their case against completion of the Cross Florida Barge Canal.

In January 1964, President Johnson referred to the Ocklawaha River as a natural resource to be exploited for the benefit of man. Within a few short years, however, the American people's tolerance for pork-barrel projects that destroyed the environment while benefiting local developers had started to wane. *Silent Spring* paved the way for citizen engagement in localized, single-issue campaigns that challenged government or corporate projects that privileged profits over environmental stewardship. Environmentalists' weapon of choice would be the environmental impact statement, which exposed the disastrous consequences of projects designed without consideration of their ecological consequences. One such project was the colossal Miami jetport that the Dade County Port Authority planned to erect in the Big Cypress Swamp, located 6 miles upstream from Everglades National Park. The Port Authority planned to build one of the largest airports in the world there, complete with a "super-train" that would ferry travelers through the Everglades. South Florida's growth was considered to be an inevitable fact of life, and the Port Authority did not perceive any conflict between the urban sprawl that would accompany the billion-dollar, 39-square-mile "jetport of the future" and its chosen location inside the vulnerable, ecologically important Everglades ecosystem.[2]

The Miami jetport would have deprived the northwestern portion of Everglades National Park and the Ten Thousand Islands of their main source of freshwater. The proposed airport's runways would accommodate the largest jets the industry could produce and stretch for 6 miles. Acting on behalf of the National Audubon Society, Joe Browder patched together a coalition that included the Miccosukees, alligator poachers (who realized that the airport threatened their livelihood), hunters, and environmentalists. He convinced Marjory Stoneman Douglas to serve as the movement's figurehead, transforming the seventy-nine-year-old author of *The Everglades: River of Grass* into an environmentalist for the first time in her life. *River of Grass*—along with Leopold's *A Sand County Almanac*; Wallace Stegner's *This Is Dinosaur*, on the opposition to the proposed Echo Park Dam on the Utah-Colorado border; and Carson's *Silent Spring*—helped set the stage for the environmental movement. Although *River of Grass* offered no solutions to the environmental problems of Florida or the nation, it articulated the benefits of a healthy Everglades to life—including human life—and became the bible of Florida environmentalists in the late 1960s.[3]

Although older statewide and national organizations such as the Audubon Society and the Izaak Walton League continued to play an important role in the growing environmental movement, single-issue organizations experienced greater success as they challenged the programs of conservation-minded federal organizations such as the Bureau of Reclamation and the Corps of Engineers. Another indispensable ally to Florida's new environmental movement was the Republican Party. Walter Hickel, President Nixon's interior secretary, took a personal interest in the state's wild alligator population, which had fallen from a total in the millions to an estimated twenty thousand. Hickel and Florida governor Claude Kirk—who had dug a ceremonial shovel full of dirt at the start of the jetport's construction before Nathaniel Reed convinced him to withdraw his support for the project—visited the Everglades to investigate the poaching problem. After a night of beer-fueled alligator hollering, Hickel pledged to increase funding for alligator protection and consider the implications of the jetport, which would devastate the Everglades' native flora and fauna.[4]

Meanwhile, a draft of the National Environmental Protection Act (NEPA) was working its way through Congress. Among other things, NEPA would require environmental impact statements before federal approval or funding could be made available for major development projects. Jetport opponents commissioned Luna B. Leopold (Aldo Leopold's son), a former University of Miami professor who specialized in river hydrology, to lead the Florida team as they drafted an environmental impact statement on the Everglades jetport. At the same time, Dade County commissioners requested an independent study of the jetport's impact, and the National Academy of Sciences provided sixty scientists with a grant to conduct a study of south Florida's planning and water needs with a special emphasis on the implications of the jetport.[5]

The Everglades jetport attracted the attention of the national media. On September 17, 1969, the Leopold report was released to the public; it suggested that the jetport would wreak havoc on the south Florida ecosystem and Everglades National Park. The following day, the National Academy of Sciences report confirmed the results of the Leopold study. The county commission's independent study was finally released in December. Predictably, the commission's report sanctioned construction of the jetport, as long as it was limited to runways only. In what would be the first of several important environmental decisions for his administration, President Richard Nixon ended the debate by ordering a halt to the jetport's construction. The Port Authority begrudgingly entered into negotiations with the Departments of the Interior and Transportation and Governor Kirk's office, resulting in the creation of the "Jetport Pact," through which the Port Authority agreed to a new location for the jetport in exchange for federal reimbursement of the $12 million the agency had already invested in the project.[6]

The American public began to question the soundness of the Corps of Engineers' manipulation of the Everglades ecosystem. The change in public opinion from unquestioning acceptance of Corps projects to suspicion came as a shock to this elite organization. The Corps was a fraternity whose engineering expertise had traditionally commanded respect and authority. Since the nineteenth century, the Corps had applied its technical expertise to state and federal projects that utilized and "improved" natural resources. The Corps was not accustomed to having its engineering decisions questioned. However, the blossoming environmental movement, which had come to be symbolized by Florida's opposition to the desecration of the Everglades and the Ocklawaha River, was composed of experts of a different sort, who were no longer willing to defer to the expertise of the Corps or other conservation-minded agencies.[7]

When the Corps of Engineers formed its initial plans for construction of a barge canal along the Ocklawaha, St. Johns, and Withlacoochee Rivers, no government agency questioned the organization's designs. In fact, the Corps maintained complete oversight over the planning, construction, and evaluation of its own projects. Over the years, Herbert Hoover, Dwight Eisenhower, and other presidents had recommended various solutions to remedy this inherent conflict of interest, but their proposals were never acted upon. When Route 13-B was selected as the most appropriate path for the barge canal, the Budget Bureau (which later became the Office of Management and Budget) and the Board of Engineers for Rivers and Harbors (which was composed of two Corps of Engineers officers and five regional engineers) were the only "external" agencies charged with reviewing Corps projects. Marjorie Carr brought the agency's lack of legitimate independent oversight to the attention of the media, identifying this problem as one of the reasons why the Corps had consistently failed to consider the impact of its projects on the environment.[8]

As the 1966 public hearing had clarified, the Corps of Engineers was unable to admit the environmental consequences of the barge canal—including its potential impact on the Floridan Aquifer—and had expressed little concern for the canal's effects on the Ocklawaha ecosystem. The hearing also demonstrated that the Audubon Society was not the ideal organization to coordinate the Ocklawaha campaign, although it would continue to provide financial and organizational support. The defenders of the Ocklawaha needed to found a new, independent agency that would be dedicated exclusively to the campaign to protect the river valley from the Cross Florida Barge Canal. This new organization would continue to utilize tried-and-true grassroots methods such as letter writing and public education, but these methods would be supplemented by sophisticated ecological studies and federal lawsuits. Founding one central organization to direct an environmental campaign at the state and national levels would help activists overcome the logistical problems they had encountered previously when their campaign was splintered and too regional in focus. After the fiasco of the 1966 public hearing on an alternate route for the canal, Carr and her colleagues realized that federal intervention was needed.

Marjorie Carr, David Anthony, and other Ocklawaha supporters contacted Environmental Defense Fund (EDF), which had just won a major lawsuit against the producers of DDT. Carr convinced EDF's leaders that the opposition to the barge canal had accumulated enough scientific and economic evidence to challenge the Corps of Engineers in court for breach of public interest. EDF advised the Ocklawaha activists to form an ad hoc committee to continue their investigation of the canal and its potential effects on the environment. In July 1969, Florida Defenders of the Environment (FDE, or EDF reversed) was born. Although the organization's leadership consisted of current and former Audubon Society members—including Carr (FDE's founding vice chairman and longtime president, and Alachua Audubon Society's copresident), Anthony (FDE's second president, and Alachua Audubon Society's copresident), and Bill Partington (who took leave from his position as Florida Audubon Society's assistant executive director to serve as FDE's founding chairman)—FDE's sole focus in its early years was to protect the Ocklawaha River Valley from the barge canal. Carr described the organization as a "coalition of scientists, lawyers, economists, and other specialists who volunteer their expertise to defend a quality environment in Florida."[9]

FDE's strongest source of intellectual support stemmed from its core membership of University of Florida (UF) professors, who contributed the majority of the reports for the organization's environmental impact statement for the barge canal. Carr encapsulated FDE's strategy in the Ocklawaha campaign—which she considered to be a successful recipe for any environmental campaign—as follows: "Solutions to environmental problems may result from the education of the general public through the press, new legislation at the state and federal levels, action by governmental agencies or through the influence of the courts. Most often a combination of methods is the most successful. Whatever the method, the essential ingredient will be a thorough and accurate knowledge both of the problem and the opponent."[10]

FDE's first task was to research the environmental and economic effects of the Cross Florida Barge Canal, which also involved getting to know as much as possible about the inner workings of the U.S. Army Corps of Engineers. At the time, the Corps, which was a branch of the Defense Department, was the world's largest construction organization and the biggest developer of water-control structures. The Corps was composed of two hundred regular U.S. Army officers and forty thousand civil employees. Its annual expenditures exceeded $1 billion of what Carr loved to refer to as the "taxpayers' money." She credited the Corps (along with the Bureau of Reclamation) with developing scores of dams and other waterways projects that appeared to serve a purpose in the nineteenth century, but which were no longer needed in the late twentieth century. By then, Carr argued, the Corps had resorted to colluding with waterways organizations such as the National Rivers and Harbors Congress (NRHC) and construction interests to undertake water-resource projects that would justify the Corps of Engineers' existence, help politicians please their constituents, and pad developers' pockets at the expense of the environment. The NRHC, an independent organization with tremendous clout in Congress, shaped most successful rivers and harbors legislation. Canal boosters including Tom Adams, Florida senator Spessard Holland, and Florida representative Robert Sikes served as national vice presidents of the organization. Longtime canal proponent Henry Buckman, a Jacksonville engineering consultant, served as president of the NRHC throughout much of the 1960s, helping to push barge canal appropriations through Congress. In 1953, the Hoover Commission—a nonpartisan economic study group—

pointed out that NRHC members shared close connections with contractors' lobbyists, but at the time, this alliance was not investigated further.[11]

Throughout the continuing campaign to save the Ocklawaha, Carr remained optimistic. She reminded supporters that Corps of Engineers projects only lived from appropriation to appropriation; therefore, FDE formulated a plan that was intended to bring an end to the barge canal's congressional funding. By 1969, the Corps of Engineers had completed approximately one-third of the barge canal. To secure funding for FDE's legal expenses, Carr sought the assistance of Roland Clement of the National Audubon Society, who helped her set up an account for donations to the Ocklawaha fund. She hoped that the FDE lawsuit would teach the Corps a lesson. "The mere fact of the public taking the Corps into Court for betrayal of public interest may in itself have a therapeutic effect on the Corps, the Bureau of Reclamation and similar groups," Carr wrote Clement. "And it would certainly stimulate Congressional action necessary to prevent such enormous and arrogant squandering of public assets by governmental agencies."[12]

On September 15, 1969, EDF filed suit in U.S. District Court in Washington, D.C., on behalf of FDE. The organizations charged the Corps of Engineers with violating the constitutional rights of the American people by destroying a natural treasure, the Ocklawaha River. The premise of EDF's lawsuit—that citizens have environmental rights that cannot be violated by government or private entities—was a revolutionary concept. EDF further alleged that the Corps failed to report objections to the Cross Florida Barge Canal to Congress; misrepresented benefit-cost ratios; grossly underestimated maintenance costs; and failed to consider the ecological value of the loss of the Ocklawaha River when calculating the canal's benefit-cost ratio. By this time, several state agencies had lent their support to the campaign to save the Ocklawaha. The Florida Department of Air and Water Pollution Control issued a report that described the canal as "the most devastating project ever undertaken in Florida." The Florida Senate Committee on Natural Resources voted 5-0 for an investigation to determine whether the state should withdraw its support of the canal.[13]

FDE's legal experts—including EDF at the national level, and a team of law professors from UF and other state schools at the local level—helped the organization make the best use of a stream of new environmental legislation that President Nixon signed into law. Although President Johnson's Great Society programs ushered in the first wave of antipollution legislation in the 1960s, between 1970 and 1974, Nixon signed into law an arsenal of environmental legislation that enabled the environmental movement to mount a series of successful campaigns in that decade and beyond. In Nixon's first years in office, Congress enacted an updated Endangered Species Conservation Act (December 1969), which increased the number of flora and fauna it protected; the National Environmental Policy Act (January 1970), which made environmental impact studies a requirement for major government projects; the Clean Air Act (1970), which improved upon the previous air-quality standards of the 1967 Air Quality Act; and the Clean Water Act (1972), which extended protection to wetlands. Symbolizing Nixon's commitment to the environment—at least in the first years of his administration—in July 1970, the president established the Environmental Protection Agency (EPA) to coordinate and enforce the volumes of new federal policies designed to protect the environment. In 1972, a decade after the publication of Rachel Carson's *Silent Spring*, the EPA banned the use of DDT within the United States, although chemical companies continued to export the pesticide to neighboring countries. The new federal environmental legislation was complemented at the state level by the pioneering 1972 Land Conservation Act, which provided up to $240 million in state bonds for the acquisition of large tracts of Florida real estate for preservation. Only California, New York, and Washington would enact similar legislation, making Florida one of the nation's leading states in the practice of land preservation.[14]

In the late 1960s and early 1970s, in response to *Silent Spring* and the public's increasing awareness of deteriorating environmental conditions, the national conservation organizations—Sierra Club, National Audubon Society, Wilderness Society, and others—struggled to adapt themselves to the new environmental age and watched their memberships double in size. Gaylord Nelson launched the first national Earth Day celebration on April 22, 1970, with an estimated 20 million Americans participating in environmental activities ranging from tree planting to public protests. The science of ecology had permeated the American consciousness, replacing the human-centered conservation ethos with an appreciation of humans' tiny part in a larger series of ecosystems that made up Spaceship Earth. During Nixon's first term in office, Congress laid the institutional framework for the environmental movement, which was in full bloom at the time of FDE's founding.[15]

As America became more attuned to the consequences of human manipulation of the environment, the science of ecology gained more credence in the media, shaped public opinion, and informed new legislation at the local, state, and federal level. Ecology played a central role in redefining the Ocklawaha campaign, which experienced a major turning point with the March 1970 publication of Florida Defenders of the Environment's environmental impact statement. FDE's evidence was clear: if construction of the Cross Florida Barge Canal continued, Florida would experience an environmental catastrophe. The impact statement's language echoed the message put forth in *Silent Spring*: "Although man evolved as part of the natural biosphere, much of his effort has been turned toward disrupting it. So far, we have managed to survive our ecologic errors, but there are signs that we may be reaching the limits of our immunity. Such a sign is the lack of any sound assessment of the long-term values and ecologic options at stake in the Oklawaha regional ecosystem. It is the purpose of this report to give a brief account of those values and options." The impact statement examined conditions in the Ocklawaha regional ecosystem, which the report defined as "all communities within the drainage basin of the Oklawaha River," before construction of the barge canal began, the current state of the ecosystem after partial construction of the canal, and the predicted state of the ecosystem after the proposed completion of the canal. The report considered physical factors (geology, hydrology, climate, and soils) and biological systems (plants, animals, and people), in addition to probable interactions among these systems (the relationships within the Ocklawaha ecosystem).[16]

Carr and Partington were among the members of the board of editors who directed the environmental impact study. The majority of the study's contributors were UF faculty members from a variety of relevant disciplines. The study featured extensive data on the barge canal's observed and expected impact on the Ocklawaha and the Floridan Aquifer, including ecological, economic, and land-use studies that FDE maintained "should properly have been undertaken before the project was initiated." FDE's volunteer experts studied the canal from the viewpoints of ecology, hydrology, geology, economics, land-use planning, anthropology, and environmental quality. Their findings indicated that a completed Cross Florida Barge Canal would pollute the Floridan Aquifer and contaminate all surface water in the ecosystem, including the popular Silver Springs nature park; would require extensive additional pumping facilities to maintain canal operations during natural drought conditions; would fail to provide alleged flood-control benefits; would destroy a unique natural region that supported the full spectrum of plant and animal life native to north central Florida; and would promote the growth of masses of water weeds in the shallow Rodman and Eureka Pools. Furthermore, the report suggested that the controversy surrounding the proposed barge canal emphasized the need for long-range regional land-use planning, which had not been done in central Florida. No agency then existed to direct long-term land-use planning at the regional level. More than forty years after FDE made the case for regional land-use planning, decisions pertaining to Florida's long-term growth continue to be made primarily at the local level, and there is little cooperation or planning at the regional level. Where regional agencies do exist, as in the case of Florida's water-management districts, policies often favor the interests of private industry and developers over environmental considerations.[17]

From an economic perspective, FDE's experts determined that the discount rate used by the U.S. Army Corps of Engineers to calculate the benefit-cost ratio of the canal was unrealistic. If realistic interest rates were applied, the canal's benefit-cost ratio would no longer exceed the cost. In addition, the amount of traffic that the Corps estimated would use the canal and the freight savings per ton-mile appeared to be "unjustifiably inflated," according to FDE's impact study. The report also challenged canal proponents' claims that the canal would enhance land values and improve recreational values in the region affected by construction. Moreover, FDE pointed out an important oversight in the Corps of Engineers' benefit-cost ratio. Successful operation of the canal depended upon the completion of the Intracoastal Waterway from St. Marks southward along the northwest coast of Florida (a section of the Intracoastal Waterway known as the "missing link"). However, the Corps had not included construction costs for the proposed waterway in its benefit-cost ratio for the barge canal. Even when considering the amount of money already invested in the barge canal project, the impact study suggested that an impartial economic restudy of the project "would result in its rejection as unsound, on a purely economic basis, without any consideration of the environmental values to be lost."[18]

Although FDE was adamant that there was no economic justification for the canal, its main interest resided in preserving the integrity of the unaffected areas of the Ocklawaha regional ecosystem and restoring what had already been damaged. Carr served as one of the primary editors and coordinators of the environmental impact statement. In a section of the report with no byline—but bearing the same writing style and some of the exact phrasing from the ecological study of the Ocklawaha River that appeared in Carr's 1965

Florida Naturalist essay—FDE stressed the environmental value of the Ocklawaha River. Within an 85-mile radius of Eureka on the Ocklawaha River
(where two proposed reservoirs would be located), there were 875 lakes, but
just seven rivers. If the barge canal were completed, three of these rivers—the
Ocklawaha, Withlacoochee, and St. Johns—would be modified severely or
essentially destroyed. "For this loss," the report stated, "the creation of two
artificial reservoirs is offered in restitution." FDE maintained that the Corps
of Engineers' claims regarding the increased recreational values that the canal
would provide were greatly exaggerated.[19]

Among the many experts Marjorie Carr recruited to contribute to the
environmental impact statement was Archie Carr, who joined UF ecology
professor Ariel Lugo in arguing that the Ocklawaha regional ecosystem was
a reservoir of ecological stability that was "still relatively unruined by human
exploitation," and which should be considered an incomparable asset, especially since the region's natural environments were disappearing quickly. The
two ecologists explained that the ecosystem's treasure trove of diverse, native
flora and fauna—including the endangered Florida panther—was only part
of its charm; what was even more valuable was the ecosystem's vast, uninterrupted size. "The Oklawaha Ecosystem is an investment in the ecologic
future of man, a big expanse of uncommitted, undisrupted biological landscape, left as a buffer against human ecological error," they concluded. "In a
region that is fast becoming fit habitat only for man, and perhaps is not long
destined to remain even that, such an asset is one to be treasured."[20]

FDE's impact statement conceded that construction of the Cross Florida
Barge Canal had already altered the Ocklawaha ecosystem drastically. Nonetheless, FDE's experts observed that much of the Ocklawaha River and its valley remained unimpaired, and if construction of the barge canal were to stop,
the damaged areas would recover dramatically within ten to twenty years.
FDE recommended a cessation of further federal and state funding for construction of the canal and requested its deauthorization. FDE suggested that
the canal right-of-way along the Ocklawaha River be transferred to the U.S.
Forest Service or another appropriate agency for recreation and other appropriate multiple-use management. FDE requested that the Ocklawaha River
be designated as a scenic river, which would guarantee its protection as part
of the national wild and scenic rivers system. One of FDE's most adamant
recommendations was that the Rodman Reservoir be drained immediately
so that the river could return to its original free-flowing condition from the

Silver River to the St. Johns River. In order to prevent similar ecological mistakes in the future, FDE's report indicated the need for the establishment of a regional environmental planning council to consider the needs of conservation, environmental protection, recreation, and development throughout the Ocklawaha regional ecosystem. Throughout the 1970s and 1980s, Marjorie Carr organized several conferences to promote the idea of land-use planning at the local and regional levels.[21]

In addition, FDE recommended that benefit-cost analyses for future projects be conducted by an impartial agency, and that full consideration be given to environmental values in the planning and evaluation of such projects. FDE also pointed out a major flaw with the congressional authorization and appropriations process, which had permitted a long gap between the canal's authorization in 1942 and the start of construction in 1964. The report recommended that all authorized public-works projects be started within five years of their authorization, and that a full restudy be required of all projects that are not completed within ten years of their original authorization date. Not surprisingly, FDE also recommended that official public hearings be held near the site of the proposed public-works project within a year prior to authorization and initial funding in order to determine whether the project is in the public interest. FDE suggested that public hearings were a necessity given the "rapid environmental, economic, and social changes currently being experienced in the United States."[22]

In September 1969, EDF charged the Corps of Engineers with violating the constitutional rights of the people of the United States by destruction of natural resources. The lawsuit sought to enjoin the Corps from proceeding further with construction of the Cross Florida Barge Canal as presently planned. FDE's environmental impact statement would serve as the backbone of the legal case against the Corps of Engineers. FDE modeled its environmental impact statement after the Leopold report commissioned by opponents of the Miami jetport. At the same time that FDE prepared the impact statement, it also conducted a poll of Florida candidates running for state or federal office in 1970. The results indicated that 81 percent favored a moratorium or abandonment of the barge canal; only 1 percent favored completion of the canal as planned. In addition to having the support of most state politicians running for office in 1970, FDE benefited from the spate of environmental legislation Nixon signed into law at the beginning of the decade, including NEPA, which—as mentioned previously—would soon require environmental impact statements for all projects receiving federal authorization or funding.[23]

EDF accused the Corps of Engineers of violating the Fish and Wildlife Coordination Act, Water Pollution Control Act, and Migratory Bird Act. When NEPA was signed into law in 1970, the Corps of Engineers' ignorance of the environmental impact of the barge canal strengthened FDE's case immensely. "The minute [NEPA] passed we used it in our lawsuit," Carr recalled. On February 16, 1970, EDF filed an amended complaint that sought to require that the Corps of Engineers comply with various federal statutes and executive orders that protect the environment. The passage of NEPA and the release of FDE's environmental impact statement prompted Secretary of the Interior Walter Hickel to order the Bureau of Sport Fisheries and Wildlife to evaluate the barge canal's impact on the environment. Hickel had been inundated with letters from Florida residents and state officials who expressed their opposition to the canal. State Representative Roger Wilson of St. Petersburg was among the officials who wrote Hickel, asking him to take action to protect Florida's natural resources from the destruction the canal was causing. "Furthermore, there also seems to be some question as to the benefit-cost ratio," Wilson added. In light of the fact that the Corps of Engineers had not considered the environmental impact of the canal before commencing construction, Hickel concluded that "a new appraisal of this project and its effects on the environment of northern Florida is in order." In the interim, Hickel called for a moratorium on construction.[24]

FDE had begun courting the Nixon administration in earnest soon after the president expressed an interest in improving the quality of the American environment in his 1970 State of the Union address. On February 6, 1970, FDE sent President Nixon a letter requesting a moratorium on construction of the barge canal. More than 150 scientists and other experts signed the letter, which was forwarded to Nixon's Council on Environmental Quality, which he had created on January 29, 1970. The letter thanked Nixon for emphasizing his concern over the "alarming degradation of natural environment in America" in his recent State of the Union address. FDE requested the president's assistance in "preventing further degenerative manipulation of one of the most valuable natural ecosystems of Florida, the Oklawaha River Valley, and in averting probable attendant changes in the quality of the subsurface water supply of Central Florida." In addition, FDE identified problems with the lengthy gap between the Cross Florida Barge Canal's authorization and the

start of its construction, and a questionable benefit-cost ratio that had fluctu-
ated over the years.[25]

When FDE sent its letter to Nixon, the canal was approximately one-third
complete; only 25 miles of the 107-mile-long channel of the canal had been
excavated. A completed canal, FDE's letter to Nixon advised, would "drastically alter ecosystems" associated with the Ocklawaha and Withlacoochee
Rivers. "Moreover, excavation of the channel of the cross-state canal will be
carried out in a section of the peninsula in which the great Floridan Aquifer
comes closest to the ground surface," FDE warned. In addition, central Florida's high incidence of sinkhole formation further demonstrated the perme-
ability and unstable nature of the aquifer along the canal route. FDE also
faulted the Corps of Engineers for using outdated construction plans that
were both impractical (the locks were too small to accommodate modern
barges) and failed to meet the environmental standards required by recent
environmental legislation. FDE informed the president that its experts were
completing a study of the barge canal's effects on the Ocklawaha River ecosystem that would be similar in scope and form to the environmental impact
study of the "Big Cypress Jetport" that the U.S. Department of the Interior
prepared in September 1969. FDE concluded the letter by congratulating
Nixon and his administration for resolving the Miami jetport issue and asking for his help "in avoiding a major, national ecological disaster."[26]

The letter included the signatures of several of the nation's most important
ecologists, including Eugene P. Odum (coauthor of *Fundamentals of Ecology*);
Paul R. Ehrlich (author of *The Population Bomb*); Rene Dubos (author of *So
Human an Animal*, which won the 1969 Pulitzer Prize for General Nonfic-
tion); David R. Ehrenfeld (author of *Principles of Biological Conservation*);
Barry Commoner (author of *Science and Survival*); G. Evelyn Hutchinson
(author of *The Enchanted Voyage* and *The Ecological Theatre and Evolutionary
Plays*); Raymond F. Dasmann (author of *Different Kind of Country* and *Environmental Conservation*); Marston Bates (author of *The Prevalence of People*
and *Man in Nature*); Archie Carr, who was listed as an ecologist and author;
and Harvard University ecologist E. O. Wilson. The list also included many
members of the National Academy of Sciences. Approximately one-quarter of
the scientists hailed from UF, and nearly one-third of the rest of the signatures
came from professors at other Florida universities and colleges. Several of the
Carrs' former colleagues from the UF biology department lent their support
to the cause as well, including Theodore Hubbell (who had returned to the

University of Michigan); Horton Hobbs (who was then the Smithsonian Institution's senior scientist with the Department of Invertebrate Zoology); and Harley Sherman (a retired UF professor of zoology).[27]

Marjorie Carr coordinated the production of the scientists' letter to Nixon, and she continued to solicit their support and the support of other scientists as FDE's campaign to save the Ocklawaha progressed. Because she had earned a master's degree in zoology from UF, Carr considered herself a colleague of UF's specialists in the environmental field. "In talking to my colleagues I realized that an awful lot of scientists are just as upset—or even more so—over the destruction of the environment [as members of conservation organizations]," she recalled. Carr called upon scientists at the local level and across the nation to contribute to FDE's efforts to save the Ocklawaha by sharing their expertise. On May 1, 1970, in a letter addressed to "Dear Fellow Scientist" that accompanied a complimentary copy of FDE's recently released environmental impact statement, Carr directed the recipients to contact Secretary Hickel and the Honorable Russel Train, chairman of the President's Environmental Council, as soon as possible to express their expert opinion on the environmental effects of the barge canal project. Carr also informed the recipients of the letter that FDE was working to add its environmental impact study to the official record of the Public Works Subcommittee of the Appropriations Committee, as part of its ongoing effort to end congressional funding for the canal. Although the campaign to save the Ocklawaha had already lasted for the better part of a decade, Carr's letter displayed her unflagging confidence in an eventual victory over the Corps of Engineers and its supporters. "We are encouraged with the progress of our effort and we will press right on until we have satisfactorily resolved the problem," she concluded.[28]

Science was central to FDE's legal case. The Corps of Engineers had not conducted thorough studies of central Florida's geology or hydrology. At the time of the 1966 public hearing, a representative of the Corps of Engineers admitted to Carr that the Corps had never had a biologist on staff before. The Corps had commissioned only limited studies of the Floridan Aquifer. The barge canal's potential effects on the aquifer were not clearly understood. "They had not involved the geological survey people in the studies on the middle part of the state," Carr explained. "But in the barge canal they had something that was designed to float on the aquifer waters. And yet they had not made the studies. They did not know about the aquifer." Nathaniel Reed, who served President Nixon as the assistant secretary of the Department of the Interior, accused canal proponents and the Corps of Engineers of gambling with Florida's environment. "Since nobody knew whether [the canal] would or wouldn't destroy the Floridan Aquifer, well, why not take the chance?" Reed mused. "The opposite side was, why take the chance? But that was the drumbeat in the 1960s. We were still growing up. We were still the land of conquest. We're going to conquer this land. And this is true not only in Florida, but right across the country."[29]

The Floridan Aquifer is an intricate system of highly porous limestone that stores water and facilitates its movement underground. The Floridan Aquifer system, formed over millions of years as carbonate sediments were deposited and dissolved, is among the world's most productive aquifer systems. It underlies all of Florida, varying in depth from a few feet below the surface to 1,000 feet underground. When the Corps of Engineers completed its plans for the barge canal, it relied upon inadequate surveys of select sections of the aquifer. Corps planners were unaware that the depth of the aquifer varied from one end of the proposed route to the other, and the organization failed to consider the consequences of dredging and routine barge operations along the aquifer.[30]

By the close of 1969, construction of the Cross Florida Barge Canal had fallen seven years behind schedule. Congress had scaled back appropriations by several million dollars each year, which increased the total estimated cost of construction. In 1962, the canal was expected to cost $147 million to complete. Seven years later, the estimated total cost of construction had risen to $177 million—a calculation that was based upon a 1977 date of completion. Any delay in construction would elevate the estimated cost of completion to $200 million when factoring in unpaid interest rates. The barge canal would cost one dollar for every ninety-two cents of estimated benefits. Canal proponents had touted the canal as a river of gold that would create new sources of industry such as docking facilities and manufacturing plants. At the same time, the Corps of Engineers inflated the recreation benefits that would originate from the industrial canal. Fishermen, recreational boaters, campers, and swimmers would have to compete with westbound barge traffic that would enter the St. Johns River at Jacksonville, travel south to Palatka, move into the 12-foot-deep canal, pass through five locks and enter the Gulf of Mexico at the small fishing village of Yankeetown. In 1936, Congress changed the Corps of Engineers' planning formula from navigation and flood-control values to the benefit-cost ratio. In calculating the barge canal's benefits to central Florida, the Corps of Engineers had overlooked the canal's impact on the environment and the communities that would be affected by the canal.[31]

Change proceeded rapidly after FDE distributed its environmental impact statement on the effects of the Cross Florida Barge Canal. In June 1970, just three months after the release of the impact statement, Secretary Hickel responded to FDE's recommendation for a moratorium on construction by asking the Corps of Engineers to halt construction for fifteen months while further study of the canal's environmental impact was completed. "We have known for a long time that if this project was ever examined closely, it would collapse," Carr announced after Hickel requested a moratorium on construction. "Our opponents know it, too."[32]

FDE bolstered its federal lawsuit against the Corps with allegations that the agency had not reported objections to the canal to Congress (including those voiced at the infamous 1966 public hearing). The lawsuit also blamed the Corps for misrepresenting the benefit-cost ratio, grossly underestimating maintenance costs, and failing to include the environmental value of the Ocklawaha River in its calculations. The Corps failed to comply with Hickel's request for a moratorium, but on January 15, 1971, the federal court issued a temporary injunction halting further construction work on the canal project, pending the outcome of the lawsuit. After nearly a decade of painful losses, the defenders of the Ocklawaha witnessed a relatively speedy victory in federal court. It took eighteen months for FDE to attain the preliminary injunction. "It ended this Corps project in mid-flight," Carr recounted, adding that the Corps had a difficult time believing the judgment when it was released.[33]

On January 19, 1971, Carr and FDE experienced an even greater surprise when President Nixon ordered a separate halt to the canal's construction. Mimi Carr recalled that her mother—a staunch Democrat—was both grateful to Nixon and a little disappointed that a Republican president would receive credit for stopping the canal. FDE continued to press its federal lawsuit against the Corps of Engineers after Nixon ordered a halt to the canal's construction. Nixon's Council on Environmental Quality had recommended the construction halt because of the threat the canal posed to the Ocklawaha River Valley's "unusual and unique natural beauty." The president called the Ocklawaha a natural treasure that would be destroyed if construction continued. Although $50 million had been invested in the project—which was estimated to cost approximately $180 million to complete—Nixon explained that the economic return from the project's completion did not justify its cost, including the environmental costs of the canal. In calculating the economic return of the canal, Nixon contended, "the destruction of natural, ecological values was not counted as a cost, nor was a credit allowed for actions preserving the environment. The step I have taken will prevent a past mistake from causing permanent damage." He asked the secretary of the army to work with the Council on Environmental Quality to develop recommendations for the Ocklawaha's future. Nixon's action stunned canal proponents and energized environmentalists. Moreover, Nixon's defense of the Ocklawaha River gave the terms "environment" and "ecology" new political currency.[34]

Carr commended the president for intervening on behalf of the Ocklawaha. "It was a very forthright action by the President and his Council on Environmental Quality," she told reporters immediately following Nixon's order to halt construction of the canal. "We have telegraphed our thanks on behalf of the thousands of Floridians who have been engaged for years in the battle to prevent degradation of this beautiful valley." Nixon's decision was a crucial victory for environmentalists. For canal boosters and the Corps of Engineers, however, the construction halt represented a painful loss. Canal proponents claimed that the president did not have the authority to cancel a project that had received congressional authorization and appropriations. Within days of Nixon's announcement, the White House was inundated with telegrams pleading with the president to reverse his decision. Carr was well aware that the battle for the Ocklawaha River was far from over. Although construction of the Cross Florida Barge Canal had ended, the war over the Ocklawaha's restoration had only just begun.[35]

Now that the construction phase of the Cross Florida Barge Canal was over, Carr and FDE pushed for its immediate deauthorization. "We don't want this thing to sit around for another twenty years and then be revived again," Carr told reporters and supporters, referring to the canal's rebirth in the 1960s, decades after its initial authorization in 1942 as a World War II defense measure. Carr speculated that the best way to make sure that the project was halted permanently was for FDE to continue its lawsuit against the Corps of Engineers. Just four days before Nixon's order, U.S. District Judge Barrington Parker had suspended work on the canal by granting a preliminary injunction requested by EDF's attorneys. Parker ruled that the Corps of Engineers had failed to comply with the newly enacted NEPA. President Nixon's subsequent order to halt construction of the Cross Florida Barge Canal enraged the canal boosters who had worked for decades to gain congressional support and funding for the canal. Seeking to nullify FDE's legal victory against the Corps of Engineers—and to challenge the president's authority in stopping the canal—canal proponents filed several countersuits in U.S. District Court.[36]

The Corps of Engineers' reaction to Nixon's order to halt construction of the Cross Florida Barge Canal was less than enthusiastic. Their second in command, Lieutenant Colonel John R. McDonald, informed the press that the agency would obey President Nixon's order to halt construction. "This is a directive from the President, who is also commander in chief," McDonald announced. "The Corps of Engineers obviously will abide by the directive. Until we receive further instructions from our Washington office, we will be unable to make any further comment on the announcement." Congressman Don Fuqua was less diplomatic. He complained that Florida's congressional delegation had been unable to meet with the president before he issued his executive order to suspend the canal's construction. Former senator Spessard Holland accused Nixon of acting on bad advice. "Stopping the canal is entirely unnecessary and can be extremely expensive," Holland told reporters. Former interior secretary Walter J. Hickel said he was pleased with the president's decision. "It's the kind of action we recommended months ago," Hickel explained. "This is a step in the right direction for all America."[37]

Congratulatory letters and telegrams soon flooded the FDE office in Gainesville. Carr responded with a call to action. "There is, of course, a great deal yet to be done before this Florida project can be considered closed," she wrote the National Coalition to Save the Ocklawaha, a collection of scientific and economic experts and concerned citizens dedicated to stopping construction of the Cross Florida Barge Canal. Carr highlighted several items that required immediate attention, including restoration of the Ocklawaha River Valley; taking the required measures to include the river in the national system of Wild and Scenic Rivers; developing a comprehensive land-use plan for the Ocklawaha Regional Ecosystem; and determining the environmental impact of other water resource projects on the Ocklawaha. Carr encouraged FDE's supporters to act upon the environmental mandate presented by the barge canal victory. "Everyone engaged in the effort to save the Oklawaha has realized the broader implications of this fight," she wrote. "The effort truly stands as a classic example of concerned citizens' determination to defend the natural environment from needless destruction. President Nixon has made a dramatic and positive response. We urge you to take the initiative in encouraging an overwhelming public response so that Mr. Nixon will know, beyond a shadow of a doubt, that he has public support when he defends the environment."[38]

FDE had established two major legal precedents. First, the court ruled against the Corps of Engineers' claim that it had sovereign immunity in relation to projects authorized by Congress. Second, FDE had shattered the notion that a Corps of Engineers project could not be stopped once it was under way. FDE member Herbert Kale II, a U.S. Army veteran and vertebrate ecologist who had studied with Eugene Odum at the University of Georgia and later became the Florida Audubon Society's vice president for ornithology, commended Carr for her fortitude during the fight to stop construction of the canal, a battle he had believed to be futile. "Please allow me to eat humble pie," Kale implored her, "with all the others who thought that trying to stop the Cross Florida Barge Canal was akin to one of Don Quixote's impossible dreams." Although Carr would have been the last to claim credit for FDE's victory, her unwavering dedication to the cause had produced a momentous victory for environmentalists. "Even though some of us continued to write impossible letters, give impossible talks, and attend impossible hearings we never really felt that our time was not being wasted, that our efforts couldn't even put a dent in the economic armor of the canal's proponents," Kale admitted.[39]

Congressman Fuqua wrote FDE to reiterate his support for the canal, claiming that the Corps had already demonstrated that the canal posed no threat to the environment. "The U.S. Army Corps of Engineers has had the responsibility for the construction of this waterway and exhaustive studies have shown that the construction would not present any irrevocable disturbances to the surrounding area," Fuqua stated. "I have called on the Secretary of the Interior to conduct additional studies into the ecological effects of this construction and I regret that these studies were not undertaken before the President issued his termination orders."[40]

One month after Nixon halted construction of the canal, Florida governor Reubin Askew observed that the dream of the canal project was over. "If it's not completely dead," he told reporters, "it's in the last stages of gasp." Askew insisted that the president's decision on the canal was final, and that Florida needed to address the problem of dealing with the completed sections of the canal and tying up loose ends. "The state cannot finance it alone," he concluded. "I don't think Congress is going to beat the President on this, and after all the ecology facts are in[,] Florida might not want it anyway." The governor agreed with longtime canal proponent Tom Adams that Nixon's decision to kill the canal was purely political, but he did not support Adams's suggestion that the State of Florida or the Florida Canal Authority should challenge the president in court. Askew conceded that a growing segment of Florida's population had expressed dissatisfaction with the barge canal and cautioned against proceeding with the project "without the support of the people."[41]

Despite the governor's assurance that the barge canal was dead, some members of Congress were reluctant to walk away from it. By the time the canal project was halted in 1971, $73 million had already been expended on it, and the canal was approximately 35 percent complete. Although construction of the canal had stopped, the existing barge-canal structures had not been removed. Rodman Dam still blocked 16 miles of the Ocklawaha River. Eureka Dam and Lock were constructed between 1965 and 1970, but the dam was never closed and the structures were never operational. Although FDE's scientists were confident that the basin under Rodman Reservoir could be replanted and a developing forest would be present within twenty-five to thirty years, the approximately 10,000-acre Rodman Reservoir and Dam still remained intact. In addition, Buckman Lock—which opened December 14, 1968—was still operational. Located approximately 5 miles to the northeast of Rodman Dam, the lock lifts boats from the level of the St. Johns River to the level of the Rodman Reservoir. There have been several documented cases of endangered West Indian manatees dying while attempting to pass through Buckman Lock and Rodman Dam.[42]

More than a year after construction of the canal had officially stopped, none of the steps Carr recommended in her letter to the National Coalition to Save the Ocklawaha had been accomplished. She expressed her frustration to the president. "It is springtime in Florida and another growing season has started," Carr lamented. "When will restoration begin in the Oklawaha River Valley?" She forwarded copies of the letter to Florida's Department of Pollution Control, the EPA, the U.S. Forest Service, the U.S. Department of the Interior, the Florida section of the Society of American Foresters, the National Audubon Society, and a host of other national and statewide environmental organizations, signaling that the campaign to restore the Ocklawaha River Valley required immediate assistance.[43]

The collective efforts of FDE and a coalition of state and national conservation organizations soon resulted in a federal court order to lower the Rodman

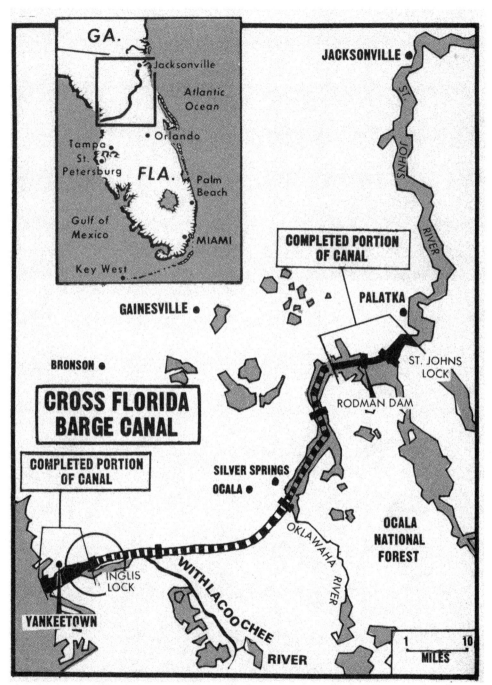

This 1971 map highlights the completed sections of the Cross Florida Barge Canal. Courtesy of the State Archives of Florida.

A completed section of the Cross Florida Barge Canal near Palatka on Florida's eastern coast. Photo by Peggy Macdonald.

Rodman Dam (now George Kirkpatrick Dam) continues to interrupt the natural flow of the Ocklawaha River. Trees killed when Rodman Reservoir flooded the Ocklawaha River Valley in 1968 still drift toward the dam. Photo by Peggy Macdonald.

Anglers fish near Rodman Dam. Photo by Peggy Macdonald.

Reservoir by 5 feet in order to save a significant number of trees at the edge of the reservoir. "It's quite a major victory," said Carr, who became FDE's president in 1972. "It's long overdue and could be the first big step into restoration of the area." However, instead of bringing about the permanent removal of Rodman Reservoir, the drawdown was only temporary. Although the reservoir's water level was lowered by 5 feet, reducing its size from 10,000 acres to 4,300 acres until December 1, 1972, all this accomplished was a short-term reduction in algae and water weeds in the reservoir. The Corps of Engineers sought to return Rodman's water level to its previous depth of 18 feet. Using the media as a public-education tool, Carr explained that raising the water level that much would put the lives of approximately twenty-five thousand hardwood trees and 600–700 hundred acres of land back in jeopardy. FDE

A great egret competes with anglers for fish that pass through Rodman Dam. Photo by Peggy Macdonald.

planned to push for incremental drawdowns of the reservoir until it would finally be drained completely, but this strategy never succeeded.[44]

In the spring of 1972, while the battle over Rodman Reservoir's water level continued, canal boosters sought to revive the canal by any means necessary. Proponents distributed pro-canal bumper stickers in Washington, D.C., before a House Appropriations Committee vote on a three-hundred-thousand-dollar appropriation for another study of the canal's effects on the environment. Boosters contended that the canal would divert water southward from the Ocklawaha and Withlacoochee Rivers, which would help the Everglades. FDE's scientists countered that a completed barge canal would not alter the northward and northeastward flows of the respective rivers. The real purpose of the study was to keep the canal project alive with a fresh injection of federal study funds. The bumper stickers, which were produced by the Jacksonville Chamber of Commerce, said "Save the Everglades—complete the Cross-Florida Canal." Carr was outraged at canal proponents' blatant attempt to secure new funding for the project by conflating it with the popular movement to save the Everglades. "Saving the Everglades has become a national battle cry," she said. "It's an unfair tactic. They wouldn't dare distribute those stickers in Florida. But in Washington, they might actually mislead a Congressman into thinking the Everglades would benefit." Congressmen who supported the new canal study included Don Fuqua, Robert Sikes, Bill Chappell, and Charles Bennett. Carr criticized Fuqua for joining his three Florida colleagues—who had been some of the barge canal's most ardent supporters—in the request for a new canal appropriation. "He has twenty-six counties in his district," Carr pointed out, "and only Putnam County is pressing him. He can't say he is doing what the vast majority of constituents want. The day of rubber stamping every project of the vested interests is past. That's not what Florida wants."[45]

At the start of the 1970s, Nixon's involvement in the barge canal dispute appeared to have resolved the issue. However, by the decade's close, little progress had been made toward the restoration of the Ocklawaha. Throughout the 1970s, Carr and FDE continued to push for deauthorization of the Cross Florida Barge Canal and restoration of the Ocklawaha River Valley. Meanwhile, canal proponents remained steadfast in their belief that the court would rule in their favor. The Corps of Engineers conducted its own environmental impact statement so that the canal project would be in compliance with NEPA. This restudy was completed in February 1977. Contrary to initial expectations, the results prompted the chief of engineers to recommend against completion of the barge canal, "in view of its marginal economic justification and potential adverse environmental impacts." This was exactly what FDE had argued for years.[46]

When President Jimmy Carter took office in 1977, Carr and her allies thought that deauthorization was just around the corner. In 1978, Carter asked Congress to deauthorize the Cross Florida Barge Canal. The president recommended extending the borders of the Ocala National Forest in order to protect the Ocklawaha River in the future. He urged Congress to consider how to dispose of the barge-canal lands and structures. Most importantly, he called for the restoration of the Ocklawaha River and suggested that the river be designated as a Wild and Scenic River. On January 27, 1978, the secretaries of agriculture and the army, the Department of the Interior, the EPA, and the governor and cabinet of Florida responded to the president's request for congressional deauthorization of the barge canal. They estimated that the cost (at January 1978 price levels) of enacting the president's proposals for restoring the Ocklawaha River and disposing of canal lands and facilities would be slightly more than $30 million. By contrast, they predicted that the cost of completing the canal would be approximately $367 million.[47]

Although President Carter had called for the deauthorization of the barge canal and the restoration of the Ocklawaha, Congress took no action on either matter. There was no end in sight for FDE's battle for deauthorization and restoration. "We find ourselves in the very peculiar position of having won our fight but not our prime objective," Carr complained to Fuqua. "An impressive array of elected officials vigorously recommend deauthorization of the canal project, including the Florida Legislature, Governor Graham, the Florida Cabinet, Senators Chiles and Stone, you [Fuqua] and twelve other Florida Representatives, and President Carter. And yet because Mr. Chappell and Mr. Bennett, representing a small group of vested interests in Jacksonville, oppose the legislation, the bill to legally terminate the canal project is stalled."[48]

Unless the barge canal was deauthorized at both the federal and state levels, it could be restored to active status with ease. Carr expressed her frustration with the slow pace of the barge canal's deauthorization to Representative Fuqua:

Today the canal project is alive and only needs appropriation of construction funds to continue on its destructive path. And we citizens are in the anomalous position of having won every battle but not succeeded in saving the Oklawaha and Withlacoochee Rivers, ensuring the protection of the central Floridan Aquifer, and preventing a great waste of tax-payers' dollars. The canal project is in limbo and as long as it remains in this state of suspended animation, sixteen miles of the Oklawaha River remain flooded, the lower Withlacoochee's flow is reduced to a damaging level, nearly a million dollars a year are spent maintaining the canal structures, and thousands of acres of right-of-way lands are tied up that might be used for public and/or private ventures.[49]

Throughout the 1970s, Congress and the Florida Legislature considered legislation calling for the deauthorization and restoration of the Ocklawaha River and the incessant requests of a small but vocal group of barge canal supporters. In 1974, Carr advised the Florida Senate's Committee on Natural Resources and Conservation to issue a favorable report on a deauthorization bill, citing the Florida Canal Authority's "lack of responsiveness to the citizens of Florida" because the agency "still envisages its promotion of the canal as an ongoing project." She reminded the committee that the Florida cabinet had suspended its support for the canal project in 1972, pending the completion of an updated environmental impact study. Although the cabinet had rescinded its support for any future canal plans that passed through the Ocklawaha River Valley, the Canal Authority's plans continued to include the Ocklawaha.[50]

Carr was certain that the barge canal was dead when a 1976 study indicated that the completion of the Cross Florida Barge Canal would have little impact on industrial growth in the region. "I would think it would remove the last bit of genuine support for the canal," she said, adding that many "very reasonable people" had supported the canal on the assumption that it would stimulate industrial development and boost Florida's economy (although FDE had long maintained that the opposite was true). Carr thought that support for the barge canal would wane upon the release of the independent study, conducted by the Cambridge, Massachusetts, firm Meta Systems, Inc., as part of a $1.8 million court-ordered study on the environmental and economic impacts of the canal. In February 1974, as the Watergate scandal was in full bloom, U.S. Senior Circuit Judge Harvey M. Johnsen ruled that only Congress had the authority to determine whether the canal should be completed or terminated, and that President Nixon had overstepped his authority in halting the canal. Johnsen further ordered that separate environmental and economic studies be conducted to serve as a guide for Congress in determining whether the canal should be completed or terminated. According to the economic study, which was financed by the EPA, the canal would be located too far from major markets to withstand competition from established industrial centers. Moreover, there were not enough raw materials in the canal area to sustain substantial economic growth in central Florida.[51]

Meta Systems' findings failed to kill boosters' dream of a completed canal. Carr argued that a completed canal would benefit only a small group of Jacksonville businessmen at the expense of the public good. "The Florida public is very concerned about the wasteful and destructive project," she told the press, stressing that it was unlikely that the Corps would be able to justify the revival of the project. "The evidence is so overwhelming that it seems to us there isn't any way they can come out saying the project isn't an economic loser." Carr hoped that the time had finally come for the Ocklawaha's restoration. "This area, even though damaged in small areas, can be restored and be a very valuable and productive area for all Floridians," she argued. Carr attempted to persuade Floridians that restoration would be more profitable than completing the canal. "Economically, there will be more jobs in restoration than there would be in construction of the canal," she explained. "Also, there will be more long-term economic gains from recreation in the [restored river] than there would have been from a canal."[52]

Carr likened the continuing battle for deauthorization and restoration to the Energizer bunny. "It's like that pink rabbit," she said. "It keeps going and going." Carr believed that the outcome of the battle for the Ocklawaha would be indicative of the success of environmental struggles around the globe. "This is really symptomatic of any other conservation problem," she suggested. "The way the Ocklawaha goes is the way the world goes."[53]

Carr did not know if she would live to see the restoration of her beloved river, but she was determined to persevere until the barge canal was deauthorized. In 1980, state senator Dempsey Barron, who had repeatedly blocked FDE's efforts to deauthorize the barge canal, told Carr that there was no "real public support for your point of view." After their confrontation, Carr returned to her Tallahassee office and made five phone calls. The following day, five major Florida newspapers published editorials calling for deauthorization of the barge canal. "We had been sending these papers information right along and keeping them up with developments," Carr explained. "So all I had to do was call the editors and let them know the current state of the [deauthorization] bill." A state legislator once claimed that Carr's mere presence at the Florida State Capitol persuaded legislators to take action on the barge canal issue. "All you have to do is walk the halls," the legislator told Carr. "You don't have to say a word. Just be seen there, and every legislator who sees you will say to himself, 'Oh, yes. The Barge Canal.'"[54]

Despite Carr's influence in Tallahassee, a handful of powerful state politicians had succeeded in protecting the interests of a relatively small number of Floridians who wanted to resurrect the canal. These politicians—including Barron, Bennett, Chappell, and state senator George Kirkpatrick—managed to railroad FDE's numerous attempts to deauthorize the canal. "Well, we almost won," Carr wrote FDE members after another failed attempt at deauthorization in the fall of 1978. "But since we didn't we will have to start all over again with the new 96th Congress when it convenes on January 15, 1979." Year after year, Carr remained unwilling to accept defeat in FDE's quest to restore the Ocklawaha River. According to former FDE public-relations worker JoAnn Myer Valenti, "Marjorie didn't take no for an answer." Carr urged FDE members to assist the campaign by writing or telephoning their congressmen and persuading them to support deauthorization.[55]

In the 1980s, although there was continued support for deauthorization at the highest levels of the state and federal government, canal boosters succeeded in stalling a final vote on deauthorization at the federal level for more than a decade after Carter's initial request to Congress. Canal backers continued to postpone deauthorization with the idea that the political climate would eventually shift in favor of the completion of the barge canal. U.S. senator Paula Hawkins supported a canal restudy championed by Bill Chappell and Charles Bennett. The proposed $450,000 restudy would reexamine the canal's economic benefits. Chappell claimed that the economic restudy would be valuable "even if you wanted to blow [the barge canal] up like Mrs. Carr wants to do." Carr called the proposed restudy a "slice of pork" and laid much of the blame for delaying deauthorization upon Chappell. She claimed that the new study was "a waste of money and could be completed with a pocket calculator or a piece of paper and a pencil." Carr accused Hawkins of contributing to the delay by failing to clarify her position on the canal. She contended that Hawkins only supported environmental issues if they benefited her politically.[56]

Carr also opposed Hawkins's plan to preserve the canal right-of-way for recreational use without deauthorizing the canal since this would leave open the possibility that the canal project could be revived at any time in the future. Carr called Hawkins's plan "frivolous, ridiculous, and nonsensical," adding, "the only reason not to deauthorize the canal is to build it." Hawkins's stance on deauthorization of the Cross Florida Barge Canal became a campaign issue in 1986, when she lost her bid for reelection to the Senate to former governor Bob Graham, a longtime supporter of deauthorization of the canal and restoration of the Ocklawaha.[57]

At the same time that Carr challenged Hawkins on her views on deauthorization, Carr placed Bill Chappell between a rock and a hard place when she crafted a measure to use a section of canal right-of-way as the site of a national veterans' cemetery. In order for the barge canal lands to be used for the cemetery, the canal project would have to be deauthorized. FDE's proposal outraged Chappell, who had fought for years to establish a national veterans' cemetery at a different location near the Withlacoochee River. The proposed $30 million Florida National Cemetery on a section of former canal right-of-way would accommodate nearly three hundred thousand grave sites. Carr hoped that the cemetery proposal would finally lead to the canal's deauthorization. "The state can't wait any longer," she said.[58]

Chappell mobilized veterans' groups behind his original plan for a cemetery near the Withlacoochee, capitalizing upon their concerns that the politics of deauthorization might jeopardize the new national veterans' cemetery. With close to 1.5 million veterans living in Florida, the state's three national veterans' cemeteries were unable to accommodate the growing number of World War II veterans who had retired to the state. In the end, this unorthodox effort to secure deauthorization of the barge canal failed. In 1988, the new cemetery was dedicated in Bushnell, close to the Withlacoochee River. It was actually in the best interest of the Ocklawaha that the cemetery was located elsewhere. This way, when deauthorization finally became a reality, none of the former canal lands were sacrificed to development.[59]

FDE's grassroots strategy eventually paid off. In March 1990, U.S. senators Bob Graham and Lawton Chiles sponsored deauthorization legislation with the assistance of Marjorie Carr and Jack Kaufmann, both of whom made specific recommendations for the initial drafts of the deauthorization legislation. Finally, on October 27, 1990, Senate Bill 2740 deauthorized the canal at the federal level. On November 28, 1990, President George H. W. Bush, who wished to be remembered as an environmental president, signed the bill into law.[60]

On January 22, 1991, the governor and cabinet of the State of Florida signed a resolution agreeing to the terms of federal deauthorization, an act that officially deauthorized the Cross Florida Barge Canal. The Florida Legislature

A section of the Marjorie Harris Carr Cross Florida Greenway, an uninterrupted wilderness corridor located on the lands formerly designated as barge canal right-of-way. Photo by Peggy Macdonald.

had previously enacted a deauthorization bill that conformed to a bill passed simultaneously in the U.S. Senate, but the state deauthorization could not go into effect until the canal was first deauthorized at the federal level. On the date of the canal's deauthorization, the lands that had formerly been set aside as canal right-of-way became the Cross Florida Greenway, a 107-mile nature park.[61]

Marjorie Carr never imagined that she would have to fight for so long to help deauthorization of the Cross Florida Barge Canal come to pass. When the canal was finally deauthorized, she recalled a conversation she had had two decades earlier, when the canal's construction was halted. "Bill Partington, who was our president back in 1971, told me at the time, 'You know, now we have another twenty-year fight ahead of us,'" Carr recalled. "And I said, 'Bill, you're crazy.' But he was right."[62]

Carr attributed her success to her grassroots organization's ability to harness the power of the democratic process. "We had gained the attention of the decision makers," she explained. "I think elected officials listen to the public, if the public speaks loudly. Furthermore, the results of not doing what's right for the environment are dreadful, and they will happen fairly quickly. And the rascals will get turned out if they are perceived as neglecting the environment."[63]

In the last half of her life, protecting and restoring the Ocklawaha River had become Marjorie Carr's raison d'être. Although FDE continued to encounter obstacles to restoration in the final years of her life, Carr remained optimistic about the future of Florida's environment. "I think we are at a watershed time," she surmised. "One reason I'm encouraged is that I do believe that the economic well-being of the state is tied to its environmental well-being. I think the big businesses realize if you don't have a good environment here in Florida, then businesses will go down the drain. When more people realize that, you will have the business community coming in right behind the environmentalists to work on behalf of the environment." Referring to the common practice of condemning land for the construction of an Interstate highway, Carr asked, "If they can condemn land for a road, why can't we condemn land for conservation? Our society has already accepted condemnation of land in the public good. I think we just have to define what is the public good."[64]

Marjorie Carr and Florida Defenders of the Environment convinced the public and politicians that unchecked growth and development in environmentally sensitive areas was not in the public good. Using scientific and economic facts as weapons, they defeated the Cross Florida Barge Canal. To Carr, FDE's success was indicative of the power of the democratic process. "In the environmental effort," Carr said at an environmental conference in Key West, "I am constantly made aware of the advantages of a democracy." Her speech touted the benefits of an involved, educated, and outspoken public to the environmental movement. Environmental progress, Carr argued, is most likely to occur when the citizenry accepts the responsibility of stewardship and when a democratic government responds to the public's requests. "I think that's why the U.S. is extraordinary in the field of the environment," she maintained, "and where Florida is a leader, too."[65]

Conclusion

The battle over the Ocklawaha River had important implications for later environmental struggles in Florida and across the nation. In the late twentieth century, the creation of a new, national environmental infrastructure contributed to the development of an environmental ethos. Marjorie Harris Carr helped shape the discourse of the modern environmental movement by being among the first leaders of a single-issue organization to apply the science and language of ecology to a complex environmental problem. In the process, she helped prevent the nation's most prestigious engineering organization, the U.S. Army Corps of Engineers, from completing a project that was grounded in nineteenth-century views of progress and failed to consider the environmental consequences of its construction. Although the Cross Florida Barge Canal was approximately one-third complete before Carr and her allies were able to achieve the unprecedented feat of forcing the Corps of Engineers to stop a major project while it was already under way, one woman's committed leadership of a pioneering environmental campaign grounded in the male-dominated fields of science, economics, and law prevented an environmental tragedy from permanently altering Florida's landscape on a catastrophic level.

Carr's leadership of the movement to protect and restore the Ocklawaha River Valley set a precedent for future environmental campaigns. A firm believer in the power of the democratic process, Carr championed a new breed of environmental leadership that blended grassroots activism, public education, the science of ecology, and legal action. In the early to mid-twentieth century, Carr's participation in the predominantly male field of science was limited by her gender. However, by the close of the twentieth century, Carr provided an example of how citizens could use science to protect the earth from senseless destruction. In the tumultuous 1960s and 1970s, when Americans grappled with the antiwar movement, race riots, Watergate, and the assassination of some of the nation's greatest leaders, Carr and Florida Defenders of the Environment (FDE) restored the public's faith in the power of representative democracy.

Historian Lee Irby observed that the battle over the Cross Florida Barge Canal and its remnants represents the intersection of "two diametrically opposed views of nature and the human place in the natural world." The controversy over the canal's construction began as a contest over the best use of Florida's natural resources. Canal proponents exerted their right to shape nature according to human will, while the defenders of the Ocklawaha River Valley employed a "not in my backyard" approach; instead of calling for an end to the canal's construction, they simply requested that the Corps of Engineers select an alternate route that would not affect the Ocklawaha. However, the debate was gradually transformed into a dispute over the meaning of the word "ecosystem." Whereas environmentalists contended that the Ocklawaha Regional Ecosystem merited protection based upon its unique ecological features, those who favored the preservation of the most controversial remaining canal structure, Rodman Dam, countered that the reservoir—which they referred to as Rodman Lake—was also worthy of protection as a functional, if not natural, ecosystem.[1]

In 2012, FDE continued its efforts to restore the Ocklawaha. In February, seeking to transcend the debate over the merits of a natural ecosystem versus a built one, FDE—in partnership with the Florida Wildlife Federation—filed notice of intent to sue the U.S. Forest Service in order to protect manatees and shortnose sturgeon, whose migration in the Ocklawaha River is blocked by Rodman Dam. The manatee and shortnose sturgeon are protected under the U.S. Endangered Species Act (ESA); in December 2012, the National Oceanic and Atmospheric Administration (NOAA) Fisheries Service decided to add the Atlantic sturgeon—another species blocked by the dam—to the list of species protected under the ESA. Erin Condon, executive director of FDE, is optimistic that the U.S. Forest Service and Florida Game and Fresh Water Fish Commission, which have previously expressed support for draining Rodman

Impoundment and restoring the Ocklawaha River, will agree to develop a plan that will include at least partial removal of Rodman Dam.[2]

If restoration will ever take place, it will likely come as a result of FDE's continued dedication to the approach that Carr and her colleagues first developed in 1969. FDE's original strategy, which has changed little over the years, utilizes scientific research and professional expertise; fosters cooperation among local, state, and national environmental groups; harnesses the power of the media to sway public opinion and influence lawmakers; and utilizes the muscle of the legal system to enact change.

As a founding member and longtime leader of FDE, Carr learned to use the media both to educate the public and to shame politicians into doing the right thing for the environment. "People at every level were intimidated by her," Carr's former public relations consultant David Godfrey recalled, "because she could put their name in the papers the next day." In an article published two weeks after FDE's monumental victory over the U.S. Army Corps of Engineers, *Time* magazine observed that the demise of the Cross Florida Barge Canal was indicative of the increasing role ecology was beginning to play in national politics.[3]

At the beginning of the Ocklawaha campaign, most news publications supported the barge canal project. FDE's lawsuit against the Corps of Engineers—supplemented by its pathbreaking environmental impact statement—transformed the media's interpretation of the barge canal debate into a battle between sound environmental practices and ecologically questionable canals and dams. The media had become more critical of Corps of Engineers pork projects that satisfied shipping interests, construction interests, and the needs of others who would exploit the earth for profit. However, congressmen continued to court Corps projects that would direct money and jobs to their districts, and the Corps remained the nation's leading director of waterways projects.[4]

Although environmental concerns were the driving force behind the demise of the barge canal, FDE's economic argument set an important national precedent for other public-works projects. "It is the first real confirmation that the 'benefit-cost ratio philosophy' has been challenged," University of Florida professor of engineering Olle I. Elgerd noted. "It could conceivably have as a result that the whole value system which in the past has laid at the base of all hydro projects will come up for review on a national scale. In this respect the victory on Oklawaha could be as fundamental in the annals of conservation as was Carson's work for turning the pesticide tide." For decades, the Corps of Engineers had relied upon the benefit-cost ratio to justify its manipulation of the land. After FDE's victory over the Corps of Engineers, federal agencies would be required to consider the environmental impact of a proposed project when deciding if it was in the public's best interest. Moreover, FDE revealed that the Corps was guilty of exaggerating the economic benefits of the canal project in order to receive congressional funding.[5]

At the time of FDE's victory over the Corps of Engineers, environmental law was still in its infancy. The Miami jetport case was the first environmental lawsuit in Florida. The only environmental laws in existence in 1970 were antipollution and antidumping laws; no laws were designed specifically to protect the environment, according to David Gluckman, who filed the first environmental lawsuits on behalf of the Sierra Club in Florida in the late 1960s. In 1970, only five national environmental cases served as precedents for environmental litigation. "It was the beginning of the movement," Gluckman reflected. FDE's lawsuit against the Corps of Engineers resulted in the termination of one of the nation's largest public-works projects. "You have to remember, the Cross Florida Barge Canal was the biggest deal since the digging of the Panama Canal," Nathaniel Reed explained. "Marjorie was eventually able to prove that, economically, the barge canal was nineteenth-century thinking."[6]

During the Great Depression, when construction of the barge canal began as a public-works project, many parts of Florida—unlike the rest of the United States—had escaped the process of industrialization in the nineteenth century. Florida was hot, humid, and undeveloped; inland Florida was inhospitable to tourists and residents alike. With the advent of air-conditioning and a massive influx of new residents after World War II, this would all change. Veterans who had trained in Florida returned to the state to start a new life after the war. Florida was transformed from the least populous state in the South (and one of the poorest) before the war, to the fourth-most-populous state in the nation by the century's close. In the absence of any significant efforts to develop regional land planning, developers' plans received little scrutiny.[7]

In the postwar era, the proposed barge canal generated debate over the best use of Florida's rivers. Although state leaders had championed the Cross Florida Barge Canal as a means to achieve economic growth, an increasingly vocal group of Floridians contested the state's dominant discourse of industrialization and promoted a competing discourse grounded in ecology. While canal proponents viewed the Ocklawaha, St. Johns, and Withlacoochee Rivers as transportation routes that should be utilized to facilitate commerce in central Florida, Carr and her colleagues argued that rivers—particularly the undisturbed Ocklawaha River—were central to the health of their respective ecosystems, and that industry threatened the stability of these ecosystems.

Carr succeeded in translating the complex new language of ecology to the masses. She influenced the media, which initially supported construction of the barge canal as a means to foster economic growth in central Florida, to inform the public about the importance of preserving the integrity of the Ocklawaha regional ecosystem. After suffering a crushing defeat at a 1966 public hearing in the state's capital, Carr transformed a local campaign to reroute the barge canal around the Ocklawaha River Valley to a national effort to prevent the U.S. Army Corps of Engineers and similar federal agencies from completing pork-barrel projects planned without considering their effects on the environment. FDE's environmental impact statement challenged the conservation ethos of federal agencies that manipulated natural resources for profit and furthered the nation's transition to an environmental awareness grounded in the science of ecology.

Once construction of the Cross Florida Barge Canal was halted, when the official court-ordered economic and environmental impact studies had been completed, and even after the Corps of Engineers recommended against completing the canal, proponents continued to sponsor legislation authorizing expensive economic restudies designed to keep the dream of the canal alive until the political climate shifted in favor of finishing the partially constructed canal, until the barge canal project was finally deauthorized nearly a half century after its initial authorization during World War II.

The strategies FDE employed in its struggle to save the Ocklawaha River Valley served as a guide for other environmental battles across the nation. To this day, environmental groups continue to adapt the model of FDE's environmental impact statement to suit the requirements of their own projects. Carr's resolve inspired other environmentalists to persevere in their own seemingly unwinnable campaigns. Environmental organizations from other states sought her expert counsel in their respective battles with nuclear power plants, phosphate mines, industrial pollution, river restoration, and other complex environmental issues. Carr served on the boards of state and local land-planning councils, state and national environmental organizations, cooperative efforts between environmentalists and businesses, and environmental education foundations. She was a firm believer in the power of coop-eration between government, industry, and the citizenry. Unlike the confron-tational activists of later environmental groups such as Earth First!, Carr and FDE promoted civil dialogue.

Carr attempted to branch out in new directions in the 1980s and 1990s, but FDE's efforts to deauthorize the Cross Florida Barge Canal and restore the Ocklawaha River Valley continued to demand most of her time. FDE's mem-bership had expanded from fewer than four hundred members at the start of the Ocklawaha campaign to approximately two thousand members, with Carr still at the helm of the organization of volunteer experts. In addition to leading the Ocklawaha campaign, Carr and FDE directed efforts to manage growth in Florida and worked to restore and preserve threatened wetlands and rivers, including the Apalachicola, Suwannee, Wekiva, and St. Johns, which—like the Ocklawaha—were in need of restoration. She envisioned FDE taking a leading role in the drive to preserve as much as possible of what remained of natural Florida. "To keep samples of our original landscapes here in Florida, whether in hammocks, coastlines, scrubs, wetlands or swamps . . . that's a worthwhile goal," Carr maintained. She looked forward to the day when Florida would restore the Kissimmee River, Lake Okeechobee, and the Everglades.[8]

Carr emphasized the importance of maintaining close relationships with government and industry in order to craft responsible solutions for the envi-ronment. This was the primary motivation behind FDE's establishment of the Environmental Service Center in Tallahassee, where FDE could monitor legis-lation and involve its coalition of volunteer specialists in solving any problems that might arise. Instead of antagonizing developers and industrialists, Carr partnered with them where appropriate to further her environmental goals. Because a strong economy in Florida depends upon a healthy environment and sustainable development, she was confident that businesses would make decisions that were in the best interests of the environment. Carr believed that citizens, government, and industry should work together to protect Florida's future. For example, she suggested that the Florida Chamber of Commerce, the Department of Natural Resources, and local and state departments of tourism assume a leading role in teaching new residents and tourists about the environment by using the media to coordinate a public education program. Florida's long-running debate over economic growth versus environmental stewardship continues in the twenty-first century.[9]

Carr believed that local citizen action was the key to environmental stewardship. In 1970, she reflected upon the role environmentalists had played in defending the environment from unregulated development. "Although the last few years have seen the adoption of a growing amount of legislation designed to curb the mindless destruction of the land, the time has grown so late," she cautioned. "So little is left and destructive forces have become so strong, that if the remaining American landscapes are to be saved, it will only be because groups of conservationists—the 'little-old-ladies-in-tennis-shoes'—have learned to take prompt and effective action." Lack of citizen support for the barge canal was a key factor in the eventual cancellation of the project.[10]

Carr's opposition to the barge canal stemmed from a personal connection to the natural beauty of north central Florida, which was her home for sixty years. Whenever she left home, she traveled along U.S. Highway 441. Heading north, she passed through Paynes Prairie on the way to Gainesville, taking in changing scenery that included prehistoric animals such as alligators when heavy rains flooded the prairie, and an assortment of native and migratory birds such as sandhill cranes, egrets, ibises, and hawks soaring above the prairie in search of food. Even if there was not enough time to stop the car and listen to the frogs singing in the tall grasses or the clicking of cicadas in the trees, a short drive through the prairie was enough to recharge Carr's soul and remind her what she was fighting for. In 1964, when Interstate 75 replaced these sounds with the roar of thousands of automobiles cutting through her own backyard, she became determined to stand up for the north central Florida environment.

Carr's strong sense of place kept her involved in science, conservation, and environmental activism in spite of the powerful institutional barriers that had prevented her from maintaining a formal career in zoology. Her affiliation with the University of Florida, where she was both an alumna of the school's graduate program in zoology and an associate of the Florida Museum of Natural History, and her status as the wife of one of the world's leading turtle experts and a pioneer in the field of conservation biology, provided her with the resources she would draw upon over the course of a nearly forty-year career in conservation and environmental activism that ultimately preserved not only the Ocklawaha River, but also much of what remains of the north central Florida landscape.

Although Archie Carr lent whatever support he could to his wife's conservation and environmental activities, he was preoccupied with his own research and conservation agenda. Archie credited his wife with being "the militant

one" whose optimism, dedication, and persistence were responsible for preserving and restoring Paynes Prairie and Lake Alice; stopping the University
of Florida from building a four-lane throughway and two-thousand-car parking garage that would have destroyed Lake Alice; preventing the construction
of a Jacksonville-Tampa turnpike that would have further damaged Paynes
Prairie, disrupted the rural charm of historic Micanopy, and damaged other
environmentally sensitive lands in central Florida; and saving the Ocklawaha
River. Marjorie Carr contributed to the awakening of Florida's environmental
consciousness by making ecology accessible to the citizenry, and she inspired
citizens across the nation to use the activist science of ecology to improve
the environment in their own communities, at the local level, by gathering
relevant scientific and economic information and using the media to convey
that information to the public and politicians.

Carr's approach to environmental activism was cutting-edge. Beginning
with her 1965 *Florida Naturalist* essay, she conveyed a complex ecological
message in plain words that anyone could understand, elucidating the threat
that ill-conceived development posed to Florida's fragile ecosystems. Carr
understood the ecological ramifications of the Corps of Engineers' proposal
to build a canal along the Ocklawaha River, including the damage it would
cause to the Floridan Aquifer. Moreover, she felt a personal connection to
the river, which she had known most of her life. She was outraged that the
river would be sacrificed in the name of (dubious) economic progress. "It's
the same outrage one feels upon hearing that a man took a hammer and
wrecked the Pieta," Carr explained. "It should be saved because it is a beautiful, unique river."[11]

Throughout Marjorie Carr's long career as a conservationist and environmental activist, she sometimes felt compelled to play the part of the housewife. Marjorie projected the image of domesticity by emphasizing her status
as Archie's wife, referring to herself as "Mrs. Carr" in her dealings with the
media and politicians. Bob Graham, Florida's former governor and a retired
U.S. senator, worked closely with Marjorie Carr on legislation to deauthorize
the barge canal and other environmental issues. Yet he did not immediately
recognize her name in a 2005 conversation on the University of Florida campus. After being reminded of Carr's efforts to stop construction of the Cross
Florida Barge Canal, the name Marjorie Carr still did not ring a bell. Upon
hearing that she was the wife of Archie Carr, however, Graham responded
animatedly, "Ohhh . . . *Mrs. Carr!*"[12]

Although Florida's older generation of environmental activists still remembers Marjorie Carr's name, Carr—and the Ocklawaha River itself—is not well known among younger environmentalists. Moreover, Carr's leadership of the campaign to save the Ocklawaha River is seldom addressed in national histories of the environmental movement, although her campaign served as a model for other environmental campaigns across the United States. Buddy MacKay, who worked to dismantle the barge canal project as a U.S. congressman and state lawmaker, described the death of the canal as "one of the real happy endings in the entire American environmental movement." He was instrumental in urging the Florida Legislature to name the Cross Florida Greenway after Marjorie Carr.[13]

Although she was honored by this gesture, Carr would have been more pleased if the legislature had resolved to restore the Ocklawaha River. Restoration remained plagued by problems of financing and contesting visions of the Ocklawaha's future. Estimates of the total cost of removing the existing barge canal structures—including Rodman Dam and Reservoir—and restoring the river to its natural course varied wildly, but with a likely price tag in the millions, the expense was too great for private charities and environmental organizations to cover without government assistance. Not only was restoration expensive, it was controversial as well. Bill Chappell and George Kirkpatrick prevented the passage of deauthorization and restoration legislation at the federal and state levels year after year, touting the reservoir's benefits as a bass fishery. Carr claimed that very few people opposed the Ocklawaha's restoration, but those who did were "obsessed" with maintaining Rodman Reservoir. She further maintained that bass anglers who opposed restoration "ought to be ashamed of themselves." Restoring the Ocklawaha would not detract from local fishing, Carr argued, since nearby Lake George provided excellent fishing and recreation opportunities in a more natural setting than the artificial Rodman impoundment, which was expensive to maintain.[14]

Marjorie and Archie Carr continued to work well past the traditional age of retirement. Their relationship began and ended with science. "They were for most of their lives rather happy people, I believe," Mimi observed. "Towards the end of their lives they were very driven." While Marjorie continued to lead FDE's efforts to deauthorize the canal, Archie remained immersed in his sea turtle research. In the mid-1980s, he was diagnosed with stomach cancer. "I don't think he had any inkling the cancer was coming on," Mimi reflected. Archie had a fear of doctors, which might have been caused by the traumatic

Marjorie and Archie Carr both won the New York Zoological Society's Gold Medal for achievement in biological conservation in 1978; in 1988, the society made Marjorie a Scientific Fellow. Courtesy of Mimi Carr.

development of osteomyelitis in his youth. By the time doctors discovered Archie's stomach cancer, it was too late to start an aggressive course of treatment. On May 21, 1987, Archie died at home in Micanopy. Soon after Archie's death, Marjorie's health began to deteriorate. "Mother was, of course, just slowly destroying herself with the smoking," Mimi recalled.[15]

Carr developed emphysema, a smoking-induced disease that results in irreversible lung damage. The disease progresses slowly, culminating in what is commonly referred to as end-stage emphysema, in which only 30 percent of the patient's lungs are still able to function and the risk of contracting lung infections such as pneumonia and bronchitis is elevated.[16] Emphysema reduced Carr's mobility rapidly. In the early 1990s, she moved from the family farm in Micanopy to a Gainesville duplex developed by Rodman Reservoir proponent George Kirkpatrick. Mimi left behind an acting career in Oregon and moved in with her mother, who required full-time care. Carr continued to campaign on behalf of the Ocklawaha from home, remaining optimistic that she would live to see its restoration.

In the final years of her life, Carr was tethered to an oxygen tank. Emphysema restricted her travel and sapped her energy. Nonetheless, she remained the symbolic leader of FDE's fight for restoration of the Ocklawaha, lobbying over the phone and through letters to politicians, including Senator Bob Graham, who made house calls to discuss proposed legislation. In order to continue her work as FDE's president emeritus, Carr converted her bedroom into a working office with a desk, filing cabinet, and telephone. "The centers of power," she reminded supporters, are only a phone call away. Carr continued to harness the powerful tool of the media, contributing fact-filled commentaries to Florida newspapers. In November 1996, Carr was inducted into the Florida Women's Hall of Fame, but she was too ill to attend the ceremony. Shortly afterward, she endured a month-long hospitalization for respiratory distress. Upon her release, Carr gradually resumed her efforts to remove Rodman Dam and secure restoration.[17]

Carr was confident that there was still time to save the Ocklawaha River. She envisioned a time after the dam was breached and the reservoir was drained when the springs underneath the flooded section of the river would help it resume its original course, the forested valley would return to its former glory, the Ocklawaha's water quality would improve, and the water creatures that were unable to pass through the dam (and often died trying) would resume their normal migration along the river. "Once the dam is gone," Carr predicted, "the manatees will be able to come up there during the winter. What a sight that will be. How lovely that will be."[18]

Tragically, it was a vision that Carr would never see come to fruition. On October 10, 1997, after living with end-stage emphysema for two years, she lost her battle with the disease. Carr died at age eighty-two without having the chance to see her beloved river run free again. Each of her five children remained involved in conservation and environmental activism after their parents' deaths. Mimi supplemented a professional acting career with documentary projects and public appearances for FDE. Longtime FDE activist Joe Little has observed that engaging Mimi in a conversation is like talking with Marjorie Carr. Chuck followed in his parents' footsteps closely. Like his mother, he earned a bachelor of science degree at Florida State University and a master of science degree at the University of Florida. He completed a doctorate in estuarine ecology at the University of Michigan. Chuck became a regional coordinator for the Wildlife Conservation Society and directed conservation projects in Central America and the Caribbean. Steve worked to restore the sturgeon, a primitive and highly endangered fish, to the Suwannee River. Tom produced aerial surveys of mega fauna—including native species such as manatees and sea turtles—for several national and international organizations. David served as FDE's research director in the 1980s and worked as the executive director of the Caribbean Conservation Corporation (now known as the Sea Turtle Conservancy) before embarking upon other conservation activities. In 1999, he founded the Conservation Trust for Florida, a nonprofit land trust modeled after FDE and dedicated to the preservation of the state's rural landscapes. All the Carr children still reside in Alachua County.[19]

In 1998, the Florida Legislature dedicated the former canal right-of-way to Carr, renaming it the Marjorie Harris Carr Cross Florida Greenway. Stretching from the Gulf coast to the Atlantic, the greenway's uninterrupted span of habitat supports a diverse assortment of native flora and fauna and provides Floridians and tourists with a variety of recreational opportunities. However, the Ocklawaha River remains blocked by Rodman Dam, which was renamed the George Kirkpatrick Dam to honor its greatest supporter. The dam costs between $150,000 and $500,000 annually to maintain. In the absence of Marjorie Carr's leadership, the battle for restoration continues while the Ocklawaha River Valley holds its breath.[20]

Marjorie Carr bridged the gap between conservation and environmentalism. Like many other women in the early twentieth century, Carr first participated in conservation activities through the Woman's Club, Garden Club, and Audubon Society. Carr's activist career provided her with an acceptable way to make use of her scientific training. As Carr came to embrace ecology over conservation, her undergraduate and graduate studies in zoology, ornithology, ichthyology, and bacteriology provided her with a level of expertise that proved to be indispensable as she took the helm of an environmental organization that used the science of ecology to mount its opposition to a colossal Corps of Engineering project that would have disastrous consequences for Florida's environment.

Carr was uniquely poised to assume leadership of the movement to save the Ocklawaha. Although not a native Floridian, Carr spent the majority of her life in the state, and she witnessed the profound impact that the rapid pace of postwar development had had on the state's ecosystems. Although Carr had been powerless to stop the construction of a federal interstate highway in her own backyard, she learned a powerful lesson from this experience and applied it successfully to two subsequent proposals for highway projects that would have destroyed ecologically sensitive lands.

Although Carr was a mother to five children, her activist career was based upon her understanding of science, not her experiences as a woman. Nonetheless, when it suited her purposes, Carr was willing to use her presumed status as a "housewife" to gain entry into public spaces that were reserved for men and to shield her from any negative repercussions of her environmental activism. Indeed, being married to one of the world's most prominent zoologists offered Carr distinct advantages over her unmarried contemporaries. For more than four years, Carr balanced career and family with the help of a cadre of domestic servants who cared for her children and managed the household while she and her husband explored the Honduran rain forests.

Unlike many other wives of accomplished scientists, Carr had established her scientific credentials before she met her spouse. In fact, at the beginning of her marriage, Carr was forced to conceal her status as a married woman from her employer so that she would not lose her job. At the Bass Biological Laboratory, Carr was subjected to sexual harassment and gender discrimination. In addition, Carr had to stave off her employer's repeated attempts to engage her in secretarial tasks instead of scientific activities. As a Phi Beta Kappa student at Florida State College for Women, Carr had actually planned to double major in zoology and secretarial science so that she would be more marketable to male employers after graduation. Instead, Carr was hired as the nation's first federal female wildlife technician at the Welaka Fish Hatchery. Through this position, Carr first encountered the Ocklawaha River, nearly three decades before it was scarred by the Rodman Dam.

The Welaka position also steered Carr toward the University of Florida, where she met the love of her life. Although Marjorie Harris had already made science her life before she met Archie Carr, together, they would support and strengthen each other's professional growth through education, research, travel, and lively discussions of many of the most important scientific books to emerge in the twentieth century. Archie provided Marjorie with an avenue to a graduate education in science that had been denied to her because of her gender. Moreover, Archie's financial, intellectual, and emotional support sustained Marjorie's activist career, and he frequently lent his expertise and reputation to her various conservation and environmental battles.

Marjorie was Archie's muse. Equally comfortable in the laboratory and the field, she joined him on adventurous research and collecting trips in Florida, Mexico, and Central America throughout much of their marriage. Together with their five children, Marjorie and Archie lived close to the land in rural Micanopy, where they enjoyed an enduring love affair with Florida's wild things and scenic places. There was room in Marjorie Carr's heart for two great loves: the Ocklawaha and her soul mate, Archie. Early in their courtship, in one of their many beautiful love letters, Archie wrote Marjorie that at the moment of his death, "When the electrons of the last atoms that have been me fly out of their orbits it will be in quest of you." More than sixty years later, Marjorie Harris Carr went to her death without seeing the cypress-lined Ocklawaha River run free. Sixteen years after her death, the river's restoration remains an unresolved issue. However, as Carr maintained until the end, "it isn't too late to save the Ocklawaha."[21]

Acknowledgments

At the University of Florida, I am grateful to Louise Newman for her mentorship and patience. She and Jack Davis provided extensive comments on an early draft of this manuscript. Along with Sheryl Kroen and Angel Kwolek-Folland, Louise Newman was instrumental in shaping my understanding of gender history. Jack Davis stimulated my interest in environmental history. Sevan Terzian provided useful suggestions for secondary sources in gender and education. Steven Noll was an important influence on this manuscript, and I am grateful to Steve and David Tegeder for sharing an early version of *Ditch of Dreams: The Cross Florida Barge Canal and the Struggle for Florida's Future*.

This manuscript also benefited from the insightful comments of the readers who reviewed it for the University Press of Florida (UPF), Frederick Rowe Davis and Lee Irby, to whom I owe my sincerest thanks. At UPF, Sonia Dickey was a great help with the process of transforming this manuscript into a book. In addition, UPF's Amy Gorelick, whom I got to know over a series of mother-baby lunches after we gave birth at the same hospital, encouraged me to stay focused on the revision process while I was also balancing the responsibilities of working at home while caring for a toddler.

Bertram Wyatt-Brown was a wonderful role model early in my graduate career. Always smiling and wearing a bow tie, he and Bill Link, who succeeded him as the Richard J. Milbauer Chair at the University of Florida, provided generous financial support when I worked as the Milbauer assistant. I am also indebted to Robert Zieger. Alan Petigny inspired me to pursue graduate studies in history at the University of Florida, where I had originally enrolled in a graduate education program.

In 2008, I had the great fortune of spending several months with the Florida Humanities Council (FHC), located just a few blocks from the Florida Studies Program at the University of South Florida St. Petersburg. As a participant in a variety of FHC Teachers Center, Speakers Bureau, and other grant-funded programs featuring Florida scholars such as Gary Mormino, Ray Arsenault, and Bruce Stephenson, I developed a deeper understanding of Florida history and culture. Janine Farver, Susan Lockwood, Ann Simas Schoenacher, Barbara O'Reilley, Patricia Putman, Laurie Berlin, Barbara Bahr, and Lisa Lennox were impeccably professional and also a great deal of fun to work with.

Leslie Kemp Poole and Everett Caudle's interviews with Marjorie Harris Carr were indispensable to my research and writing. Leslie Poole also kindly shared her interview with JoAnn Valenti, who worked for Florida Defenders of the Environment (FDE) and briefly lived with the Carrs in Micanopy. Nick Williams shared FDE's resources with me at the start of this project and pointed me in the right direction. Rosalie Leposky introduced me to a treasure trove of digitized oral history interviews. Robert Ryals of the Mildred and Claude Pepper Library in Tallahassee showed great kindness by opening the facility to me at night and during the weekend so that I could examine the Pepper Papers. I also appreciate the help of Jim Cusick, Carl Van Ness, and the staff of the P. K. Yonge Library of Florida History at the University of Florida, who provided assistance with the FDE and Archie Carr collections.

I had the pleasure of interviewing Tom Carr, David Anthony, and J. C. Dickinson Jr. while they were in their nineties. Sadly, they are no longer with us. J. C. Dickinson permitted me to examine his records at the Florida Museum of Natural History, which he directed from 1961 through 1979. These papers included earlier correspondence with the Carrs, some of Marjorie Carr's publication materials, and items pertaining to her museum work in the 1950s. Tom Carr shared correspondence between Jack Bass and Marjorie Carr, documents pertaining to Tom and Archie Carr's sailing trips on the *Virginia*, and other useful documents. David Anthony's wife, Joan Griffin Anthony, helped facilitate my interview with her husband and continues to make appearances at FDE and Alachua Audubon Society events.

Interviews with Archie (Chuck) Carr III, Joe Little, Elizabeth Wing, David Godfrey, Elizabeth Powell, and David Gluckman furthered my understanding of Carr's personal and professional life. Additional oral history material came from Darren Preston Lane's forthcoming documentary, *From Waterway to Greenway: The History of the Cross Florida Barge Canal*. Lane traveled throughout Florida to interview many of the key players from both sides of the battle over the Cross Florida Barge Canal. His interviews provide fresh insights into the continuing debate over the barge canal and restoration of the Ocklawaha River.

My son, Richard, learned to speak the language of environmental history in grade school. He has grown up with this book project. His sister, Katherine, was born into it. As I completed the final version of this manuscript, she perfected the art of climbing over a pile of books on the couch and into my lap while I was working on my laptop computer. My husband, Nick, served as my muse while I was completing this book. I am grateful to Nick, Katherine, and especially Richard for their support and understanding as I worked to meet deadline after deadline over the years.

Throughout the writing of this manuscript, my mother, Katherine (Kit) Macdonald, served as a willing sounding board. She was a former member of Marjorie Harris Carr's Girl Scout troop and is one of Mimi Carr's lifelong friends. My mother kindly helped coordinate interviews with Mimi Carr over meals at a variety of local restaurants, often picking up the tab due to my long stint in grad school. Richard patiently tolerated many of these research dinners at a young age, and years later Katherine had fun playing with Miss Mimi's doggies while we scanned and rescanned photos at her house.

I express my deepest gratitude to Mimi Carr, who shared her memories of her mother and father with me over the course of several lengthy interviews, the bulk of which took place between 2005 and 2009. She also shared original photographs of the Carr family and entrusted me with treasured family books and papers, including her parents' love letters from the fall of 1936 through the summer of 1937. It was a rare honor to read these private letters, many of which were encased in envelopes that had resealed with time and humidity. These letters and additional documents that Mimi shared offer a more complete picture of Marjorie Carr's life than the one that existed before this information was made available. Mimi Carr was exceptionally generous with her time and resources, and without her help, this book would not be possible.

Chronology

The Life of Marjorie Harris Carr

1915 On March 26, Marjorie Harris is born to Clara Louise (Haynes) Harris and Charles Ellsworth Harris in Boston, Massachusetts.

1918 The Harrises and seven other Boston families follow the Florida dream to rural Bonita Springs, where Charles Harris purchases a 10-acre orange grove near the Imperial River.

1927 On January 21, President Calvin Coolidge signs the Rivers and Harbors Act into law. Among other things, the act authorizes preliminary studies and surveys for a cross-state ship and barge canal.

1928 The Harrises relocate to nearby Fort Myers, where Marjorie Harris attends high school.

1930 Charles Harris contracts pneumonia and dies.

1932 Marjorie Harris graduates from Fort Myers High School and enrolls in Florida State College for Women in Tallahassee, where she studies biology, ecology, botany, ornithology, and bacteriology.

1933 Harris spends the first of three consecutive summers working for the National Youth Administration, a New Deal agency. In return for leading a pioneering naturalist education program she designed for Lee County youth, she receives assistance with tuition, room, and board at Florida State College for Women.

1935   On August 30, President Franklin Delano Roosevelt authorizes $5 million for construction of a 30-foot-deep, sea-level ship canal that is estimated to cost $143 million to complete. The ship canal is justified as a public-works project that will provide Floridians with much-needed relief during the Great Depression. The U.S. Army Corps of Engineers was unable to recommend construction based upon the customary economic return basis, but Roosevelt was eager to create new jobs in the state.

On September 19, a ceremony marks the official start of construction of the cross-state ship canal.

In December, President Roosevelt transfers to Congress the power to authorize grants for projects such as the ship canal.

1936   Harris graduates from Florida State College for Women with a B.S. in zoology. Her honors include membership in Phi Beta Kappa and the science honor society Sigma Xi. She also becomes a charter member of the Florida Academy of Sciences.

Cornell University declines to admit Harris to graduate school, citing her gender as the reason for its decision. The University of North Carolina at Chapel Hill admits Harris to graduate school but withdraws an initial offer of funding at the last minute.

Harris becomes the nation's first female federal wildlife technician. Through her work as a biologist at the Welaka Fish Hatchery, she is introduced to the Ocklawaha River and her future husband, herpetologist Archie Fairly Carr Jr.

Michigan senator Arthur H. Vandenberg challenges the cross-state ship canal, observing that the project had never received congressional authorization.

Thirteen million cubic yards of material have been excavated, nearly 5,000 acres of right-of-way for the ship canal have been cleared, and four large bridge piers have been erected near Ocala. Because construction funds for the cross-state ship canal are exhausted, however, construction comes to a stop.

1937   Marjorie Harris and Archie Carr elope and are married near the Everglades on New Year's Day.

Out of economic necessity, Marjorie Harris Carr conceals her marriage while starting a new position as a laboratory technician and field collector at the Bass Biological Laboratory and Zoological Research Supply Company in Englewood, Florida. During a separation that lasts for six months, she corresponds daily with her new husband, who is finishing his doctoral dissertation at the University of Florida in Gainesville.

Archie becomes the first student to receive a doctorate in biology at the University of Florida.

Marjorie and Archie spend their first summer together in Cambridge, Massachusetts, where Archie studies turtles on a Thomas Barbour fellowship to the Museum of Comparative Zoology at Harvard.

Carr enters the graduate zoology program at the officially all-male University of Florida, where Archie begins teaching biology in the fall.

1939   Marjorie and Archie lead students on the first of several research and collecting trips to Mexico.

1942   Carr graduates from the University of Florida with an M.S. in zoology. She publishes her master's thesis, "The Breeding Habits, Embryology and Larval Development of the Large-Mouthed Black Bass of Florida," in *Proceedings of the New England Zoology Club*. The same issue features "Notes on the Courtship of the Cottonmouth Moccasin," the first scientific paper Marjorie and Archie publish together.

The U.S. Congress authorizes construction of the Cross Florida Barge Canal along Route 13-B, which crosses the Ocklawaha River Valley in north central Florida. The estimated cost of the shallower barge canal is approximately $44 million.

1943   On June 20, Marjorie and Archie welcome the birth of their first child, Marjorie (Mimi).

1945   On May 10, Archibald Fairly Carr III (Chuck) is born.

The Carr family moves to Honduras, where Archie teaches biology at the Escuela Agrícola Panamericana Zamorano. Marjorie and Archie explore the tropical rainforests on daily excursions. Carr publishes her findings on the birds of Honduras in subsequent years (see below). Archie describes the Honduran ecosystems—including humans' role within the ecosystem—in *High Jungles and Low* (1953).

1946   On December 1, Stephen Carr is born.

Publishes "Notes on the Breeding Habits of the Eastern Stumpknocker, *Lepomis Punctatus Punctatus* (Cuvier)" in the *Quarterly Journal of the Florida Academy of Sciences* (now *Florida Scientist*).

1948   On March 15, Thomas Carr is born.

1949   The Carr family returns to Florida.

1951   Publishes "The San Geronimo Swift in Honduras" (coauthored with J. C. Dickinson Jr.) in the *Wilson Bulletin*.

1952   On January 1, David Carr is born.

   Volunteers as a Girl Scout leader in Gainesville (through 1954).

1954   Joins the Board of Associates of the Florida Museum of Natural History at the University of Florida. Her donation of thousands of scientific skins from Honduras—including many species that were new to the museum—improves the museum's tropical ornithology collection.

1956   The Carrs move to Costa Rica, where Marjorie teaches biology and chemistry at the Escuela Metodista in San Jose while Archie helps establish the biology department at the University of Costa Rica (through 1957). Marjorie assists Archie with his sea turtle research as he creates a research and conservation station at Tortuguero.

1957   Joins the Gainesville Garden Club and begins work on the Paynes Prairie preservation campaign. She serves on the board of directors from 1958 through 1962.

1960   Cofounds the Alachua Audubon Society. She serves on the board of directors from 1960 through 1968 and from 1972 through 1980.

1962   On November 8, Carr and fellow Audubon officer David Anthony host a meeting on the effects of the proposed Cross Florida Barge Canal. The movement to save the Ocklawaha River Valley begins.

1964   On February 27, President Lyndon Johnson ignites a ceremonial blast of dynamite near the Ocklawaha River, marking the official start of construction of the 107-mile Cross Florida Barge Canal.

1965   Publishes "The Oklawaha River Wilderness" in *Florida Naturalist*. Awarded the Florida Audubon Society's Award of Merit.

1966   Hundreds of activists travel to the annual water resources development meeting in Tallahassee to request that the proposed barge canal be rerouted to preserve the natural beauty of the river valley. State officials decide to continue construction along the current route before the public hearing even begins.

   Construction of Rodman Dam and Reservoir in the Ocklawaha River Valley commences.

1967   Publishes "What Do Users Want? Wilderness!" in the *Proceedings*

*of the Annual Meeting of the Southeastern Section of the Society of
American Foresters.*

1968   At the start of the year, three of the barge canal's five navigation
locks are complete and another is under construction, and 68
percent of the canal right-of-way has been purchased.

By the fall, 500 acres of Rodman Reservoir have been cleared,
Rodman Dam and the St. Johns Lock are complete, and Eureka
Dam is under construction.

On September 30, the U.S. Army Corps of Engineers closes
Rodman Dam and floods the Rodman Reservoir. Thousands of dead
trees float to the top of the pool. Invasive water weeds proliferate in
the shallow reservoir.

1969   Carr cofounds Florida Defenders of the Environment (FDE), which
partners with the Environmental Defense Fund in filing a lawsuit
against the U.S. Army Corps of Engineers for violating the public
interest. Carr and FDE develop a coalition of scientific, economic,
and legal experts who contribute research to its environmental
impact statement on the barge canal's effects on the Ocklawaha
regional ecosystem.

Carr spearheads the campaign to preserve Lake Alice on the
University of Florida campus after the university and the Florida Department of Transportation announce plans to build a cross-campus
highway and two-thousand-car parking lot that will destroy the lake.

1970   Publishes "Modulated Reproductive Periodicity in *Chelonia*"
(coauthored with Archie) in *Ecology*. The article reports on evidence
from fifteen years of tagging at a *Chelonia mydas* turtle nesting
ground at Tortuguero, Costa Rica.

Publishes "Recruitment and Remigration in a Green Turtle
Nesting Colony" (coauthored with Archie) in *Conservation Biology*.

Paynes Prairie State Park is created.

Awarded the Florida Governor's Award for Outstanding
Conservation Leadership.

Coordinates and edits FDE's *Environmental Impact of the Cross-
Florida Barge Canal with Special Emphasis on the Oklawaha Regional
Ecosystem*.

1971   The Cross Florida Barge Canal is halted at the judicial and executive
levels.

Presents her paper "The Fight to Save the Ocklawaha" at the Twelfth Biennial Sierra Club Wilderness Conference in Washington, D.C.

Joins the board of directors for the Florida Conservation Foundation, serving from 1971 through 1990.

1972   Publishes "Site Fixity in Caribbean Green Turtles" (coauthored with Archie) in *Ecology*.

1973   Wins the National Federation of Business and Professional Women's Club's Headline Award.

1974   Wins the Fairchild Tropical Garden's Thomas Barbour Award.

Joins the board of directors of the Institute for Social Policy Studies, serving through 1978.

1976   Writes "An Interim Report on the Cross Florida Barge Canal" and the case history section for "In Defense of Rivers, A Citizens' Workbook: Impacts of Dam and Canal Projects," which are published by the Delaware Valley Conservation Association.

Awarded the National Wildlife Federation's Conservation Service Award.

1978   Publishes "The Ecology and Migrations of Sea Turtles: The West Caribbean Green Turtle Colony" (coauthored with Archie and Anne B. Meylan) for the *Bulletin of the American Museum of Natural History*.

Awarded the New York Zoological Society's Gold Medal for achievement in biological conservation.

1980   Establishes the Environmental Service Center in Tallahassee with the goal of fostering cooperation between citizens, government, and business in developing sound environmental practices. The center closes in 1988.

1984   Awarded the Florida Audubon Society's Conservationist of the Year Award.

1986   The Cross Florida Barge Canal is officially deauthorized.

1987   On May 21, Archie Carr dies in Micanopy at age seventy-seven.

1988   Writes the preface to *Florida: Images of the Landscape*.

Becomes a scientific fellow of the New York Zoological Society.

1989   Writes the foreword to *Ecosystems of Florida*.

1990   Writes the script for the FDE video production "Restoring the Ocklawaha River" (with fellow Florida Defenders of the Environment officer Jack Kaufmann).

Cowrites and edits *Restoring the Ocklawaha River Ecosystem* (an FDE publication).

Awarded the Teddy Roosevelt Conservation Award.

1991 Edits republications of Archie's *High Jungles and Low* and *Ulendo*.

Awarded the Alexander Calder Conservation Award for Special Achievement.

Awarded the Unsung Hero Award by the Miami Hosting Committee of the United Nations Environmental Program's Global Assembly of Women and the Environment.

1992 Edits *The Case for Restoring the Free-Flowing Ocklawaha River* (with David Godfrey, Jack Kaufmann, and Jeanne Marie Zokovitch).

1994 Edits *A Naturalist in Florida: A Celebration of Eden*, a collection of Archie's essays.

1995 Publishes "Notes on the Birds of Honduras for the Years 1945–1949, with Special Reference to the Yeguare River Valley, Department of Francisco Morazán," in *Ceiba*.

1996 Inducted into the Florida Women's Hall of Fame.

1997 Inducted into the Florida Wildlife Federation's Conservation Hall of Fame.

On October 10, Marjorie Harris Carr dies in Gainesville at age eighty-two.

1998 The land formerly set aside for the Cross Florida Barge Canal is named the Marjorie Harris Carr Cross Florida Greenway.

2014 FDE's campaign to restore the Ocklawaha River Valley to its precanal state continues.

Notes

Introduction

1. Throughout this book, Marjorie Harris Carr is referred to by her maiden name (Harris) or her married name (Carr), depending upon the context of the chapter. The first chapter refers to Marjorie Harris as "Harris," whereas the other members of her family are identified by first name only. In the sections that examine Carr's life after marriage, Marjorie Harris Carr is identified as "Carr," while her husband (Archie Fairly Carr Jr.) and children (Mimi, Chuck, Stephen, Tom, and David) are identified by their first names only. When Marjorie Carr's name is used in the same sentence as another member of the Carr family, her first name is used.

2. Photographer John Moran, who covered Marjorie Harris Carr's funeral for the *Gainesville Sun*, suspects that one of her children placed the "Free the Ocklawaha" sticker on the back of the hearse, where it was taped to the window (John Moran to author, e-mail message, December 12, 2012).

3. Joan Griffin Anthony, conversation with author, November 20, 2012, after a Millhopper Library/Alachua Audubon Society presentation in Gainesville, Fla., to commemorate the fiftieth anniversary of the Alachua Audubon Society's meeting at P. K. Yonge Developmental Research School to learn more about the proposed Cross Florida Barge Canal; David Anthony, interview by author, October 3, 2008, Gainesville, Fla.

4. JoAnn Myer Valenti, interview by Leslie Kemp Poole, March 1, 2011, Tampa, Fla.

5. Smith, "Florida Population Growth: Past, Present and Future"; United States Census Bureau, "State & County QuickFacts."

6. Contemporary documents pertaining to the Cross Florida Barge Canal did not consistently hyphenate "Cross Florida." Moreover, "Cross Florida" is not hyphenated in the

title of the Marjorie Harris Carr Cross Florida Greenway. For consistency, Cross Florida Barge Canal is not hyphenated in this manuscript. In addition, the modern spelling "Ocklawaha," with a "c," is used in this manuscript, the spelling that officially replaced "Oklawaha" in 1992.

7. Nathaniel Reed, speech, 2009.

8. "Conservationist Marjorie Carr Dies," *Ocala Star-Banner*, October 11, 1997.

9. "Paula Hawkins, 82, Florida Ex-Senator, Dies," *New York Times*, December 4, 2009.

Chapter 1. Marjorie Harris Carr's Girlhood

1. Mimi Carr, interviews by author, November 11, 2005, and August 6, 2008, Gainesville, Fla.; Marjorie Harris Carr, interview by Everett Caudle, April 24, 1989, Micanopy, Fla.

2. Greater Fort Myers Chamber of Commerce, "The History of Fort Myers," www.fortmyers.org/fort-myers-history.html; Mimi Carr, interviews by author, November 11, 2005, and August 6, 2008.

3. Crist, "The Citrus Industry in Florida"; Kohen, "Perfume, Postcards, and Promises"; Porter, "An Eighteenth-Century Flower Child."

4. Kohen, "Perfume, Postcards, and Promises"; Andrews, *A Yank Pioneer in Florida*, 239; Bigelow, *Frontier Eden*; Crist, "The Citrus Industry in Florida"; Porter, *John James Audubon*; Mormino, *Land of Sunshine*.

5. Marjorie Harris Carr, interview by Caudle; Mimi Carr, interviews by author, November 11, 2005, and March 7, 2007.

6. Marjorie Harris Carr, interview by Caudle; Mimi Carr, interviews by author, November 11, 2005, and March 7, 2007.

7. Mimi Carr, interviews by author, November 11, 2005, March 7, 2007, and November 16, 2012; Marjorie Harris Carr, interview by Caudle.

8. Hoffman and Libecap, "Institutional Choice and the Development of U.S. Agricultural Policies in the 1920s"; Mimi Carr, interview by author, August 6, 2008.

9. The 1920 U.S. Census listed all residents of Bonita Springs as "white," including the town's two Hispanic households (Southwest Florida Pioneers Historical Society, "Fourteenth Census of the United States 1920—Population," www.rootsweb.ancestry.com/~flswphs/records/census/boni1920_full.htm).

10. Marjorie Harris Carr, "Chiquita"; Mimi Carr, interview by author, August 6, 2008; "Sand in Her Shoes, River in Her Blood," *St. Petersburg Times*, November 18, 1996; Town of Fort Myers Beach Florida, "Island History," www.fortmyersbeachfl.gov/index.aspx?nid=60; Mormino, *Land of Sunshine*.

11. Marjorie Harris Carr's letters to Archie Carr, November 1936 through July 1937, in the private collection of Mimi Carr; Marjorie Harris Carr, "Chiquita"; Town of Fort Myers Beach Florida, "Island History." Unless otherwise noted, all letters cited are in the private collection of Mimi Carr.

12. Newman, "Rosewood Revisited"; Dye, "The Rosewood Massacre"; Dye et al., "A Documented History of the Incident Which Occurred at Rosewood."

13. The Southwest Florida Pioneers Historical Society, "Fourteenth Census of the United States 1920—Population"; Mimi Carr, interviews by author, November 11, 2005, and March 7, 2007.

14. Mimi Carr, interviews by author, November 11, 2005, and March 7, 2007; Cohen, *Protestantism and Capitalism*. William Cronon and other environmental historians paint an entirely different portrait of New Englanders, who treated the land as property to be "improved" upon for the benefit of proto-capitalist colonists. Carr expressed her interpretation of a Puritan sense of stewardship in her oral history interview by Leslie Kemp Poole, October 18, 1990.

15. Elman, *America's Pioneering Naturalists*; Marjorie Harris Carr, interview by Caudle.

16. J. E. Davis, "Alligators and Plume Birds," 243.

17. Marjorie Harris Carr, interview by Caudle; J. E. Davis, "Alligators and Plume Birds"; Poole, "The Women of the Early Florida Audubon Society"; Price, *Flight Maps*; Merchant, "Women of the Progressive Conservation Movement."

18. Vanderblue, "The Florida Land Boom"; Mormino, *Land of Sunshine*, 45–62. Florida's first land boom lasted from 1782 to 1784, when British Loyalists sought solace along the northeastern coast of Florida, where the British population increased from six thousand to seventeen thousand.

19. Marjorie Harris Carr, "Chiquita," 2–4; Andrews, *A Yank Pioneer in Florida*.

20. Marjorie Harris Carr, interview by Caudle; J. E. Davis, *An Everglades Providence*, 383.

21. Grunwald, *The Swamp*, 143; J. E. Davis, *An Everglades Providence*; Marjorie Harris Carr, interview by Caudle; Mormino, *Land of Sunshine*, 185–228.

22. Marjorie Harris Carr, interview by Caudle; Graham, "What Matters Most," 94.

23. Andrews, *A Yank Pioneer in Florida*.

24. Shofner, "The Legacy of Racial Slavery"; J. E. Davis, *An Everglades Providence*; Marjorie Harris Carr, interview by Caudle.

25. Marjorie Harris Carr, "Chiquita," 4; Andrews, *A Yank Pioneer in Florida*, 107–8; Marjorie Harris Carr, interview by Caudle.

26. Mimi Carr, interviews by author, August 6, 2008, and November 11, 2005; Marjorie Harris Carr, interview by Caudle.

27. Mimi Carr, interview by author, March 7, 2007; Graham, "What Matters Most," 96; Mimi Carr, interview by author, August 6, 2008.

28. Rossiter, *Women Scientists in America*, vol. 1.

29. McComb, *Great Depression and the Middle Class*; Rury, *Education and Women's Work*; Wyer et al., eds., *Women, Science, and Technology*, 1–78; Rossiter, *Women Scientists in America*, vol. 1; Janice Law Trecker, "Sex, Science, and Education," in *Women, Science, and Technology*, ed. Wyer et al., 88–98; Rich and Phillips, eds., *Women's Experience and Ed-*

ucation; Goldin, Katz, and Kuziemko, "The Homecoming of American College Women"; Kwolek-Folland, *Incorporating Women*.

30. Napier, "The Southern State College for Women."

31. FSCW annual, *Flastacowo*, vol. 21; Clarke, *Ellen Swallow*; Solomon, *In the Company of Educated Women*; Peril, *College Girls*; Bordin, *Women at Michigan*; Horowitz, *Alma Mater*; Feldman, *Escape from the Doll's House*; Rossiter, *Women Scientists in America*, vol. 1; Hubbard, *The Politics of Women's Biology*; Napier, "The Southern State College for Women"; "History," Florida State University website, www.fsu.edu/about/history.html.

32. Marjorie Harris Carr, *Special Voices, Two Florida Women*; Mimi Carr, interview by author, January 30, 2009.

33. Tigert, "Co-ordination in Florida."

34. Graham, "What Matters Most," 96. Herman Kurz was well published in the fields of botany and ecology. His publications include: "Influence of Sphagnum and Other Mosses on Bog Reactions," *Ecology* 9, no. 1 (January 1928): 56–69; "Cypress Buttresses and Knees in Relation to Water and Air," *Ecology* 15, no. 1 (January 1934): 36–41; "Factors in Cypress Dome Development," *Ecology* 34, no. 1 (January 1953): 157–64 (with Kenneth A. Wagner); "Hydrogen Ion Concentration in Relation to Ecological Factors," *Botanical Gazette* 76, no. 1 (September 1923): 1–29; "Northern Aspect and Phenology of Tallahassee Red Hills Flora," *Botanical Gazette* 85, no. 1 (March 1928): 83–89; "The Relation of pH to Plant Distribution in Nature," *American Naturalist* 64, no. 693 (July-August 1930): 314–41; and "Cypresses Change Shape According to Water Depth," *Science News-Letter* 21, no. 562 (January 16, 1932): 37.

35. FSCW annual, *Flastacowo*, vol. 21; UF annual, *The Seminole*.

36. Graham, "What Matters Most," 96; Marjorie Harris Carr, interview by Caudle.

37. Bowler, *The Norton History of the Environmental Sciences*.

38. Ibid.

39. McCandless, *The Past in the Present*, 97. Marjorie Harris Carr, foreword to *Ecosystems of Florida*, ed. Myers and Ewel, xi–xiii. Marjorie Harris Carr, interviews with Poole and Caudle; FSCW annual, *Flastacowo*; Marjorie Harris Carr, curriculum vitae, n.p., n.d., box 33, FDE Papers.

40. Bordin, *Women at Michigan*; The Cornell Women's Handbook, "History of Women at Cornell."

41. Rossiter, *Women Scientists in America*, vol. 1.

42. Solomon, *In the Company of Educated Women*; Peril, *College Girls*; Eisenmann, *Higher Education for Women in Postwar America*; Bordin, *Women at Michigan*; McCandless, *The Past in the Present*; Horowitz, *Alma Mater*; Rury, *Education and Women's Work*; Wolfe, ed., *Women, Work, and School*; Rich and Phillips, eds., *Women's Experience and Education*; Feldman, *Escape from the Doll's House*.

43. McCandless, *The Past in the Present*; Peril, *College Girls*; Rury, *Education and Women's Work*; Wolfe, ed., *Women, Work, and School*; Rich and Phillips, eds., *Women's Experience and Education*; Horowitz, *Alma Mater*; Rossiter, *Women Scientists in America*, vol. 1.

44. Graham, "What Matters Most," 97; Ezda Mae Deviney to Marjorie Harris, July 22, 1936.

45. Graham, "What Matters Most," 97.

Chapter 2. Blending Science and Marriage in the New Deal Era

1. U.S. Fish & Wildlife Service website, www.fws.gov/fisheries/; "Men from the World War I Veterans Labor Camp Building Cages and Houses for the Aviary at the Welaka Fish Hatchery," Florida State Archives, www.floridamemory.com/items/show/152515; Welaka National Fish Hatchery website, www.fws.gov/welaka/index.html.

2. Kwolek-Folland, *Incorporating Women*; Milkman, *Gender at Work*; Kessler-Harris, *In Pursuit of Equity*.

3. Kwolek-Folland, *Incorporating Women*; Milkman, *Gender at Work*; Kessler-Harris, *In Pursuit of Equity*; Ware, *Beyond Suffrage*.

4. Ware, *Beyond Suffrage*.

5. Ibid., 61; Rose, *Limited Livelihoods*; Rury, *Education and Women's Work*; McComb, *Great Depression and the Middle Class*.

6. Ware, *Beyond Suffrage*.

7. Graham, "What Matters Most," 96.

8. "Men from the World War I Veterans Labor Camp Building Cages and Houses for the Aviary at the Welaka Fish Hatchery," Florida State Archives, www.floridamemory.com/items/show/152515; Marjorie Harris Carr, *Special Voices, Two Florida Women*.

9. Dick Franz, conversation with author, February 27, 2009, Tallahassee, Fla.

10. Marjorie Harris to Archie Carr, November 8, 1936; Rossiter, *Women Scientists in America*, vol. 1; Tom Carr, interview by author, August 13, 2008, Gainesville, Fla.

11. Archie Carr to Marjorie Harris, December 6, 1936; Carr letters, December 1936 through January 1937; Mimi Carr, interviews by author.

12. Archie Carr to Marjorie Harris, December 1936.

13. Archie Carr to Marjorie Harris, mid-December 1936; Archie Carr to Marjorie Harris, dated simply "Sunday." This letter was never mailed; it was likely written in mid-December, the day after the previous excerpt.

14. Tom Carr, interview by author.

15. Ibid.

16. Archie Carr to Marjorie Harris, dated simply "Sunday."

17. Archie Carr to Marjorie Harris, December 22, 1936, afternoon.

18. Archie Carr to Marjorie Harris, December 22, 1936, evening; "Bass Biological Laboratory brochure, Englewood, Florida, c. 1933," DSpace at Mote Marine Laboratory, https://dspace.mote.org/dspace/handle/2075/165.

19. Archie Carr to Marjorie Harris, December 22, 1936, evening; Archie Carr to Stewart Springer, December 10, 1936, DSpace at Mote Marine Laboratory, https://dspace.mote.org/dspace/handle/2075/823.

20. Archie Carr to Marjorie Harris, December 22, 1936, evening; Archie Carr to Marjorie Harris, December 23, 1936; Archie Carr to Marjorie Harris, December 25, 1936.

21. Archie Carr to Marjorie Harris, December 27, 1936.

22. Jack Bass to Archie Carr, December 14, 1936, DSpace at Mote Marine Laboratory, https://dspace.mote.org/dspace/handle/2075/823; Archie Carr to Marjorie Harris Carr, March 26, 1937; Tom Carr, interview by author.

23. Archie Carr to Louise Carr, early January 1937.

24. Marjorie Harris Carr to Archie Carr, May 24, 1937.

25. Rossiter, *Women Scientists in America*, vol. 1.

26. Archie Carr to Marjorie Harris Carr, January 4, 1937.

27. Marjorie Harris Carr to Archie Carr, January 5, 1937; Marjorie Harris Carr to Archie Carr, February 16, 1937.

28. Marjorie Harris Carr to Archie Carr, dated simply "Thursday" (with no postmarked envelope).

29. Marjorie Harris Carr to Archie Carr, another letter dated "Thursday"; Marjorie Harris Carr to Archie Carr, January 1937.

30. Tom Carr, "A Voyage to Remember."

31. Marjorie Harris Carr to Archie Carr, January 1937.

32. Ibid.; Marjorie Harris Carr to Archie Carr, early January 1937. Although Marjorie saved most of Archie's envelopes, which include the postmarked date, Archie usually saved the letters only. Without the postmark, the only date available is the day of the week, at best. This letter had no date.

33. Marjorie Harris Carr to Archie Carr, June 5, 1937.

34. Archie Carr to Marjorie Harris Carr, January 10, 1937.

35. Tom Carr, interview by author. As a minister's wife, Louise Carr was disappointed that her son had forgone a traditional church wedding ceremony. Several months after the elopement, Louise Carr and Marjorie Harris Carr's aunts orchestrated a formal wedding ceremony performed by Archie Fairly Carr Sr.

36. Louise Carr to Marjorie Harris Carr, January 19, 1937.

37. Tom Carr, interview by author; Louise Carr to Marjorie Harris Carr, January 19, 1937.

38. The emphasis is Louise Carr's. Louise Carr to Marjorie Harris Carr, March 20, 1937.

39. Archie Carr to Marjorie Harris Carr, late March 1937; Marjorie Harris Carr to Archie Carr, late March 1937. Kenneth's last name is not mentioned in the Carrs' letters.

40. Archie Carr to Marjorie Harris Carr, April 3, 1937.

41. Archie Carr to Marjorie Harris Carr, April 1, 1937; Archie Carr to Marjorie Harris Carr, March 14, 1937.

42. Marjorie Harris Carr to Archie Carr, early April 1937; Archie Carr to Marjorie Harris Carr, April 5, 1937.

43. Marjorie Harris Carr to Archie Carr, April 13, 1937.

44. Marjorie Harris Carr to Archie Carr, early April 1937; Archie Carr to Marjorie Harris Carr, March 24, 1937; Archie Carr to Marjorie Harris Carr, March 27, 1937.

45. Louise Carr to Marjorie Harris Carr, April 21, 1937.

46. Archie Carr to Marjorie Harris Carr, April 16, 1937; Archie Carr to Marjorie Harris Carr, March 26, 1937; Mimi Carr, interview by author, March 7, 2007.

47. Marjorie Harris Carr to Archie Carr, May 28, 1937; Marjorie Harris Carr to Archie Carr, June 1937.

48. Marjorie Harris Carr to Archie Carr, June 24, 1937.

49. Marjorie Harris Carr to Archie Carr, June 3, 1937.

50. Marjorie Harris Carr to Archie Carr, February 16, 1937.

51. Marjorie Harris Carr to Archie Carr, April 5, 1937; Marjorie Harris Carr to Archie Carr, April 9, 1937.

52. Marjorie Harris Carr to Archie Carr, June 1937.

53. F. R. Davis, *The Man Who Saved Sea Turtles*; F. R. Davis, "A Naturalist's Place."

54. F. R. Davis, *The Man Who Saved Sea Turtles*; F. R. Davis, "A Naturalist's Place." Archie Carr chronicled his visit to Harvard and meetings with Barbour and other renowned herpetologists in a series of letters to Marjorie Carr in January 1937.

55. F. R. Davis, *The Man Who Saved Sea Turtles*, esp. 52–56.

56. Tom Carr, interview by author.

57. Archie Carr to Marjorie Harris Carr, January 8, 1937.

58. Graham, "What Matters Most," 97; Thomas Barbour to Archie Carr, January 24, 1934; Thomas Barbour to Archie Carr, April 30, 1937.

59. Marjorie Harris Carr to Archie Carr, April 9, 1937.

60. Marjorie Harris Carr to Archie Carr, May 24, 1937.

61. Mimi Carr, interview by author, January 13, 2013; Tom Carr, interview by author; Marjorie Harris Carr, "Speech by Marjorie Harris Carr about Responsible Industry and Protecting the Keys," in Florida International University Everglades Digital Library Collection, "A Tale of Two Women: Marjory Stoneman Douglas and Marjorie Carr"; Marjorie Harris Carr to Archie Carr, June 14, 1937; Marjorie Harris Carr to Archie Carr, June 2, 1937.

62. Marjorie Harris Carr to Archie Carr, June 22–23, 1937.

63. Burg et al., eds., *Women at the University of Florida*, 33–40.

64. Marjorie Harris Carr to Jack Bass, November 12, 1937.

65. Jack Bass to Marjorie Harris Carr, December 6, 1937.

66. Ibid.

67. Archie Carr to Jack and Else Bass, April 28, 1937; "Bass Personal Papers," DSpace at Mote Marine Laboratory, https://dspace.mote.org/dspace/handle/2075/2400. The Bass Lab ceased operations in 1944, sat dormant for decades, and fell into disrepair. "Cookie House," a small cabin that housed a laboratory and Jack Bass's office, was relocated to the Cedar Point Environmental Park in Englewood, Florida, in 2006 ("Charlotte County Historical Markers: Bass Biological Labs/Cookie House," Charlotte County Board of County Commissioners website, www.charlottecountyfl.com/Historical/HistoricalMarkers/Bass-Cookie.asp). The Mote Marine Laboratory in Sarasota, Florida, acquired the Bass records,

which have been partially digitized and can be viewed at https://dspace.mote.org/dspace/handle/2075/163.

Chapter 3. Honduras in the 1940s

1. Graham, "What Matters Most," 97.
2. Ibid.
3. F. R. Davis, *The Man Who Saved Sea Turtles*, 32–63.
4. Graham, "What Matters Most," 98.
5. J. C. Dickinson Jr., interview by author, February 22, 2008, Gainesville, Fla.
6. Mimi Carr, interview by author, November 16, 2012.
7. F. R. Davis, *The Man Who Saved Sea Turtles*, 32–62.
8. Tom Carr, interview by author; Marjorie Harris Carr, foreword to *High Jungles and Low*, by Archie Carr, xiii.
9. J. C. Dickinson Jr., interview by author.
10. F. R. Davis, *The Man Who Saved Sea Turtles*, 32–62; Mimi Carr, interview by author, January 13, 2013.
11. Archie Carr, *High Jungles and Low*, xix.
12. Malo, *El Zamorano*, 222, 413; Archie Carr, *High Jungles and Low*; Graham, "What Matters Most"; Archie Carr to Thomas Barbour, January 10, 1945.
13. Graham, "What Matters Most," 98; Archie Carr, *High Jungles and Low*, xx; Malo, *El Zamorano*.
14. Archie Carr, *High Jungles and Low*, xx–xxi.
15. Ibid., xix.
16. Ibid., xxi.
17. Zamorano did not graduate its first female students until 1983 (Malo, *El Zamorano*, 343). For information on Zamorano's mission and early history, see ibid., 19–33.
18. Ibid., 213–21; Marjorie Harris Carr, interview by Poole, October 18, 1990.
19. Marjorie Harris Carr to Thomas Barbour, March 9, 1945; Thomas Barbour to Marjorie Harris Carr, March 12, 1945; Marjorie Harris Carr to Clara Haynes Harris, October 7, 1945.
20. Archie Carr to Thomas Barbour, June 3, 1945.
21. Marjorie Harris Carr to Clara Haynes Harris, July 9, 1945; F. R. Davis, *The Man Who Saved Sea Turtles*, 66.
22. Malo, *El Zamorano*, 433–34; Archie Carr, *High Jungles and Low*, 162; F. R. Davis, *The Man Who Saved Sea Turtles*; Barrow, *A Passion for Birds*.
23. Marjorie Harris Carr to Thomas Barbour, July 17, 1945; Marjorie Harris Carr to Thomas Barbour, July 31, 1945.
24. Marjorie Harris Carr to Clara Haynes Harris, October 7, 1945; Marjorie Harris Carr to Clara Haynes Harris, July 15, 1945; Marjorie Harris Carr to J. C., Lucy, and Dick Dickinson, April 13, 1948.

25. Marjorie Harris Carr to Clara Haynes Harris, July 30, 1945; Marjorie Harris Carr to Clara Haynes Harris, October 31, 1945; Archie Carr to J. C. Dickinson Jr., January 16, 1948.

26. Archie Carr, *High Jungles and Low*, xxii; Graham, "What Matters Most," 101.

27. Marjorie Harris Carr to Thomas Barbour, n.d.; Marjorie Harris Carr to Clara Haynes Harris, July 22, 1945; Marjorie Harris Carr to Thomas Barbour, July 31, 1945.

28. Archie Carr, *High Jungles and Low*, 25; Malo, *El Zamorano*, 434; Archie Carr, *High Jungles and Low*, 30, 34–35.

29. Malo, *El Zamorano*, 434.

30. Marjorie Harris Carr to Lucy Dickinson, November 23, 1945.

31. Mimi Carr, interview by author, March 7, 2007.

32. Marjorie Harris Carr to Clara Haynes Harris, September 8, 1945. The paper Carr referred to in the letter she wrote her mother was "Notes on the Breeding Habits of the Eastern Stumpknocker." Carr's paper was cited repeatedly in David K. Caldwell, Howard T. Odum, Thomas R. Hellier Jr., and Frederick H. Berry, "Populations of Spotted Sunfish and Florida Large-Mouth Bass In a Constant-Temperature Spring," *Transactions of the American Fisheries Society* 85 (1957): 120–34; moreover, this paper and Carr's 1942 paper on Florida's large-mouthed black bass continue to be cited by biologists today.

33. Malo, *El Zamorano*, 22–33.

34. Marjorie Harris Carr to Clara Haynes Harris, October 23, 1945.

35. Marjorie Harris Carr to Clara Haynes Harris, August 17, 1945.

36. Marjorie Harris Carr to Clara Haynes Harris, July 3, 1945.

37. Marjorie Harris Carr to Clara Haynes Harris, July 15, 1945.

38. Archie Carr to J. C. Dickinson Jr., July 11, 1946.

39. Mimi Carr, interview by author, March 7, 2007; Archie Carr to J. C. and Lucy Dickinson, January 16, 1948.

40. Marjorie Harris Carr to Lucy Dickinson, December 7, 1946; Marjorie Harris Carr to Lucy Dickinson, March 18, 1948.

41. Tom Carr, interview by author.

42. Marjorie Harris Carr to J. C. and Lucy Dickinson, July 28, 1949.

43. Marjorie Harris Carr to Clara Haynes Harris, September 17, 1945; Marjorie Harris Carr to Clara Haynes Harris, November 18, 1945.

44. Marjorie Harris Carr to Clara Haynes Harris, September 11, 1945; Marjorie Harris Carr to Sara Beard, April 18, 1946; Marjorie Harris Carr to Lucy and J. C. Dickinson, July 28, 1949; Marjorie Harris Carr to Lucy Dickinson, August 9, 1948; Mimi Carr, interview by author, November 16, 2012.

45. F. R. Davis, *The Man Who Saved Sea Turtles*.

46. Ibid., 84–85; Archie Carr, *High Jungles and Low*; Marjorie Harris Carr, *High Jungles and Low*, by Archie Carr, xiv.

47. F. R. Davis, *The Man Who Saved Sea Turtles*, 84–86.

48. Chuck Carr to author, e-mail message, November 5, 2012; Costa Rica Exotica Nat-

ural (CREN), "Sea Turtles of Tortuguero National Park," www.tortugueroinfo.com/usa/
sea_turtles_tortuguero.htm.

49. Marjorie Harris Carr, foreword to *High Jungles and Low*, by Archie Carr, xiv–xv;
Chuck Carr, interview by author, March 18, 2009, Gainesville, Fla.; *Pittsburgh Post-Gazette*, July 1, 1991; Chuck Carr to author, e-mail message, November 5, 2012.

50. Archie Carr, *High Jungles and Low*, 37–43.

51. Ibid., 46.

52. Ibid., 47–48.

53. Malo, *El Zamorano*, 442.

54. Ibid., 437–46.

55. Marjorie Harris Carr to J. C. Dickinson Jr., November 20, 1948; Marjorie Harris Carr
and J. C. Dickinson Jr., "The San Geronimo Swift in Honduras."

Chapter 4. Marjorie Harris Carr's Early Conservation Career

1. Marjorie Harris Carr, review of *The Diligent Destroyers*, by Laycock.

2. Irby, "A Passion for Wild Things"; Mormino, *Land of Sunshine*.

3. "Looking for Marjorie," *Ocala Star-Banner*, October 24, 1997.

4. J. E. Davis, *An Everglades Providence*; Lear, *Rachel Carson*; Lytle, *The Gentle Subversive*; Tarr, ed., *The Private Marjorie*.

5. Platt, "Jane Addams and the Ward Boss Revisited."

6. Flanagan, "The City Profitable, the City Livable," 164–65; Poole, "The Women of the
Early Florida Audubon Society"; J. E. Davis, "Alligators and Plume Birds"; Derr, *Some Kind
of Paradise*, 136–37.

7. Tom Carr, interview by author; Marjorie Harris Carr to Archie Carr, June 18–19, 1937.

8. Archie Carr to Marjorie Harris Carr, January 25, 1937.

9. "Sand in Her Shoes, River in Her Blood," *St. Petersburg Times*, November 18, 1996;
Chuck Carr, interview by author; Graham, "What Matters Most," 98–100; Mimi Carr, interviews by author, March 6, 2009, and July 8, 2006.

10. Mimi Carr, interview by author, July 8, 2006.

11. Chuck Carr, interview by author; Archie Carr, "Wewa Pond," 2–9.

12. Mimi Carr, interviews by author, July 8, 2006, and July 23, 2005.

13. "The Family Carr," *Gainesville Sun*, December 6, 1993.

14. Elizabeth Powell, interview by author, March 11, 2006; Mimi Carr, interview by
author, January 13, 2013.

15. Chuck Carr, interview by author; "The Family Carr," *Gainesville Sun*, December 6,
1993.

16. "The Family Carr," *Gainesville Sun*, December 6, 1993.

17. Archie Fairly Carr, "Thirty Years with Sea Turtles"; Bates, Ehrenfeld, Odum, Commoner, Dasmann, and Ehrlich were among the prominent authors who lent their names
to a January 27, 1970, letter to President Richard Nixon signed by more than 150 scientists.

The letter, orchestrated by Marjorie Carr, requested that Nixon take action to save the Ocklawaha River from catastrophic environmental damage.

18. Chuck Carr, interview by author; Mimi Carr, interview by author, March 7, 2007; Archie Carr's curriculum vitae, Dickinson Papers.

19. H. B. Sherman (acting head of biology department) to Marjorie Harris Carr, May 1, 1947, Dickinson Papers.

20. John S. Allen (University of Florida vice president) to Marjorie Harris Carr, March 20, 1954, Dickinson Papers.

21. J. C. Dickinson Jr., interview by author, February 22, 2008.

22. Ibid.; Archie Carr to J. C. Dickinson Jr., October 1, 1948.

23. Chuck Carr, interview by author; Archie Carr's curriculum vitae, Dickinson Papers; Graham, "What Matters Most"; David Godfrey, interview by author, December 19, 2008, Gainesville, Fla.; "The Family Carr," *Gainesville Sun*, December 6, 1993; F. R. Davis, *The Man Who Saved Sea Turtles*; Mimi Carr, interview by author, March 7, 2007.

24. "Rambler's Round-Up," *Ocala Star-Banner*, August 25, 1963.

25. Chuck Carr, interview by author.

26. "The Family Carr," *Gainesville Sun*, December 6, 1993; "Skyway Financing Scheme without Justification," *St. Petersburg Independent*, April 18, 1958; "All's Not Rosy: Here's Some of the More Darker Corners," *Times Daily*, October 25, 1960.

27. "The Family Carr," *Gainesville Sun*, December 6, 1993.

28. Ibid.; *St. Petersburg Independent*, April 18, 1958; "All's Not Rosy: Here's Some of the More Darker Corners," *Times Daily*, October 25, 1960.

29. "Environmental Group to Fight Tampa-Jacksonville Turnpike," *St. Petersburg Times*, November 25, 1988; "State Ponders Building a Turnpike between Jacksonville and Tampa," *Gainesville Sun*, May 15, 1987. See also "The Incredible DOT," *Gainesville Sun*, December 1, 1988; "Area Residents give DOT Plan a Cool Reception," *Ocala Star-Banner*, December 16, 1988; and "Toll Road Study Deadline Extended," *Ocala Star-Banner*, December 16, 1988.

30. "Butterworth Is One of Many against Road," *Ocala Star-Banner*, March 1, 1989; "Ex-DOT Head's Firm Gets State Bonanza," *Ocala Star-Banner*, October 11, 1990; "Managing Growth in State Leads Environmentalist's Concerns," *Gainesville Sun*, December 11, 1988.

31. "Ex-DOT Head's Firm Gets State Bonanza," *Ocala Star-Banner*, October 11, 1990.

32. "Restoring Heritage: Barbecue, Breakfast Attract Local Crowd," *Gainesville Sun*, November 18, 2002.

33. Chuck Carr, interview by author.

34. Archie Carr, *Ulendo*, 160–61.

35. Ibid., 205–6, 161; Graham, "What Matters Most," 92; Archie Carr, "Armadillo Dilemma," in *A Naturalist in Florida*, ed. Marjorie Harris Carr, 204–5.

36. Archie Carr, "Armadillo Dilemma," 206–9.

37. Graham, "What Matters Most," 91–92.

38. Andersen, *Paynes Prairie*, 128–39.

39. Ibid.

40. Ibid., 134–39; Marjorie Harris Carr, interview by Caudle.

41. Andersen, *Paynes Prairie*, 129–39.

42. "Recharging Florida Forever: Rising Land Prices and a Flat Budget Have Eroded the State's Leading Conservation Program," *Florida Trend*, October 1, 2006; Bruce Ritchie, "Florida Could Run Out of Land-Buying Money by Oct. 1," *Environmental News from Florida's Capital*, http://bruceritchie.blogspot.com/2009_08_01_archive.html.

43. Andersen, *Paynes Prairie*, 134–39; Porter, "An Eighteenth-Century Flower Child."

44. Archie Carr, "Water Hyacinths," in *A Naturalist in Florida*, ed. Marjorie Harris Carr, 216.

45. Ibid., 218–19.

46. Ibid., 219; Marjorie Harris Carr, Notes to Archie Carr, *A Naturalist in Florida*, 252.

47. "Road to Divide UF Campus Already Divisive," *St. Petersburg Times*, October 19, 1969.

48. Ibid.

49. Ibid.; Archie Carr to Stephen C. O'Connell, October 17, 1969, series 4, box 41, folder 16, Archie F. Carr Papers.

50. "Road to Divide UF Campus Already Divisive," *St. Petersburg Times*, October 19, 1969.

51. "Society Seeks to Block Road," *St. Petersburg Times*, November 13, 1971.

52. Joe Little, interview by author, December 19, 2008, Gainesville, Fla. Little became active in the Alachua Audubon Society, serving as president in 1973. He served as FDE's legal chairman starting in 1970, as a trustee from 1977 to the present, and has served for several years as FDE's vice president.

53. Ibid.

54. Jack Kaufmann, interview, Florida International University Everglades Digital Library, "A Tale of Two Women: Marjory Stoneman Douglas and Marjorie Harris Carr."

55. Marjorie Harris Carr, interview by Caudle.

56. Marjorie Harris Carr, foreword to *Protecting Paradise*, by Cavanaugh and Spontak, 3–4.

57. "Micanopy Honors Its Three 'Great Floridians' with Historic Markers," *Gainesville Sun*, May 4, 2000.

Chapter 5. Protecting Paradise: Marjorie Harris Carr
Launches the Campaign to Save the Ocklawaha River

1. Mimi Carr, interview by Darren Preston Lane, director of *From Waterway to Greenway: The History of the Cross Florida Barge Canal*, DVD, forthcoming, www.aabstractproductions.com/Cross-Florida-Barge-Canal.htm.

2. Carter, *The Florida Experience*, 279.

3. Partington, "History of the Cross-Florida Barge Canal"; Bennett, "Early History of the Cross-Florida Barge Canal"; Sewell, "Cross-Florida Barge Canal." For a thorough ex-

amination of the origins, construction, and demise of the Cross Florida Barge Canal, see Noll and Tegeder, *Ditch of Dreams*.

4. U.S. Army Corps of Engineers, *Army Corps of Engineers Summary of Civil Works Projects under Construction and Surveys in Progress*. January 1964, 8, series 301, box 29A, folder 1, Mildred and Claude Pepper Library; *Summary of Civil Works Projects under Construction and Studies in Progress*, December 1965, series 301, box 29A, folder 4, Mildred and Claude Pepper Library.

5. Simpson, *A Provisional Gazetteer of Florida Place-Names of Indian Derivation*; Loughridge and Hodge, *English and Muskokee dictionary*; Marjorie Harris Carr, "The Oklawaha River Wilderness"; FDE, *Restoring the Ocklawaha River Ecosystem*; "Ocklawaha River," United States Department of Agriculture Forest Service website, www.fs.usda.gov/recarea/ocala/recreation/recarea/?recid=40317; "Learn about your Watershed: Ocklawaha River Watershed," Florida Department of Environmental Protection website, www.protectingourwater.org/watersheds/map/ocklawaha/.

6. Steven Noll and David Tegeder examine the history of the Ocklawaha steam boat industry in *Ditch of Dreams*. Marjorie Harris Carr, "The Oklawaha River Wilderness"; FDE, *Restoring the Ocklawaha River Ecosystem*.

7. "Sand in Her Shoes, River in Her Blood," *St. Petersburg Times*, November 18, 1996; David Anthony, interview by author; Marjorie Harris Carr, interview by Caudle; Marjorie Harris Carr, interview by Poole, October 18, 1990.

8. David Anthony, interview by author; Marjorie Harris Carr, interview by Caudle; Marjorie Harris Carr, interview by Poole, October 18, 1990. The date of the Alachua Audubon Society meeting on the Cross Florida Barge Canal's environmental impact on the Ocklawaha River has been reported two different ways. Carr informed Poole that the meeting was held on November 2, 1962, in their 1990 interview. A 1971 newspaper article stated that the meeting was held on November 8 (see Ed Pavelka, "Fame Has Come to Marjorie Carr but to Her, It's a Family Affair," *Gainesville Sun*, January 25, 1971).

9. Mimi Carr, interview by author, July 23, 2005; Marjorie Harris Carr, interview by Poole, October 18, 1990; Marjorie Harris Carr, "The Fight to Save the Ocklawaha"; Marjorie Harris Carr, interview by Caudle.

10. "Sand in Her Shoes, River in Her Blood," *St. Petersburg Times*, November 18, 1996.

11. Marjorie Harris Carr, "The Fight to Save the Ocklawaha"; F. R. Davis, "Get the Facts—and Then Act," 50; Marjorie Harris Carr, interviews by Caudle and Poole.

12. "Fame Has Come to Marjorie Carr but to Her, It's a Family Affair," *Gainesville Sun*, January 25, 1971.

13. "Fight That Blocked Canal Work Started in Gainesville in 1962," *Sarasota Herald-Tribune*, January 24, 1971.

14. Laycock, *The Diligent Destroyers*, 52–66.

15. Marjorie Harris Carr, interview by Poole, October 18, 1990.

16. F. R. Davis, "Get the Facts—and Then Act," 53; James Lewis, "Canal Recreation Decision Due," *Marion Times*, undated, box 8, FDE Papers.

17. Margie Bielling, interview by Darren Preston Lane, director of *From Waterway to Greenway: The History of the Cross Florida Barge Canal*, DVD, forthcoming, www.aabstractproductions.com/Cross-Florida-Barge-Canal.htm. Citizens for Conservation was incorporated in 1964. Marjorie Harris Carr to Mrs. Forrest, February 12, 1965, in FDE Papers; Frederick R. Davis, "Get the Facts—and Then Act," 54; Irby, "The Big Ditch," 388.

18. *Ocala Magazine*, June 29, 2007, www.ocalamagazine.com/specPubsNews/templates/cityscape.aspx?articleid=1159&zoneid=12; Noll and Tegeder, *Ditch of Dreams*, 149–50. John Couse's influence would prove helpful in convincing Nathaniel Reed to take a stand against the Cross Florida Barge Canal. In turn, Reed would help sway President Richard Nixon to halt construction of the canal.

19. Bielling, interview by Lane; F. R. Davis, "Get the Facts—and Then Act," 58.

20. Michael Blumenfeld, Assistant Secretary of the Army (Civil Works), and Bob Bergland, Secretary, Department of the Army, to Honorable Walter F. Mondale, President of the Senate, and Honorable Tip O'Neill, Speaker of the House of Representatives, April 11, 1979, box 8, FDE Papers.

21. Marjorie Harris Carr, interview by Caudle.

22. "Right of Way for Canal," *Ocala Star-Banner*, October 3, 1965; "In Heated Session— Foes of Canal Question Route," *Tampa Tribune*, October 5, 1965.

23. Hackney and Adams, "Aquatic Communities of the Southeastern United States"; Sewell, "Cross Florida Barge Canal"; Shallat, *Structures in the Stream*; Laycock, *The Diligent Destroyers*.

24. Marjorie Harris Carr, interview by Poole, October 18, 1990.

25. Nathaniel Reed, interview by Darren Preston Lane, director of *From Waterway to Greenway: The History of the Cross Florida Barge Canal*, DVD, forthcoming, www.aabstractproductions.com/Cross-Florida-Barge-Canal.htm.

26. "Right of Way for Canal," *Ocala Star-Banner*, October 3, 1965.

27. "Eppes, Kirkpatrick Shoot for State Senate," *Gainesville Sun*, September 2, 1982; "Senator Admits He's a Bully, but He Gets Things Done," *Gainesville Sun*, July 16, 1995; "About George: Will He or Won't He?" *Gainesville Sun*, November 27, 1994; "Voter Sues Senator for Switch," *Sarasota Herald-Tribune*, August 21, 1998; "George's Way," *Gainesville Sun*, February 7, 2003; "Paula Fickes Hawkins: Senator, 1981–1987, Republican from Florida," http://womenincongress.house.gov/member-profiles/profile.html?intID=103); "Paula Hawkins, 82, Florida Ex-Senator, Dies," *New York Times*, December 4, 2009; "Paula Hawkins, First Woman Senator from South, Dies at 82," *Gainesville Sun*, December 5, 2009.

28. "Paula Hawkins, First Woman Senator from South, Dies at 82," *Gainesville Sun*, December 5, 2009.

29. Hawkins's community activism commenced shortly after her arrival in Florida, where she volunteered for the Republican Party. Her campaign involvement included serving as the cochair of Richard Nixon's presidential campaign in Florida. The political connections

she formed through her campaign work helped her win election to Florida's public service commission from 1972 to 1979 (Women in Congress, "Paula Fickes Hawkins: Senator, 1981–1987, Republican from Florida," http://womenincongress.house.gov/member-profiles/profile.html?intID=103).

30. For excellent discussions of the concept of performing femininity, see Margadant, ed., *The New Biography*; and Roberts, *Disruptive Acts*.

31. *Atlanta Journal and Constitution Magazine*, August 14, 1966.

32. Barbara Laxson to Marjorie Harris Carr, January 31, 1971, box 8, FDE Papers. This January 31, 1971, letter referred to the article "Woman Took on Army Engineers to Save River in Florida," *Houston Chronicle*, date unknown.

33. "Housewife Who Roared," *Christian Science Monitor*, July 1974.

34. *Atlanta Journal and Constitution Magazine*, August 14, 1966; Barbara Laxson to Marjorie Harris Carr, January 31, 1971, box 8, FDE Papers (this January 31, 1971 letter referred to the *Houston Chronicle* article "Woman Took on Army Engineers to Save River in Florida," date unknown); "Housewife Who Roared," *Christian Science Monitor*, July 1974.

35. Laycock, *The Diligent Destroyers*.

36. Sam Eisenberg, interview by Darren Preston Lane, director of *From Waterway to Greenway: The History of the Cross Florida Barge Canal*, DVD, forthcoming. www.aabstractproductions.com/Cross-Florida-Barge-Canal.htm.

37. Laycock, *The Diligent Destroyers*; "Barge Canal: Boon or Boondoggle?," *Daytona Beach Morning Journal*, December 20, 1969; FDE, *Environmental Impact of the Cross-Florida Barge Canal with Special Emphasis on the Oklawaha Regional Ecosystem*; "Aquatic Plant Management," Southwest Florida Water Management District website, www.swfwmd.state.fl.us/projects/aquaticplants/.

38. Laycock, *The Diligent Destroyers*; Lear, introduction to *Silent Spring*, by Rachel Carson, xvii.

39. *Congress Appropriates $1,220,400,200 for Fiscal Year 1965 Army Engineers Civil Works Program*, 1, report issued by the Office of the Chief of Engineers, Department of the Army, August 1964, series 301, box 29, folder 5, Mildred and Claude Pepper Library.

40. U.S. Army Corps of Engineers, *Army Corps of Engineers Summary of Civil Works Projects under Construction and Surveys in Progress*, January 1964, 8, series 301, box 29A, folder 1, Mildred and Claude Pepper Library; *Summary of Civil Works Projects under Construction and Studies in Progress*, December 1965, series 301, box 29A, folder 4, Mildred and Claude Pepper Library.

41. Marjorie Harris Carr, "The Oklawaha River Wilderness"; FDE, *Restoring the Ocklawaha River Ecosystem*; see also Marjorie Harris Carr, "An Interim Report on the Cross-Florida Barge Canal."

42. M. M. Nelson, Deputy Chief, U.S. Department of Agriculture, Forest Service, to William M. Partington, Florida Defenders of the Environment, April 7, 1970, box 33, FDE Papers.

43. Marjorie Harris Carr, interviews by Caudle and Poole; Sewell, "Cross-Florida Barge Canal," 378–82; "The Other Canal Issue . . . and Its Offspring," *Lakeland Ledger*, May 16, 1978.

44. "Much about Marion: Tossed Salad," *Orlando Sentinel*, September 28, 1965.

45. "Opposition to Barge Canal Voiced by Alachua Group," *Ocala Star-Banner*, July 21, 1965.

46. Ibid.

47. "Canal Opponents Want Hearing," *St. Petersburg Times*, October 5, 1965.

48. FDE, "Environmental Impact of the Cross-Florida Barge Canal with Special Emphasis on the Oklawaha Regional Ecosystem," 55; "Canal Opponents Want Hearing," *St. Petersburg Times*, October 5, 1965.

49. *Florida Times-Union*, October 5, 1965.

50. "Right of Way for Canal," *Ocala Star-Banner*, October 3, 1965.

51. U.S. Army Corps of Engineers, *Water Resources Development by the U.S. Army Corps of Engineers in Florida*, U.S. Army Engineer Division, South Atlantic, 1 January 1965, series 301, box 29A, folder 4, Mildred and Claude Pepper Library; "Barge Canal Progress Is Discussed," *Florida Times-Union*, September 30, 1965.

52. Worster, *Nature's Economy*; J. E. Davis, *An Everglades Providence*, 412–17; Flippen, *Nixon and the Environment*; Chuck Carr, e-mail to author, November 5, 2012; "Curriculum vitae for Howard T. Odum," George A. Smathers Libraries website, University of Florida, http://ufdc.ufl.edu/UF00101105/00001/2x.

53. J. E. Davis, *An Everglades Providence*, 412–17.

54. Ibid.

55. Archie Carr to Miss Lore Rensoy-Otzen, February 12, 1971, box 33, FDE Papers. Archie received and responded to letters from readers from around the world. Rensoy-Otzen wrote from Norway to express her concerns about human indifference to the environment and pollution.

56. J. E. Davis, *An Everglades Providence*, 407–19, 500–528; "Presbyterian College Seeks Land in Bay," *St. Petersburg Times*, September 17, 1959; "A Wilderness Transformed: Eckerd's Campus Then and Now," Eckerd College website, www.eckerd.edu/50/index.php?f=labrant. In 1972, Florida Presbyterian College was renamed Eckerd College after Jack Eckerd, the founder of Eckerd Drug Stores, made a substantial donation to the school.

57. Carr, "The Oklawaha River Wilderness."

58. Ibid; FDE, *Restoring the Ocklawaha River Ecosystem*.

59. "Audubon Joins Stand against Barge Canal," *St. Petersburg Times*, May 10, 1965.

60. "Barge Canal Hearing Plan Draws Fire," *St. Petersburg Times*, December 12, 1965; "Early Decision May Come on Holding Canal Hearing," *Ocala Star-Banner*, December 6, 1965. The newspaper articles only identified Mrs. Kenneth D. Morrison, the leader of Florida Bi-Partisans, by her husband's name. In the early days of the Ocklawaha campaign, Marjorie Carr signed most of her letters to politicians "Mrs. Archie Carr, Co-Chairman for

Conservation, Alachua Audubon Society," but as the campaign wore on, she switched to "Marjorie H. Carr," updating her official title as it changed to "Co-President of Alachua Audubon," "Vice-Chairman of Florida Defenders of the Environment (F.D.E.)," and later "President of F.D.E."

61. "Citizens Attack Florida Barge Canal Project," *Sarasota Journal*, July 26, 1965; "Canal a Surprise to Housewife Who Led Fight," *Lakeland Ledger*, January 24, 1971.

62. "Citizens Attack Florida Barge Canal Project," *Sarasota Journal*, July 26, 1965; "Canal a Surprise to Housewife Who Led Fight," *Lakeland Ledger*, January 24, 1971; "Early Decision May Come on Holding Canal Hearing," *Ocala Star-Banner*, December 6, 1965; "Barge Canal Foes to Have Their Innings," *St. Petersburg Times*, January 24, 1966. See also FDE, "Environmental Impact of the Cross-Florida Barge Canal with Special Emphasis on the Oklawaha Regional Ecosystem," 55.

63. Marjorie Harris Carr, interview by Caudle; "Canal a Surprise to Housewife Who Led Fight," *Lakeland Ledger*, January 24, 1971; "Early Decision May Come on Holding Canal Hearing," *Ocala Star-Banner*, December 6, 1965; "Oklawaha River Backers Speak Up at Hearing," *St. Petersburg Times*, January 26, 1966; FDE, "Environmental Impact of the Cross-Florida Barge Canal"; *Pork Barrel and Pheasant Feathers*, dir. Holly Fisher, video.

64. Marjorie Harris Carr, interview by Caudle; "Canal a Surprise to Housewife Who Led Fight," *Lakeland Ledger*, January 24, 1971; "Oklawaha River Backers Speak Up at Hearing," *St. Petersburg Times*, January 26, 1966; *Pork Barrel and Pheasant Feathers*, dir. Holly Fisher, video.

65. "Early Decision May Come on Holding Canal Hearing," *Ocala Star-Banner*, December 6, 1965; Marjorie Harris Carr, interview by Caudle; *Pork Barrel and Pheasant Feathers*, dir. Holly Fisher, video.

66. Nathaniel Reed, interview by Lane.

67. "Canal a Surprise to Housewife Who Led Fight," *Lakeland Ledger*, January 24, 1971.

68. *Summary of Civil Works Projects under Construction and Studies in Progress*, December 1965, 49, series 301, box 29A, folder 4, Mildred and Claude Pepper Library. The FDE Papers contain an entire folder concerning problems and strategies related to the Freedom of Information Act.

69. Marjorie Harris Carr, interview by Poole, October 18, 1990. Gregg later supervised the creation of a series of artificial lakes and underground tunnels for Walt Disney World. F. Browne Gregg, interview by Darren Preston Lane; FDE, *Environmental Impact of the Cross-Florida Barge Canal*.

70. *Burlington County Times*, January 20, 1971; *Miami Herald*, January 21, 1971.

71. "Fame Has Come to Marjorie Carr but to Her, It's a Family Affair," *Gainesville Sun*, January 25, 1971.

72. F. R. Davis, *The Man Who Saved Sea Turtles*, 206–9.

73. Gottlieb, *Forcing the Spring*, 209.

74. See ibid., esp. 206–30.

Chapter 6. Florida Defenders of the Environment
and the Death of the Cross Florida Barge Canal

1. For an excellent analysis of barge canal boosterism, see Noll and Tegeder, *Ditch of Dreams*.

2. J. E. Davis, *An Everglades Providence*, 485; Grunwald, *The Swamp*, 254.

3. J. E. Davis, *An Everglades Providence*, 459–85; J. E. Davis, "Up from the Sawgrass," 148; Grunwald, *The Swamp*, 254–56; Flippen, *Nixon and the Environment*, 50–58.

4. J. E. Davis, "Up from the Sawgrass," 148, *An Everglades Providence*, 463–88; Grunwald, *The Swamp*, 254–56; Flippen, *Nixon and the Environment*, 50–58; Nathaniel Reed, speech, 2009.

5. J. E. Davis, *An Everglades Providence*, 463–88.

6. Ibid.

7. Ibid., 489.

8. Marjorie Harris Carr, review of *The Diligent Destroyers*, by Laycock.

9. Marjorie Harris Carr curriculum vitae, n.d., box 33, FDE Papers.

10. Ibid.

11. Marjorie Harris Carr, review of *Diligent Destroyers*, by Laycock; "Tom Adams in Dual Role on Florida's Barge Canal," *St. Petersburg Times*, January 9, 1966.

12. Marjorie Harris Carr to Roland C. Clement [vice president of biology, National Audubon Society], March 8, 1969, box 33, FDE Papers; U.S. Army Corps of Engineers, "Specifications for Job No. 8" (Department of the Army), in author's private collection.

13. "A Second Look at the Canal," *St. Petersburg Times*, September 18, 1969; "Fight That Blocked Canal Work Started in Gainesville in 1962," *Sarasota Herald-Tribune*, January 24, 1971.

14. J. E. Davis, *An Everglades Providence*, 488–504; Flippen, *Nixon and the Environment*, 1–6. Flippen contends that Nixon experimented with environmental reforms for political gain during his first term in office but abandoned them after his election to a second term. From 1972 on, Flippen argues, Nixon became increasingly conservative and rejected environmental legislation as something that was no longer politically viable (for instance, in 1972, Nixon vetoed the Clean Water Act, although Congress overrode his veto). Nonetheless, Nixon set the stage for the environmental age.

15. Flippen, *Nixon and the Environment*, 1–16.

16. FDE, *Environmental Impact of the Cross-Florida Barge Canal*, 6–7.

17. Ibid., iii–2.

18. Ibid., 2–3.

19. Ibid., 16.

20. Ibid., 29, 34.

21. Ibid., 3–5.

22. Ibid.

23. "Housewife Halted Florida Barge Canal," *Bradenton Herald*, January 24, 1971; Flip-

pen, *Nixon and the Environment*, 50–58; FDE, *Environmental Impact of the Cross-Florida Barge Canal*.

24. "Hickel Orders Review of State Canal Impact," *Tampa Tribune*, February 24, 1970.

25. Letter signed by 150 scientists to President Nixon, January 27, 1970, box 33, FDE Papers; FDE, *Environmental Impact of the Cross-Florida Barge Canal*, 58–59.

26. Letter signed by 150 scientists to President Nixon, January 27, 1970, box 33, FDE Papers.

27. Ibid.

28. Marjorie Harris Carr, interview by Poole, October 18, 1990; Marjorie Harris Carr to "Dear Fellow Scientist," May 1, 1970, box 33, FDE Papers. In the letter, Carr asked the scientists to read the recently released FDE environmental impact statement and then forward their opinions to the news media, state and federal elected officials, government agencies, and the public "as soon as possible."

29. Marjorie Harris Carr, interview by Caudle; Nathaniel Reed, interview by Darren Preston Lane.

30. Alden et al., *National Audubon Society Field Guide to Florida*, 19; Marjorie Harris Carr, interview by Caudle.

31. "Barge Canal: Boon or Boondoggle?" *Daytona Beach Morning Journal*, December 20, 1969.

32. "Professors Wage Battle to 'Kill' Barge Canal," *Sarasota Herald-Tribune*, June 10, 1970.

33. "Housewife Halted Florida Barge Canal," *Bradenton Herald*, January 24, 1971; Marjorie Harris Carr, interview by Poole, October 18, 1990.

34. "Housewife Halted Florida Barge Canal," *Bradenton Herald*, January 24, 1971; *Philadelphia Evening Bulletin*, January 20, 1971.

35. *Burlington County Times*, January 20, 1971.

36. "Politicians React as Canal Sinks," *St. Petersburg Times*, January 20, 1971; Marjorie Harris Carr, review of *The Diligent Destroyers*, by Laycock; "End of the Barge Canal," *Time*, February 1, 1971.

37. "Politicians React as Canal Sinks," *St. Petersburg Times*, January 20, 1971.

38. Marjorie Harris Carr to the National Coalition to Save the Oklawaha, February 1, 1971, box 8, FDE Papers.

39. Herbert W. Kale II to Marjorie Harris Carr, February 5, 1971, box 33, FDE Papers.

40. Don Fuqua to Helen Strathearn, January 19, 1971, box 8, FDE Papers.

41. "Barge Canal Issue 'Dead,'" *St. Petersburg Times*, February 27, 1971.

42. "End of the Barge Canal," *Time*, February 1, 1971; "Fact Sheet (Eureka, Rodman, Buckman)," Florida Department of Environmental Protection website, www.dep.state.fl.us/gwt/cfg/pdf/FACT%20SHEET.pdf; "Canal Forest Areas Return to Wild Asked," *Times Daily*, January 20, 1971; *The Effects of Proposed Restoration of the Ocklawaha River in the Vicinity of the Rodman Basin on Manatees and Manatee Habitat*, Report for the Office of Greenways and Trails, July 1997, Florida Department of Environmental Protection, http://myfwc.com/media/415372/Manatee_rodman.pdf.

43. Marjorie Harris Carr to President Richard M. Nixon, March 9, 1972, box 8, FDE Papers.

44. "Lake Oklawaha Ordered Lowered," *Lakeland Ledger*, July 25, 1972; "Barge Canal Still Gasping," *Evening Independent*, October 14, 1972.

45. "Cross-Florida Barge Canal 'Revived' in Washington," *Sarasota Herald-Tribune*, May 3, 1972.

46. Michael Blumenfeld, Assistant Secretary of the Army (Civil Works), and Bob Bergland, Secretary, Department of the Army, to Walter F. Mondale, President of the Senate, and Tip O'Neill, Speaker of the House of Representatives, April 11, 1979, box 8, FDE Papers.

47. Ibid.

48. Marjorie Harris Carr to Don Fuqua, October 19, 1979, box 8, FDE Papers.

49. Ibid.

50. "Senators Back Measure to Kill Canal Authority," *Sarasota Herald-Tribune*, May 14, 1974.

51. "Judge: Nixon Barge Canal Halt Illegal," *Palm Beach Post*, February 5, 1974; "Barge Canal Report Hailed by Environmental Leader," *Sarasota Herald-Tribune*, March 16, 1976.

52. "Canal Opponents to Fight Corps," *Palm Beach Post*, December 5, 1976.

53. "The Family Carr," *Gainesville Sun*, December 6, 1993.

54. Graham, "What Matters Most," 93–94.

55. Marjorie Harris Carr, President to FDE members, November 1, 1978, box 8, FDE Papers; JoAnn Myer Valenti, interview by Poole.

56. "New Funding for Barge Canal Tucked into Bill," *Ocala Star-Banner*, August 18, 1982; "Group Criticizes Hawkins' Environmental Record," *Ocala Star-Banner*, October 17, 1986; "Graham for U.S. Senate," *Orlando Sentinel*, October 5, 1986; "Graham Welcomes Hawkins' Attack on Environment," *Gainesville Sun*, February 2, 1986; "Paula Hawkins Rebuked over Remarks about Cross-Florida Barge Canal Land," *Lakeland Ledger*, August 3, 1984.

57. "Hawkins Aides Unveil Barge Canal Proposal," *Lakeland Ledger*, August 4, 1984.

58. "New Move Putting Chappell in a Spot on U.S. Cemetery," *Sarasota Herald-Tribune*, September 7, 1979; "Groups Want Barge Canal Land for New VA Cemetery," *St. Petersburg Times*, January 10, 1983.

59. "Nation's Newest Veterans Cemetery in Bushnell," *Ocala Star-Banner*, March 1, 1988; "Veterans React to Cemetery Location: Spokesmen Say Sumter Site Is Best," *Ocala Star-Banner*, August 10, 1983; "VA Looks for Site for New Veterans Cemetery in Florida," *St. Petersburg Times*, June 7, 1982.

60. Marjorie Harris Carr and John H. Kaufmann to Senator Bob Graham, March 21, 1990, box 8, FDE Papers; Senator Graham's revised draft of an amendment to the Water Resources Development Act of 1986, which would provide for deauthorization of the Cross Florida Barge Canal, plus the fax cover sheet that accompanied the draft, which was faxed to Carr in March 1990, box 8, FDE Papers; Senator Bob Graham, "Florida Wins Environmental Victories," December 1990 communication to Graham's constituents, box 8, FDE Papers.

61. Senator Bob Graham, "Florida Wins Environmental Victories," December 1990 communication to Graham's constituents, box 8, FDE Papers.

62. "Managing Growth in State Leads Environmentalist's Concerns," *Gainesville Sun*, December 11, 1988.

63. Ibid.

64. Ibid.

65. "Speech by Marjorie Carr about Responsible Industry and Protecting the Keys," in Florida International University Everglades Digital Library Collection, "A Tale of Two Women: Marjory Stoneman Douglas and Marjorie Carr."

Conclusion

1. Irby, "The Big Ditch," 376.

2. "F.D.E. Files Notice of Intent to Sue to the Forest Service," FDE e-mail communication, February 21, 2012; Erin Condon, interview by author, April 13, 2012, Gainesville, Fla.

3. David Godfrey, interview by author, December 19, 2008; "End of the Barge Canal," *Time*, February 1, 1971.

4. "End of the Barge Canal," *Time*, February 1, 1971.

5. Olle I. Elgerd to Marjorie Harris Carr, January 26, 1971, box 8, FDE Papers.

6. David Gluckman, interview by author, January 21, 2009; "Sand in Her Shoes, River in Her Blood," *St. Petersburg Times*, November 18, 1996.

7. MacKay, *How Florida Happened*, xi–xv; Mormino, *Land of Sunshine*.

8. "Conservationists Oppose Highway," *Miami News*, November 25, 1988; "Managing Growth in State Leads Environmentalist's Concerns," *Gainesville Sun*, December 11, 1988.

9. Florida International University Everglades Digital Library, "A Tale of Two Women: Marjory Stoneman Douglas and Marjorie Carr."

10. Marjorie Carr, review of *The Diligent Destroyers*, by Laycock.

11. "Focus on Housewife Who Roared," *Christian Science Monitor*, July 20, 1973.

12. Senator Bob Graham, conversation with author after a July 21, 2005, forum on the founding of the Bob Graham Center for Public Service on the University of Florida campus; "Retired U.S. Senator Bob Graham to Visit UF and Discuss New Graham Center for Public Service," *InsideUF*, July 18, 2005.

13. "Park Should Be Named for Carr, Says Chiles," *Gainesville Sun*, March 2, 1994.

14. "A Restoration Effort: Activist Recalls Fight to Let the River Run," *Gainesville Sun*, June 13, 1997.

15. Mimi Carr, interview by author, July 8, 2006.

16. "Life Expectancy with End Stage Emphysema," www.babyboomercaretaker.com/funeral/life-expectancy/Life-Expectancy-With-End-Stage-Emphysema.html.

17. Marjorie Harris Carr, "The Importance of Tenaciousness as Well as Patience to Help Save Florida's Environment," in Marjorie Carr, *Special Voices: Two Florida Women*; David Godfrey, interview by author; Mimi Carr, interview by author, July 8, 2006.

18. *Gainesville Sun*, June 13, 1997.

19. "The Family Carr," *Gainesville Sun*, December 6, 1993; "Speech by Marjorie Harris Carr about Responsible Industry and Protecting the Keys," in Florida International University Everglades Digital Library, "A Tale of Two Women: Marjory Stoneman Douglas and Marjorie Harris Carr."

20. Mimi Carr, interview by author, July 8, 2006; FDE staff, "Conservationists File Notice of Intent to Sue for Enforcement of Endangered Species Act in the Maintenance of Rodman Reservoir," *Monitor* 23 (2005): 3.

21. "Audubon Joins Stand against Barge Canal," *St. Petersburg Times*, May 10, 1965.

Bibliography

Alden, Peter, Rick Cech, and Gil Nelson. *National Audubon Society Field Guide to Florida.* New York: Knopf, 1998.

Andersen, Lars. *Paynes Prairie: A History of the Great Savanna.* Sarasota, Fla.: Pineapple Press, 2001.

Anderson, Karen. *Wartime Women: Sex Roles, Family Relations, and the Status of Women during World War II.* Westport, Ct.: Praeger, 1981.

Andrews, Allen H. *A Yank Pioneer in Florida: Recounting the Adventures of a City Chap Who Came to the Wilds of South Florida in the 1890s and Remained to Grow Up with the Country.* Jacksonville, Fla.: Press of the Douglas Printing Company, 1950.

Anthony, David. Interview by the author. October 3, 2008. Gainesville, Fla.

Barbour, Thomas. *That Vanishing Eden: A Naturalist's Florida.* Boston: Little, Brown, 1944.

Barrow, Mark V. *A Passion for Birds: American Ornithology after Audubon.* Princeton, N.J.: Princeton University Press, 1998.

Bass Biological Laboratory Papers. Mote Marine Laboratory website. https://dspace.mote.org/dspace/handle/2075/163.

Bennett, Charles E. "Early History of the Cross-Florida Barge Canal." *Florida Historical Quarterly* 15 (1966): 132–44.

Bielling, Margie. Interview by Darren Preston Lane, director of *From Waterway to Greenway: The History of the Cross Florida Barge Canal.* DVD. Forthcoming. www.aabstract-productions.com/Cross-Florida-Barge-Canal.htm.

Bigelow, Gordon E. *Frontier Eden: The Literary Career of Marjorie Kinnan Rawlings.* Gainesville: University Press of Florida, 1980.

Bordin, Ruth. *Women at Michigan: The "Dangerous Experiment," 1870s to the Present.* Ann Arbor: University of Michigan Press, 1999.

Bowler, Peter J. *The Norton History of the Environmental Sciences*. New York and London: Norton, 1993.

Burg, Mary Ann, Kevin McCarthy, Phyllis Meek, Constance Shehan, Anita Spring, Nina Stoyan-Rosenzweig, and Betty Taylor, eds. *Women at the University of Florida*. Gainesville: University of Florida's 150th Anniversary Committee, 2003.

Carr, Archie Fairly, Jr. *Handbook of Turtles: The Turtles of the United States, Canada, and Baja California*. Ithaca, N.Y.: Comstock, 1952.

———. *High Jungles and Low*. Gainesville: University Press of Florida, 1992.

———. Papers. Department of Special and Area Collections, George A. Smathers Library, University of Florida, Gainesville.

———. "Thirty Years with Sea Turtles: Perspectives for World Conservation." Fairfield Osborn Address. Series 1, box 12, folder 26, Archie F. Carr Jr. Papers.

———. *Ulendo: Travels of a Naturalist in and out of Africa*. Gainesville: University Press of Florida, 1993.

———. "Wewa Pond." In *A Naturalist in Florida: A Celebration of Eden*, edited by Marjorie Harris Carr, 1–13. New Haven and London: Yale University Press, 1994.

Carr, Archie Fairly, Jr., and Marjorie Harris Carr. "Modulated Reproductive Periodicity in *Chelonia*." *Ecology* 51 (1970): 335–37.

———. "Notes on the Courtship of the Cottonmouth Moccasin." *Proceedings of the New England Zoological Club* 20 (1942): 1–6.

———. "Recruitment and Remigration in a Green Turtle Nesting Colony." *Biological Conservation* 2 (1970): 282–84.

———. "Site Fixity in the Caribbean Green Turtle." *Ecology* 53 (1972): 425–29.

Carr, Archie, Marjorie Harris Carr, and Anne B. Meylan. "The Ecology and Migrations of Sea Turtles: The West Caribbean Green Turtle Colony." *Bulletin of the American Museum of Natural History* 162 (1978): 1–46.

Carr, Archie Fairly ("Chuck") III. Interview by author. March 18, 2009. Gainesville, Fla.

Carr, Marjorie Harris. "The Breeding Habits, Embryology, and Larval Development of the Large-Mouthed Black Bass in Florida." *Proceedings of the New England Zoological Club* 20 (1942): 43–77.

———. "Chiquita." Manuscript. 1996. In the private collection of Mimi Carr.

———. "The Fight to Save the Ocklawaha." Paper presented at the 12th Biennial Sierra Club Wilderness Conference, Washington, D.C. September 25, 1971. In the private collection of Mimi Carr.

———. Foreword to *Ecosystems of Florida*, edited by Ronald L. Myers and John J. Ewel. Orlando: University of Central Florida Press, 1990.

———. "An Interim Report on the Cross-Florida Barge Canal." In *In Defense of Rivers, A Citizen's Workbook: Impacts of Dam and Canal Projects*, by Delaware Valley Conservation Association, 138–46. Pennsylvania: Delaware Valley Conservation Association, 1976.

———. Interview by Everett Caudle. April 24, 1989. Courtesy of the Samuel Proctor Oral History Program.

———. Interviews by Leslie Kemp Poole. October 18, 1990, and February 4, 1991. Courtesy of FDE.

———. "Notes on the Birds of Honduras for the Years 1945–1949, with Special Reference to the Yeguare River Valley, Department of Francisco Morazán." *Ceiba* 36 (1995): 277–334.

———. "Notes on the Breeding Habits of the Eastern Stumpknocker, *Lepomis Punctatus Punctatus* (Cuvier)." *Florida Scientist* 9 (1946): 101–6.

———. "The Oklawaha River Wilderness." *Florida Naturalist* 38 (August 1965): 3-A.

———. Papers. In the private collection of Mimi Carr.

———. Preface to *Florida: Images of the Landscape*, by Valentine, James. Englewood, Colo.: Westcliffe, 1988.

———. Review of *The Diligent Destroyers*, by George Laycock. Box 33, FDE Papers.

———. *Special Voices, Two Florida Women: Marjorie Carr, Marjory Stoneman Douglas*. VHS. Florida Atlantic University/Florida International University, Joint Center for Environmental and Urban Problems, 1985.

———. "What Do Users Want? Wilderness!" *Outdoor Recreation: Challenge and Opportunity for Southeastern Forest Managers. Proceedings of Annual Meeting, Southeastern Section, Society of American Foresters,* January 12–13, 1967, Orlando, Fla.

Carr, Marjorie Harris, and J. C. Dickinson Jr. "The San Geronimo Swift in Honduras." *Wilson Bulletin* 63 (1951): 271–73.

Carr, Mimi (Marjorie). Interviews by author, July 23, 2005; November 11, 2005; July 8, 2006; March 7, 2007; August 6, 2008; January 30, 2009; March 6, 2009; November 16, 2012; January 13, 2013. All in Gainesville, Fla.

———. Interview by Darren Preston Lane, director of *From Waterway to Greenway: The History of the Cross Florida Barge Canal.* DVD. Forthcoming. www.aabstractproductions.com/Cross-Florida-Barge-Canal.htm.

Carr, Tom. Interview by author. August 13, 2008. Gainesville, Fla.

———. "A Voyage to Remember." Manuscript. In the private collection of Tom Carr.

Carter, Luther. *The Florida Experience: Land and Water Policy in a Growth State.* Baltimore: Johns Hopkins University Press, 1975.

Cavanaugh, Peggy, and Margaret Spontak. *Protecting Paradise: 300 Ways to Protect Florida's Environment.* Fairfield, Fla.: Phoenix, 1992.

"Charlotte County Historical Markers: Bass Biological Labs/Cookie House," Charlotte County Board of County Commissioners website, www.charlottecountyfl.com/Historical/HistoricalMarkers/BassCookie.asp.

Clarke, Robert. *Ellen Swallow: The Woman Who Founded Ecology.* Chicago: Follett, 1973.

Cohen, Jere. *Protestantism and Capitalism: The Mechanisms of Influence.* Hawthorne, N.Y.: De Gruyter, 2002.

Cohen, Lizabeth. *A Consumer's Republic: The Politics of Mass Consumption in Postwar America.* New York: Knopf, 2003.

The Cornell Women's Handbook. "History of Women at Cornell." Cornell University Women's Resource Center website. http://wrc.dos.cornell.edu/aboutus/handbook/chapter_01. html.

Crist, Raymond E. "The Citrus Industry in Florida." *American Journal of Economics and Sociology* 15 (1955): 1–12.

Davidoff, Leonore, and Catherine Hall. *Family Fortunes: Men and Women of the Middle Class, 1780–1850.* Chicago: Chicago University Press, 1991.

Davis, Frederick Rowe. "'Get the Facts—and Then Act': How Marjorie H. Carr and Florida Defenders of the Environment Fought to Save the Ocklawaha River." *Florida Historical Quarterly* 83 (2004): 46–69.

———. *The Man Who Saved Sea Turtles: Archie Carr and the Origins of Conservation Biology.* New York and Oxford: Oxford University Press, 2007.

———. "A Naturalist's Place: Archie Carr and the Nature of Florida." In *Paradise Lost? The Environmental History of Florida,* edited by Jack E. Davis and Raymond Arsenault, 72–91. Gainesville: University Press of Florida, 2005.

Davis, Jack E. "Alligators and Plume Birds: The Despoliation of Florida's Living Aesthetic." In *Paradise Lost? The Environmental History of Florida,* edited by Davis and Raymond Arsenault, 235–59. Gainesville: University Press of Florida, 2005.

———. "'Conservation Is Now a Dead Word': Marjory Stoneman Douglas and the Transformation of American Environmentalism." In *Paradise Lost? The Environmental History of Florida,* edited by Davis and Raymond Arsenault, 297–325. Gainesville: University Press of Florida, 2005.

———. *An Everglades Providence: Marjory Stoneman Douglas and the American Environmental Century.* Athens and London: University of Georgia Press, 2009.

———. "Up from the Sawgrass: Marjory Stoneman Douglas and the Influence of Female Activism in Florida Conservation." In *Making Waves: Female Activists in Twentieth-Century Florida,* edited by Davis, 147–76. Gainesville: University Press of Florida, 2003.

Derr, Mark. *Some Kind of Paradise: A Chronicle of Man and the Land in Florida.* New York: William Morrow, 1989.

Dickinson, J. C., Jr. Interview by author. February 22, 2008. Gainesville, Fla.

———. Papers. Florida Museum of Natural History, Dickinson Hall, University of Florida, Gainesville.

Dye, R. Thomas. "The Rosewood Massacre: History and the Making of Public Policy." *Public Historian* 19, no. 3 (1997): 25–39.

Dye, R. Thomas, Larry E. Rivers, David R. Colburn, William W. Rogers, and Maxine D. Jones. "A Documented History of the Incident Which Occurred at Rosewood, Florida in January, 1923: A Report Submitted to the Florida Board of Regents." Tallahassee: Florida State Archives, December 1993.

Eisenberg, Sam. Interview by Darren Preston Lane, director of *From Waterway to Greenway: The History of the Cross Florida Barge Canal.* DVD. Forthcoming. www.aabstract-productions.com/Cross-Florida-Barge-Canal.htm.

Eisenmann, Linda. *Higher Education for Women in Postwar America, 1945–1965*. Baltimore: Johns Hopkins University Press, 2006.

Elman, Robert. *America's Pioneering Naturalists: Their Lives and Times, Exploits and Adventures*. Tulsa, Okla.: Winchester Press, 1982.

FDE (Florida Defenders of the Environment). *Environmental Impact of the Cross-Florida Barge Canal with Special Emphasis on the Oklawaha Regional Ecosystem*. Gainesville, Fla.: Florida Defenders of the Environment, 1970.

———. Papers. University of Florida Department of Special Collections, P. K. Yonge Library, Gainesville.

———. *Restoring the Ocklawaha River Ecosystem*. Gainesville, Fla.: Florida Defenders of the Environment, 1990.

Feldman, Saul D. *Escape from the Doll's House: Women in Graduate and Professional School Education*. New York: McGraw-Hill, 1974.

Flanagan, Maureen A. "The City Profitable, the City Livable: Environmental Policy, Gender, and Power in Chicago in the 1910s." *Journal of Urban History* 22 (1996): 163–90.

Flippen, J. Brooks. *Nixon and the Environment*. Albuquerque: University of New Mexico Press, 2000.

Florida International University Everglades Digital Library. "A Tale of Two Women: Marjory Stoneman Douglas and Marjorie Harris Carr." http://everglades.fiu.edu/two/index.htm.

Florida State College for Women (FSCW) annual, *Flastacowo*, vol. 21. Tallahassee: Florida State College for Women, 1934.

Gluck, Sherna Berger. *Rosie the Riveter Revisited: Women, the War, and Social Change*. Boston: Twayne, 1987.

Gluckman, David. Telephone interview by author. January 21, 2009.

Godfrey, David. Interview by author. December 19, 2008. Gainesville, Fla.

Goldin, Claudia, Lawrence F. Katz, and Ilyana Kuziemko. "The Homecoming of American College Women: The Reversal of the College Gender Gap." *Journal of Economic Perspectives* 20, no. 4 (2006): 133–56.

Gottlieb, Robert. *Forcing the Spring: The Transformation of the American Environmental Movement*. Washington, D.C., and Covelo, Calif.: Island Press, 1993.

Graham, Frank, Jr. "What Matters Most: The Many Worlds of Archie and Marjorie Carr." *Audubon* 84 (1982): 90–105.

Greater Fort Myers Chamber of Commerce. "The History of Fort Myers." www.fortmyers.org/fort-myers-history.html.

Grossman, Elizabeth. *Watershed: The Undamming of America*. New York: Counterpoint, 2002.

Grunwald, Michael. *The Swamp: The Everglades, Florida, and the Politics of Paradise*. New York: Simon and Schuster, 2006.

Hackney, Courtney T., and S. Marshall Adams. "Aquatic Communities of the Southeastern United States: Past, Present, and Future." In *Biodiversity of the Southeastern United*

States: Aquatic Communities, edited by Hackney, Adams, and William H. Martin, 747–60. New York: Wiley and Sons, 1992.

Harvey, Mark W. T. *A Symbol of Wilderness: Echo Park and the American Conservation Movement*. Seattle and London: University of Washington Press, 2000.

Hoffman, Elizabeth, and Gary D. Libecap. "Institutional Choice and the Development of U.S. Agricultural Policies in the 1920s." *Journal of Economic History* 51 (1991): 397–411.

Horowitz, Helen Lefkowitz. *Alma Mater: Design and Experience in the Women's Colleges from Their Nineteenth-Century Beginnings to the 1930s*. 2nd ed. Amherst: University of Massachusetts Press, 1993.

Hubbard, Ruth. *The Politics of Women's Biology*. New Brunswick, N.J., and London: Rutgers University Press, 1990.

Irby, Lee. "'The Big Ditch': The Rise and Fall of the Cross Florida Barge Canal." In *Paradise Lost? The Environmental History of Florida*, edited by Jack E. Davis and Raymond Arsenault, 375–97. Gainesville: University Press of Florida, 2005.

———. "A Passion for Wild Things: Marjorie Harris Carr and the Fight to Free a River." In *Making Waves: Female Activists in Twentieth-Century Florida*, edited by Jack E. Davis and Karl Frederickson, 177–96. Gainesville: University Press of Florida, 2003.

Kessler-Harris, Alice. *In Pursuit of Equity: Men, Women, and the Quest for Economic Citizenship in 20th-Century America*. New York and Oxford: Oxford University Press, 2001.

Kohen, Helen L. "Perfume, Postcards, and Promises: The Orange in Art and Industry." "Florida Theme" issue of *Journal of Decorative and Propaganda Arts* 23 (1998): 33–47.

Kwolek-Folland, Angel. *Incorporating Women: A History of Women and Business in the United States*. New York: Twayne, 1998.

Laycock, George. *The Diligent Destroyers*. New York: National Audubon Society and Ballantine Books, 1970.

Lear, Linda. Introduction to *Silent Spring*, by Rachel Carson. 40th anniversary edition. Boston and New York: Houghton Mifflin, 2002.

———. *Rachel Carson: Witness for Nature*. New York: Henry Holt, 1997.

Little, Joe. Interview by author. December 19, 2008. Gainesville, Fla.

Loughridge, Robert McGill, and David M. Hodge. *English and Muskokee Dictionary*. Philadelphia: Westminster Press, 1914.

Lytle, Mark Hamilton. *The Gentle Subversive: Rachel Carson, Silent Spring, and the Rise of the Environmental Movement*. Oxford and New York: Oxford University Press, 2007.

MacKay, Buddy. *How Florida Happened: The Political Education of Buddy MacKay*. With Rick Edmonds. Gainesville: University Press of Florida, 2010.

Malo, Simon E. *El Zamorano: Meeting the Challenge of Tropical America*. Manhattan, Kans.: Simbad, 1999.

Margadant, Jo Burr, ed. *The New Biography: Performing Femininity in Nineteenth-Century France*. Berkeley and Los Angeles: University of California Press, 2000.

Markell Morantz-Sanchez, Regina. *Sympathy and Science: Women Physicians in American Medicine*. New York and Oxford: Oxford University Press, 1985.

McCandless, Amy Thompson. *The Past in the Present: Women's Higher Education in the Twentieth-Century American South*. Tuscaloosa and London: University of Alabama Press, 1999.

McComb, Mary C. *Great Depression and the Middle Class: Experts, Collegiate Youth and Business Ideology, 1929–1941*. New York and London: Routledge, 2006.

Merchant, Carolyn. "Women of the Progressive Conservation Movement: 1900–1916." *Environmental Review* 8 (1984): 57–85.

Meyerowitz, Joanne, ed. *Not June Cleaver: Women and Gender in Postwar America, 1945–1960*. Philadelphia: Temple University Press, 1994.

Milkman, Ruth. *Gender at Work: The Dynamics of Job Segregation by Sex during World War II*. Urbana: University of Illinois Press, 1987.

Mormino, Gary. *Land of Sunshine, State of Dreams: A Social History of Modern Florida*. Gainesville: University Press of Florida, 2005.

Napier, T. H. "The Southern State College for Women." *Peabody Journal of Education* 18 (1941): 268–75.

Newman, Richard. "Rosewood Revisited." *Transition* 80 (1999): 32–39.

Noll, Steven, and David Tegeder. *Ditch of Dreams: The Cross Florida Barge Canal and the Fight for Florida's Future*. Gainesville: University Press of Florida, 2009.

Partington, Bill. "History of the Cross-Florida Barge Canal." In *Environmental Impact of the Cross-Florida Barge Canal with Special Emphasis on the Oklawaha Regional Ecosystem*. Gainesville: Florida Defenders of the Environment, March 1970.

Pepper, Claude. Papers. Claude Pepper Center, Florida State University Special Collections & Archives, Tallahassee.

Peril, Lynn. *College Girls: Bluestockings, Sex Kittens, and Coeds, Then and Now*. New York and London: Norton, 2006.

Platt, Harold L. "Jane Addams and the Ward Boss Revisited: Class, Politics, and Public Health in Chicago, 1890–1930." *Environmental History* 5 (2000): 194–222.

Poole, Leslie Kemp. "Let Florida Be Green: Women, Activism, and the Environmental Century, 1900–2000." Ph.D. diss., University of Florida, Gainesville, 2012.

———. "The Women of the Early Florida Audubon Society: Agents of History in the Fight to Save State Birds." *Florida Historical Quarterly* 85 (2007): 297–323.

Pork Barrel and Pheasant Feathers. Directed by Holly Fisher. Video. 1966. In the private collection of Mimi Carr.

Porter, Charlotte M. "An Eighteenth-Century Flower Child: William Bartram." In *Paradise Lost? The Environmental History of Florida*, edited by Jack E. Davis and Raymond Arsenault, 47–71. Gainesville: University Press of Florida, 2005.

———. *John James Audubon: Florida Travels, 1831–1832*. Gainesville: Florida State Museum, 1985.

Powell, Elizabeth. Interview by author. March 11, 2006. Gainesville, Fla.

Price, Jennifer. *Flight Maps: Adventures with Nature in Modern America*. New York: Basic, 1999.

Reed, Nathaniel. Interview by Darren Preston Lane, director of *From Waterway to Green-way: The History of the Cross Florida Barge Canal*. DVD. Forthcoming. www.aabstract-productions.com/Cross-Florida-Barge-Canal.htm.

Reed, Nathaniel. Speech. University of Florida, Samuel Proctor Florida History Lecture Series. 2009. Bob Graham Center for Public Service, Gainesville.

Rich, Sharon Lee, and Ariel Phillips, eds. *Women's Experience and Education*. Cambridge: Harvard Educational Review Reprint Series No. 17, 1985.

Roberts, Mary Louise. *Disruptive Acts: The New Woman in Fin-de-Siècle France*. Chicago: University of Chicago Press, 2002.

Rose, Sonya O. *Limited Livelihoods: Gender and Class in Nineteenth-Century England*. Berkeley and Los Angeles: University of California Press, 1992.

Rossiter, Margaret. *Women Scientists in America: Struggles and Strategies to 1940*. Baltimore: Johns Hopkins University Press, 1982.

Rury, John. *Education and Women's Work: Female Schooling and the Division of Labor in Urban America, 1870–1930*. Albany: State University of New York Press, 1991.

Sewell, J. Richard. "Cross-Florida Barge Canal, 1927–1968." *Florida Historical Quarterly* 46 (1968): 369–83.

Shallat, Todd. *Structures in the Stream: Water, Science, and the Rise of the U.S. Army Corps of Engineers*. Austin: University of Texas Press, 1994.

Shofner, Jerrell H. "The Legacy of Racial Slavery: Free Enterprise and Forced Labor in Florida in the 1940s." *Journal of Southern History* 47 (1981): 411–26.

Simpson, J. Clarence. *A Provisional Gazetteer of Florida Place-Names of Indian Derivation Either Obsolescent or Retained Together with Others of Recent Application*. Edited by Mark F. Boyd. Tallahassee: State of Florida State Board of Conservation, Florida Geological Survey, 1956.

Smith, Stanley K. Bureau of Economic and Business Research website. "Florida Population Growth: Past, Present and Future." www.bebr.ufl.edu/files/FloridaPop2005_0.pdf.

Solomon, Barbara Miller. *In the Company of Educated Women: A History of Women and Higher Education in America*. New Haven: Yale University Press, 1985.

The Southwest Florida Pioneers Historical Society. "Fourteenth Census of the United States 1920—Population." www.rootsweb.ancestry.com/~flswphs/records/census/boni1920_full.htm.

Tarr, Rodger L., ed. *The Private Marjorie: The Love Letters of Marjorie Kinnan Rawlings to Norton S. Baskin*. Gainesville: University Press of Florida, 2004.

Tigert, Jno. J. "Co-ordination in Florida." *Journal of Higher Education* 4 (1933): 138–41.

U.S. Army Corps of Engineers. *Army Corps of Engineers Summary of Civil Works Projects under Construction and Surveys in Progress*. January 1964. Series 301, box 29A, folder 1, Mildred and Claude Pepper Library, Florida State University, Tallahassee.

——. *Congress Appropriates $1,220,400,200 for Fiscal Year 1965 Army Engineers Civil Works Program*. Report issued by the Office of the Chief of Engineers, Department of the Army. August 1964. Series 301, box 29, folder 5, Mildred and Claude Pepper Library, Florida State University, Tallahassee.

————. "Specifications for Job No. 8." Department of the Army, n.d. In author's private collection.

————. *Summary of Civil Works Projects under Construction and Studies in Progress.* December 1965. Series 301, box 29A, folder 4, Mildred and Claude Pepper Library, Florida State University, Tallahassee.

————. *Water Resources Development by the U.S. Army Corps of Engineers in Florida, U.S. Army Engineer Division, South Atlantic.* January 1965. Series 301, box 29A, folder 4, Mildred and Claude Pepper Library, Florida State University, Tallahassee.

U.S. Census Bureau. "State & County QuickFacts." http://quickfacts.census.gov/qfd/states/12000.html.

U.S. Fish & Wildlife Service. "United States Census Data for Bonita Springs, Florida, 1920." www.fws.gov/fisheries/fisheries.html.

Valenti, JoAnn Myer. Interview by Leslie Kemp Poole. March 1, 2011. Tampa, Fla.

Vanderblue, Homer B. "The Florida Land Boom." *Journal of Land & Public Utility Economics* 3 (1927): 113–31.

Walker, Nancy A., ed. *Women's Magazines 1940–1960: Gender Roles and the Popular Press.* Boston and New York: Palgrave Macmillan, 1998.

Ware, Susan. *Beyond Suffrage: Women in the New Deal.* Cambridge, Mass., and London: Harvard University Press, 1981.

Wolfe, Leslie R., ed. *Women, Work, and School: Occupational Segregation and the Role of Education.* Boulder, Colo.; San Francisco; and Oxford: Westview Press, 1991.

Worster, Donald. *Nature's Economy: A History of Ecological Ideas.* 2nd ed. New York: Cambridge University Press, 1994.

Wyer, Mary, Donna Giesman, Mary Barbercheck, Hatice Ozturk, and Marta Wayne, eds. *Women, Science, and Technology: A Reader in Feminist Science Studies.* New York and London: Routledge, 2001.

Index

Page numbers in *italics* refer to illustrations.

PEGGY MACDONALD was born and raised in Gainesville, Florida. She is adjunct professor of history at Stetson University in DeLand, Florida. She lives in Gainesville with her children, Richard and Katherine, and her husband, Nick Demosthenous.

THE UNIVERSITY PRESS OF FLORIDA is the scholarly publishing agency for the State University System of Florida, comprising Florida A&M University, Florida Atlantic University, Florida Gulf Coast University, Florida International University, Florida State University, New College of Florida, University of Central Florida, University of Florida, University of North Florida, University of South Florida, and University of West Florida.